This is to certify that this volume of

RARE
AND
BEAUTIFUL
ANIMALS

was produced in a leather-bound limited edition
of four thousand copies

THIS COPY IS NUMBER

S-85

REGISTERED IN THE NAME OF

RARE and BEAUTIFUL ANIMALS

Francesco B. Salvadori
Pier L. Florio

RARE and BEAUTIFUL ANIMALS

illustrations by Piero Cozzaglio

Newsweek Books, New York

1978 First American Edition
® 1977 Arnoldo Mondadori Editore, Milano
All rights reserved under International and Pan American
Copyright Conventions. Published in the United States by
Newsweek, Inc., New York. Published simultaneously in
Great Britain by David & Charles Publishers, Ltd. and in
Canada by Optimum Publishing Company Ltd.

Library of Congress Cataloging in Publication Data

Baschieri Salvadori, Francesco 1921-

   Rare and beautiful animals

   Translation of Animali Che Scompaiono
   Bibliography: p.
   Includes index.
   1. Rare animals.   I. Florio, Pier Lorenzo,
joint author.   II. Cozzaglio, Piero.   III. Title
Q182. B3713   591   L.C.: 78-55595

ISBN 0-88225-260-7

Printed and Bound in Italy by A. Mondadori Editore

Contents

9 Foreword
11 Introduction

MAMMALS
14 Parma Wallaby
15 Bridled Nail-tailed Wallaby
16 Ring-tailed Rock Wallaby   Eastern Native Cat
17 Numbat
18 Scaly-tailed Phalanger *or* Opossum
19 Barnard's Hairy-nosed Wombat *or*
   Queensland Hairy-nosed Wombat
20 Thylacine
22 Cuban Solenodon
23 Verreaux's Sifaka
24 Indris
26 Black Lemur
28 Aye-Aye
30 Red Uakari
31 Woolly Spider Monkey   Douc Langur
32 Lion-tailed Macaque
34 Golden Lion Marmoset
35 Pigmy Chimpanzee
36 Orang-utan
38 Mountain Gorilla
40 Giant Armadillo
42 Giant Anteater
43 Chinchilla   Kaibab Squirrel
44 European Beaver
45 Indus Dolphin
46 Blue Whale
48 Finback Whale *or* Common Rorqual
49 Humpback Whale
50 Greenland Right Whale *or* Bowhead
52 Wolf
54 Maned Wolf
56 Spectacled Bear
58 Abruzzo Brown Bear
60 Polar Bear
62 Giant Panda

64 Black-footed Ferret
65 Giant Otter
66 Sea Otter
68 Brown Hyena
69 Ocelot
70 Spanish Lynx
72 Clouded Leopard
73 Barbary Lion
74 Asiatic Lion
76 Tiger
78 Leopard
80 Snow Leopard
81 Jaguar
82 Cheetah
84 Mediterranean Monk Seal
86 Walrus
87 Steller's Sea Cow
88 Sea Cow *or* Dugong
89 Manatee
90 Przewalski's Wild Horse
92 Tarpan   Mountain Zebra
93 Quagga
94 Asiatic Wild Ass
96 African Wild Ass
98 Malayan Tapir
99 Mountain Tapir
100 Indian Rhinoceros
102 Javan Rhinoceros
103 Sumatran Rhinoceros
104 Black Rhinoceros
    White *or* Square-lipped Rhinoceros
105 Pigmy Hippopotamus
106 Vicuña
108 Wild Camel   Persian Fallow Deer
109 Brown-antlered Deer   Sika
110 Corsican Red Deer
111 Père David's Deer
114 Tamaraw   Aurochs
115 Banteng
116 European Bison
118 Wild Yak   Giant Eland
119 Bluebuck
120 Arabian Oryx
122 Scimitar-horned Oryx   Addax
123 White-tailed Gnu
124 Slender-horned Gazelle
125 Chamois of Abruzzo
126 Takin
127 Nilgiri Tahr
128 Abyssinian Ibex
129 Markhor

BIRDS

132 Giant Moa   Elephant Bird
133 Galapagos Penguin   Short-tailed Albatross
134 Galapagos Flightless Cormorant   Japanese Crested Ibis
135 Bald Ibis
136 Hawaiian Goose
138 Trumpeter Swan
139 Cape Barren Goose
140 Californian Condor
142 Bearded Vulture
143 Monkey-eating Eagle
144 Bald Eagle
146 Mauritius Kestrel
147 Seychelles Kestrel   Prairie Chicken
148 Swinhoe's Pheasant   Edward's Pheasant
149 White-eared Pheasant
150 Elliot's Pheasant
151 Mikado Pheasant
152 Palawan Peacock Pheasant
153 Japanese *or* Manchurian Crane
154 Whooping Crane
156 Takahe
157 Kagu   Great Indian Bustard
158 Audouin's Gull
159 Great Auk
160 Dodo
162 Passenger Pigeon
163 Kakapo *or* Owl Parrot
164 Kaka
165 Carolina Parakeet   Splendid Parakeet
166 Seychelles Owl   Seychelles Paradise (*or* Black) Flycatcher
167 Ivory-billed Woodpecker

REPTILES

170 Tuatara
171 Green Turtle   Hawksbill Turtle
172 Galapagos Giant Tortoise
174 Leatherback   [Galapagos] Land Iguana
175 Indian Gavial
176 Komodo Dragon
178 Giant Salamander
179 Olm   Golden Frog

APPENDICES

183 Man and Animals in the Natural World
201 Bibliography
203 Index

"The beauty and genius of a work of art may be reconceived though its first material expression be destroyed; a vanished harmony may yet again inspire the composer; but when the last individual of a race of living things breathes no more, another Heaven and another Earth must pass before such a one can be again."

William Beebe (1877–1962)
First Curator of Birds
Bronx Zoological Park
New York Zoological Society

Preface

L IKE precious metals and stones, rare animals have always been a source of fascination. Only recently has there been much appreciation of endangered species other than as curiosity. They are still often regarded as living museum pieces which, when the pulse of the last individual has died away, can simply become preserved esoteric museum specimens, rather like the last breath of Thomas Edison collected by Henry Ford.

Now we can see, as so beautifully portrayed and eloquently chronicled in this volume, that endangerment is no isolated phenomenon. No continent is spared, nor the seas. Although large vertebrates and island forms are generally the first to be endangered, no group of animals or plants or any region is beyond the threat of extinction.

Endangered species are sounding a clarion call, alerting us that man is overreaching himself biologically. They are alarm bells telling us the biological systems on which man depends are being debased.

How blind we have been to our accelerating degradation of the natural world of which we are a part. In our rush to dominate nature, and to set ourselves apart, like human caddis flies in sterile structures of concrete, glass, and steel, we have been trying to cleanse ourselves of our relationships with the natural world as though nature was pornography.

How unintelligent it is of *Homo sapiens* to expect to know what immediate value a particular species might have. While the ability of the humble nine-banded armadillo of southern North America to always produce identical quadruplets may have been perceived to be of some use in studying problems of human reproduction, whoever could have guessed it might also have been of use in leprosy research? What important secrets of cardiac physiology are held by the cheetah? How much we have to learn from nature about ourselves, how we function, how we got here, and where we might go if we choose our course intelligently. The quality of life depends squarely on the diversity of the natural world.

It is critical to save endangered species by protecting habitats and ecosystems, and it is interesting that these pages include at least three species whose survival has depended in whole or in large part on captive propagation in zoological collections. Others, such as the Carolina parakeet and the passenger pigeon, the last individuals of which both died in a zoo, could easily have been saved in such a fashion. Zoos certainly can't save all endangered species, but they will be important in preventing a growing number of extinctions.

Only a few of the animals included in this volume are extinct. At the rate at which we are bringing pressure on our biological base, it is most likely that a future edition of this book, ten years hence, would have a larger number of extinct animals. The animals in this volume are the forward contingent of an unfortunate procession of the animal kingdom toward endangerment and extinction. The numbers and composition of those species that follow are by no means certain and are, to a great extent, dependent on all of us, how rapidly we awaken to the dangers, and how energetically we address the peril. And since with each extinction, our capacity for beauty and joy is diminished, we must ask ourselves to what extent we will allow our humanity to be tarnished.

Thomas E. Lovejoy, PhD.
Program Director
World Wildlife Fund, U.S.A.

Introduction

There are illustrations in the following pages of 144 species: 132 of them are in danger of extinction or very rare; 12 are already extinct, and their disappearance, over the last four or five centuries, can be attributed almost exclusively to the actions of man. We have limited ourselves in this book to the 'superior' animals because, both in appearance and morphologically, these are closer to man and will consequently attract the maximum amount of his attention.

The species described and illustrated are: 94 mammals (of which 6 are extinct); 39 birds (of which 6 are extinct); 8 reptiles and 3 amphibians; an indication is given of their degree of importance with regard to common numbers and rarity. There are many more species currently threatened with extinction. In the Red Data Books compiled and published by the International Union for the Conservation of Nature – the technical international organization concerned with safeguarding wildlife – 839 species and sub-species of vertebrates alone are listed. Taking into account the insects, molluscs and other invertebrates the figure jumps into the thousands. The number of species of plants in danger of extinction throughout the world can be put at around 20,000. In 1974 the British National Appeal for the World Wildlife Fund published a list of 839 animals and 68 plants in danger; this was printed on both sides of a strip of paper 1.5 metres long. If it had been possible to add to the list those animals that were a little less rare and those species shrinking because of their exploitation by man, as well as all the 20,000 plants at risk, then the strip of paper would have been longer than Nelson's Column! In all, this represents an enormous heritage, an inestimable legacy which man has reaped and plundered relentlessly, and which he may have lost forever because of his insensitivity and greed.

We have selected for this book only the rarest species of vertebrates which, because they are well known and of striking appearance, are most representative of endangered species. The book is not a scientific work but one that aims, through the illustrations and brief descriptions, to bring a greater understanding of the numbers of animals which are declining, or threatened with decline, and which, once destroyed, will be extinct forever. We have consulted the most highly qualified and up-to-date scientific publications in order to give the relevant data regarding the position of each species (the majority of this from the material of the UICN and WWF). This book aims to give a clear picture of the precarious situations of these declining species, with particular attention to those animals now threatened with extinction in the authors' own country. Italy may be a paradise for millions of tourists but is certainly not so for the animals who inhabit it in the wild or pass through in the course of their migrations. The appendix illustrates the inter-relating links between mankind and the world of nature that surrounds him. It also shows the causes of the disappearance of so many species, and of the rarification of so many others. It describes man's destruction of nature, and the first efforts to rebuild after the revival of interest in the natural world. The classifications given are those used in the Red Data Books, except for the Pinnipedia, which we have considered as a suborder of the carnivores, and not as an order in their own right. We have not always adhered rigidly to the correct sequence in our presentation of the species.

Francesco Baschieri Salvadori and Pier Lorenzo Florio

MAMMALS

Parma Wallaby

(Macropus parma)

Class: Mammals Subclass: Metatheria
Order: Marsupialia Family: Macropodidae
Subfamily: Macropodinae Genus: *Macropus*
French: *Wallaby parma* Italian: *Wallaby parma*
German: *Parma-Känguruh*

Description. The Parma Wallaby is a kangaroo characterized by a beautiful brown colouring on the dorsal area, with the belly, chest and collar all white. The muzzle is marked with two longitudinal, very evident, white stripes, one on each side. One fine stripe runs half the length of the back. The upper lip is white. The size of this wallaby, which stands about 30cm (1ft) high, in comparison to the other Macropodidae is medium to small.

Geographic distribution. Originally the area inhabited by the Parma covered a large zone in the eastern part of New South Wales. Now the species can be found on the small island of Kawau, off New Zealand; they were imported to Kawau at the end of the last century.

Habitat. Formerly this species inhabited the bush and tropical forests that surrounded the edges of Lake Illawarra, close to what is now Wolongong, to the south of Sydney. The area is now totally given over to agriculture.

Population. At the end of 1965 the position of the Parma Wallaby in its own territory was desperate. It was, in fact, thought to be extinct as, for many years, none had been captured or sighted. A colony of Parmas has since been discovered on the island of Kawau; these are the remnants of those imported from Australia. Unfortunately, both the Parma Wallaby and the similar Tammar (*Macropus eugenii*), which had also been imported to the island, were hunted relentlessly by the local farmers who considered these kangaroos to be highly injurious to agriculture. Of the 3,000 killed in a year, an estimated 2,000 were Parma Wallabys. Between 1966 and 1974, 384 specimens of the Parma were taken to various zoos where they are flourishing and multiplying. Zoos and scientific research institutes have organized the exportation of a number of this species to start up new colonies, with the aim of promoting reproduction in different environments that are quiet and protected. The species in the wild has been placed under protection, and the maritime park of the Gulf of Hauraki, in the most southern part of Kawau, where the Parma is still to be found, is now a reserve. An example of the species has been sighted in its original territory on the outskirts of Gosford in New South Wales. In 1973, in 28 zoos in Australia, Canada, the United States, Europe and Japan, there were 231 Parma Wallabys, 145 of them born in captivity.

Bridled Nail-tailed Wallaby

(Onychogalea fraenata)

Class: Mammals Subclass: Metatheria
Order: Marsupialia Family: Macropodidae
Subfamily: Macropodinae Genus: *Onychogalea*
French: *Onychogale bridé* Italian: *Wallaby dalle
Briglie* German: *Kurznagel Känguruh*

Description. The most evident somatic characteristic
that distinguishes the Bridled Nail-tailed Wallaby from
the two species similar to it, *O. unguifera* and *O. lunata*,
is the bridle – the two white stripes on the shoulders
which extend up to the neck behind the nape to the base
of the ears. The tip of the long thin tail has a horny
formation, similar to a nail, the function of which has
yet to be explained. The species differs from the others
in the shape of the incisor and premolar teeth, a
characteristic which keeps this group separate from the
rest of the same genus. In the two kindred species, the
white stripes extend as far as the upper rim of the
armpit one way and to the base of the neck the other. It
has a hairy muzzle and a dark, dense coat. All three
species are small, more or less the size of a hare.

Geographic distribution. The distribution of the three
species, all rare now, in the genus *Onychogalea*, is
limited. *O. fraenata*, Bridled Nail-tailed Wallaby, is confined to the interior of New South Wales and southern
Queensland. *O. unguifera* is found in the area from
western Dampier Land in northern Australia to the
Pacific coast of northern Queensland. *O. lunata* is
limited to the eastern and central part of southern
Australia and the area of the junction of the rivers
Murray and Darling between the states of Victoria and
New South Wales.

Habitat. The environment usually inhabited by these
kangaroos is the bush and the steppes. *O. unguifera*,
however, also lives in the shrubby savannah and the
rocky areas by rivers.

Population. The Bridled Nail-tailed Wallaby was, at one
time, the most common of these three in the above areas.
Now it is the most rare. In the past thirty-five years
there has not been a discovery of this species; the last
captured was one in 1924 in New South Wales and one
in 1929 by the Dawson river in south-east Queensland.
A discovery in 1937 has not been verified. The one thing
that would save the species from extinction (if it is not
already extinct) would be to examine the area of distribution with a view to setting up a reserve to protect any
eventual colony.

Ring-tailed Rock Wallaby

(Petrogale xanthopus)

Class: Mammals Subclass: Metatheria
Order: Marsupialia Family: Macropodinae
Genus: *Petrogale*
French: *Wallaby des rochers à queue annelée*
Italian: *Wallaby delle rocce dalla coda ad anelli*
German: *Ringschwanz-Felskänguruh*

Description. The kangaroos of the genus *Petrogale* have been given the nickname 'Australian chamois' because of their exceptional agility. This comes from the structure of the ball of the foot, which has elastic pads covered in coarse granules and surrounded by a fringe of rigid skin that gives incredible adhesion to the surfaces they cross. Another aid to maintaining balance is the tail, which is long, cylindrical and hairy with a tuft of hair on the end. When frightened, the Rock Wallaby sounds an alarm by thumping the ground.

Geographic distribution. Australia, the southern mountainous areas, north-east New South Wales and south-east Queensland.

Habitat. Rocky hills and screes.

Population. This wallaby has become rare throughout the areas of its distribution as a result of being continually hunted for its valuable hide and of competition in its natural environment. It has been protected for many years, but no other projects have been instigated to guarantee its survival. A hundred specimens, all born in captivity, have been lodged in four Australian zoos.

Eastern Native Cat

(Dasyurus quoll)

Class: Mammals Subclass: Metatheria
Order: Marsupialia Family: Dasyuridae
Subfamily: Dasyurinae Genus: *Dasyurus*
French: *Dasyure moucheté* Italian: *Dasiuro viverrino*
German: *Tüpfelbeutelmarder*

Description. The Eastern Native Cat can be distinguished from the others of its genus by the absence of flecks on its tail, which has a white apex; and by the fact that it has four toes, not five, on its forefeet. The colour of its coat varies from olive-brown to almost black speckled with white flecks. Its overall length reaches 70cm (28in), 25–30cm (10–12in) of which are the tail. As with all the dasyuri, the Eastern Native Cat is a relentless hunter, abominated by farmers for the damage it does to henhouses. Apart from poultry and eggs, it eats wild birds, insects, snakes and lizards. It is basically nocturnal, passing the day hidden between tree roots or behind stones.

Geographic distribution. This species is spread out over the south-eastern part of southern Australia, the eastern half of New South Wales, east and north Victoria, King Island and Tasmania.

Habitat. The Eastern Native Cat lives principally in the eucalyptus forests with dense dry undergrowth, and in the coastal woods.

Population. The species has become rare on the Australian continent over the last ten years but is still common in Tasmania. There have been cases of reproduction in captivity in two zoos in Australia.

Numbat

(Myrmecobius fasciatus)

Class: Mammals Subclass: Metatheria
Order: Marsupialia Family: Dasyuridae
Subfamily: Myrmecobiidae Genus: *Myrmecobius*
French: *Fourmilier marsupial rayé* Italian: *Mirmecobio*
German: *Ameisenbeutler*

Description. The body and shoulders are of a beautiful brown flecked with white hairs. The back is marked with alternate black and white bands. There is a black stripe across the eye to the base of the ear; parallel to this, above and below, run two thick white stripes. Another characteristic of the coat is that the long hairs of the tail stand straight out like a bottle-brush. The male numbat is about the size of a rat. The female is smaller and not obviously marsupian, but the area around the four nipples is covered with shaggy hair to which the young cling for the length of time they are feeding from her. The young, usually four, are born between January and May, and are carried and cared for by the mother. The numbat has five toes on the forefeet and four on the back. There are fifty-two small, overcrowded, involute teeth unequally divided between the two jaws. The numbat feeds on insects and larvae, particularly on ants and termites which it hunts, unlike most marsupials, in the daytime. The 10cm (4in) long tongue is especially well designed for its diet and can easily penetrate cracks in trees to reach the termites.

Geographic distribution. The species is spread out over the most southern part of north-eastern Australia and the eastern part of southern Australia.

Habitat. Bush and forest. The numbat has never been seen in terrain without vegetation.

Population. At one time common in all the above areas, the numbat is now limited to the most western area of eastern Australia, although not even an approximate figure of the population is known. Its continuing decline is due to the destruction of the forest trees which serve as protection, particularly from its more recent enemies introduced by man, such as the dog and the wolf. The only possible way of preserving this species would be to set up reserves in south-eastern Australia where these predators would be eliminated or at least kept at a distance. In 1975, the sole pair of numbats in captivity were in Sydney Zoo, where only the female now remains.

Scaly-tailed Phalanger or Opossum

(Wyulda squamicaudata)

Class: Mammals Subclass: Metatheria
Order: Marsupialia Family: Phalangeridae
Subfamily: Phalangerinae Genus: *Wyulda*
French: *Opossum d'Australie à queue écailleuse*
Italian: *Opossum a coda squamosa*
German: *Schuppenschwanzkusu*

Description. The Scaly-tailed Phalanger, or Opossum, looks much like the other Phalangeridae, and is the size of a squirrel. It is characterized by its tail: the base is covered with dense fur but the middle and the tip are hairless and scaly, making it similar to a lemur. The coat is short and thick, grey to grey-brown in colour. The species feeds mainly from the shoots of various vegetables. It is a solitary animal. Like most other marsupials it gives birth to one offspring at a time. In East Kimberley the young have been observed to be still naked in June and in northern Kimberley they were half-grown in December/January.

Geographic distribution. Although only a few have been captured, the diffusion of this species covers a wide area, having been sighted in East, Central and North Kimberley, Australia.

Habitat. The species seems to spend most of the day in the sandstone areas between the rocks. At night it is in search of food. The records of the habitat and environment of this species are few and scanty.

Population. The first intimation of the Scaly-tailed Phalanger came from Valley Station on the outskirts of Turkey Creek, where it was sighted in 1917. It was another twenty-five years before the second example was sighted by the missionary J. R. B. Love on the edge of his mission at Kunmunya, 250 miles north of Derby. The Worora, natives of the area, seemed to know the animal well; they said that it was common throughout their territory and was called a 'llangurra'. The third opossum was a female with its young captured in 1954 at Wotjulum, a mission halfway between Kummunya and Derby, by Ken Buller of the Western Australia Museum. A fourth was sighted by John Tapper on the outskirts of Broome, south of Dampier Land, 250 miles from where the nearest opossum had been seen. In 1965 Harry Butler, from an American natural history museum and a museum in Kimberley, discovered that the animal was not as rare as had been thought, the few sightings being attributed to the fact that the opossum seldom inhabits areas frequented by man or covered by zoologists. By 1975 there were only two females in captivity, in a zoo in Perth.

Barnard's Hairy-nosed Wombat
or Queensland Hairy-nosed Wombat

(Lasiorhinus barnardi)

Class: Mammals Subclass: Metatheria
Order: Marsupialia Family: Vombatidae
Genus: *Lasiorhinus*
French: *Wombat à narines poilues du Queensland*
Italian: *Vombato dal naso peloso del Queensland*
German: *Queensland-Haarnasenwombat*

Description. Also known as the Queensland Hairy-nosed Wombat (*Lasiorhinus latifrons*), Barnard's Hairy-nosed Wombat is the rarest of its kind in Queensland. It is distinguished from the naked-nosed wombats by the white and brown hair on its nose, and also by the long dense hair of its coat, which has a thick soft undercoat. The species feeds exclusively off certain roots and shoots. The incisor teeth are strong and chiscl-shaped, and enamel-coated on the front and sides. The teeth, which are subject to continuous growth, are without roots. A slow-witted animal of a mild disposition, the species has specially adapted to digging. No obstacle impedes its progress – fallen trees, ditches and streams are all overcome by this living tank with apparent calm and indiffer-ence. It has a pouch on its belly, inside which are two teats. Generally the wombat produces one offspring in the breeding season. It is not known what age the animal reaches in the wild; but in captivity specimens of similar species have lived for twenty-six years.

Geographic distribution. The species is found in two limited areas of mid-eastern Queensland: about 80 miles north-west of Clermont and on the coastal strip of southern Australia.

Habitat. Following recent field research by D. P. Vernon, it seems that the Barnards Wombat can be found only in a sandy area little larger than 15sq km (6sq miles). The entrances to its hole are usually by the roots of various local plants. The sand is hollowed out to where the sub-soil is more humid.

Population. This wombat has always been very rare; as yet, not even an approximate census has been taken to show how many there are. Since 1925 the species has been rigidly protected under Australian law, and in 1971 a large part of its habitat was effectively controlled when it became part of a national park. A research programme has been proposed to cover the biological and ecological aspects of the population of this little-known species. There are no examples of Barnard's Hairy-nosed Wombat in captivity, but other hairy-nosed wombats are to be found in six zoos, three of them Australian (nineteen examples).

Thylacine

(Thylacinus cynocephalus)

Class: Mammals Subclass: Metatheria
Order: Marsupialia Family: Dasyuridae
Subfamily: Thylacinidae Genus: *Thylacinus*
French: *Loup marsupial* Italian: *Tilacino*
German: *Beutelwolf*

Description. The thylacine, or Tasmanian Pouched Wolf, is also known as the Tasmanian Tiger because of the stripes across its back. It differs so much from all the other marsupials that some authorities consider it as the only species of the one genus belonging to theThylacinidae family. Others see it as the representative of the subfamily and forming a part of the family Dasyuridae. The largest of all the carnivorous marsupials, the thylacine is about as big as a medium-sized dog, reaching 1m (3½ft) in length, with the tail another 50cm (20in). It has the head, muzzle and jaw of a dog; the strong jaw-bone can open to approximately 180 degrees, the angle between the jaw-bone and the mandible being almost flat. The tail and the haunches are much stronger and more compact than those of a dog, being more like a kangaroo's. The tail cannot be used to indicate friendliness or dejection as can that of a dog. The hind feet do not have the first toe. The thylacine gives birth to four young which are carried in the mother's pouch for three months and then placed in a padded, protected nest. The young follow the mother to learn to hunt. Because they are exclusively meat-eaters, they have to be unflagging hunters, keeping pace with their prey, never rushing. Sometimes when tracking they bound along on their hind legs. Observations of the species' habits in the wild date from some time ago, when the animal was seen in its natural habitat; such reports, usually from farmers and settlers, were often wildly inaccurate or at least exaggerated. The image they put forward is of an animal which throttles its prey – kangaroos and sheep included – in order to drink the blood and devour the entrails. It is far more plausible that the thylacine – if any living examples still exist – carries on in the same way as other predators, hunting its prey in order to eat the meat. Despite this 'blood-lust' attributed to the thylacine, it is not known to be aggressive to humans, except for one case in 1900 when a half-blind and starving thylacine was found with the remains of the hand and arm of a girl.

Geographic distribution. From numerous traces it seems that over the last 10,000 years the thylacine was to be found all across Australia and New Guinea. A mummified carcass in a cave at the edge of the Nullarbor Plain was carbon-dated at between 2940 and 2240 BC. Some thylacines may possibly survive in a few woody areas of Tasmania.

Habitat. The territory inhabited by the thylacine was sparse woods, woody savannah and the eucalyptus groves near rocky areas where there were kangaroos and sheep. Persecution by the owners of domestic animals then confined them to mountains and woods – to which the species was completely unadapted. Between 1888 and 1909 2,184 were massacred.

Population. No population count is possible for this species, whose very existence is in doubt. In 1930 one was killed in the north-east coast area of Tasmania, and in 1933 the latest example was captured. Sightings were reported in 1937, 1957 and, finally, in 1961, but none resulting in capture. Since 1938 the species has been under government protection and anyone killing a thylacine is liable to be fined. The animal adapted a little to life in a zoo, but did not reproduce. The last one in captivity died in a London zoo in 1931.

Cuban Solenodon

(Atopogale cubana)

Class: Mammals Subclass: Eutheria
Order: Insectivora Family: Solenodontidae
Genus: *Atopogale*
French: *Almiqui* Italian: *Solenodonte di Cuba* or
Almiqui German: *Kuba-Schlitzrüssler*

Description. In general appearance this animal is similar to a shrew, though it is longer and its shape is less delicate. It is 45–58cm (18–23in) in length, between a third and a fifth of which is taken up by the tail. The coat is brownish, with lighter shades on the head and belly. The solenodon's main characteristic is the long conical muzzle. Its paws are large with well-developed nails. Its teeth have a unique capability. When the solenodon bites its prey, the salivary glands beneath the jaw secrete a poison to the space all round the base of the second lower incisor; from there a channel carries the poison into the wound. It eats invertebrates and small vertebrates, such as reptiles (snakes and lizards), and occa-sionally poultry, fruit and vegetables. It is basically nocturnal, hiding in holes in trees and rocks. It moves in fits and starts, continually changing direction. It can have two litters a year, but only one or two, or excep-tionally three, young are born at a time; the species does not therefore reproduce enough to maintain its numbers.

Habitat. Mountain forests and thickets; plantations.

Geographic distribution. While its one relative, *Solenodon paradoxus*, is limited to Haiti, the Cuban Solenodon is found only in Cuba, mainly in the eastern and south-eastern regions.

Population. The Solenodontidae are now limited to the above islands, being represented by one genus in each. Presumably the solenodon's decline has resulted from the destruction of the woodland and the introduction of the mongoose, as well as the domestic carnivores. The species is protected by law and is present in the Jaquani Reserve near Toa Baracoa. United States law prohibits their importation. Research into the habits and distri-bution has been proposed so as to assess what protec-tive measures are necessary. In 1886 one specimen was noted in a zoo in Philadelphia. In 1975 there was one example of the Cuban Solenodon in a zoo in Cuba; one of the Haitian genus was in San Domingo Zoo and another in Washington.

Verreaux's Sifaka
(Propithecus verreauxi)

Class: Mammals Subclass: Eutheria
Order: Primates Suborder: Proscimiae
Family: Indriidae Genus: *Propithecus*
French: *Propithèque de Verreaux* Italian: *Sifaka di Verreaux* German: *Larvensifaka*

Description. Verreaux's Sifaka is 1–1.5m (3½–4ft) in length, half of which is taken up by the tail. The muzzle is black. The rest of the body varies from white to a light grey; it has a long soft coat and a dense woolly undercoat. Truly tree-living creatures, the sifakas move from branch to branch, often leaping 10–12m (30–40ft). Only rarely do they travel along the ground, moving upright in a series of jumps on the hind legs, with their arms bent against the head to help them keep their balance. From early morning they will sun themselves, comfortably installed in the fork of a branch; with the heat of midday they move into the shade. They live in groups of three to seven or very occasionally up to nine. They gather their food in groups, calling to one another with their cackling whining note. They eat leaves, flowers, bark and certain fruits. Mating takes place in February/March. After a gestation period of five months, the single offspring is born in June/July. As well as the typical *Propithecus v. verreauxi* illustrated here, there are various sub-species: *P. v. coquereli*, *P. v. deckeni*, *P. v. coronatus* and *P. v. majori*. One of those most in danger of extinction is *P. v. majori*, which inhabits an unprotected area.

Geographic distribution. The sifaka is limited to the eastern sector of the island of Madagascar. The sub-species all live in areas which at some point overlap.

Habitat. Evergreen or deciduous forest with mixed vegetation; the Analaneia Forest.

Population. Although the figures for each sub-species vary, taken as a whole the sifaka population is in imminent danger of extinction. This is owing to the continuing destruction of their habitat – a situation made worse by frequent forest fires. The taboo systems of the local tribes, which formerly protected the sifakas, have now disappeared. Again, although the species is protected by law, in the remote areas this has little effect and is difficult to enforce. The three reserves, Andohahela, Ankarafantiska and Namoraka, together with the two private reserves near Berenty and north of Mananara, offer more or less effective protection. It would be best if a national park could be set up, with some further reserves strengthening the ones already in existence and encouraging the private ones which are most efficient. The importance of the species is realized in the USA and Britain. In 1973 there were six examples of the sub-species *Coquereli* in Durham Zoo, USA, and eleven from the four sub-species in Tenerife Zoo. The sifaka does not, however, breed easily in captivity.

Indris

(Indri indri)

Class: Mammals Subclass: Eutheria
Order: Primates Suborder: Prosimiae
Family: Indriidae Genus: *Indri*
French: *Indri* Italian: *Indri* German: *Indri*

Description. The largest of the surviving lemurs, it is ironically only 66–78cm (26–30in) long; 5–6cm (2in) of this is the tail, which can measure as little as 3cm (1¼in). The head is rounded, with a small black muzzle jutting forward and large yellow-brown eyes. The coat is thick and silky, longer on the shoulders and back. The hands, feet and ears are black, as also are parts of the back, the top of the head, the arms and the front of the legs. The rest of the body is white, grey or bright tawny colour. Colour does not vary according to sex. Completely black or white individuals have been seen, but these were probably albinos or 'melanismos' as are found in various other species of the animal. In captivity, the indris eats leaves, flowers and fruit, though there is no record of their feeding habits in the wild. Diurnal animals, they go in search of food early in the morning and late in the afternoon. They are tree dwelling, adept at climbing and jumping. Having leapt on to a tree trunk they move by a sort of punting action of their forearms and then spring to the next tree with the body held vertical for short high leaps and flat out to cover a wider distance. They will hang quite happily suspended from the trunk or branches of a tree. On the ground they move slowly, standing erect on jumping. They live in small groups of two to four. Little is known of their behaviour in the wild because it is very difficult to observe them. However, their voices can be heard in chorus, with different groups replying to each other across the forest. They have a strident call like a car horn and also make short grunts. The period of gestation is put between one and – more probably – five to six months. Like other primates in general and lemurs in particular, the indris presumably produces only one offspring at a time. The female is said to choose an isolated quiet place in which to give birth, but this is supposition based on local accounts; in tribal legends the lemurs, particularly the indris, often feature as an ancestor of man.

Geographic distribution. Exclusively in Madagascar, inhabiting the eastern part of the island between 14° and 20° latitude to the south and Antongil Bay to the north, the Masora river to the east and the boundary of the high plain forest to the west. In the past, the area certainly extended further in all directions.

Habitat. Humid rain forest.

Population. As we know the exact limits of the area inhabited by the indris and the estimated very low density of the population (three individuals for every 100 hectares [200 acres] of the area), it is easy to deduce that the species is very scarce and in grave danger of extinction. Also, it has lost the protection of tradition – the animal was taboo for the Betsimisaraka of the east coast. It is no longer sheltered by impenetrable forest. Not only has its habitat been destroyed by fire, bushwacking and the continual claims of cultivation but it is probable that the animal's birth-rate has been affected by the arrival of man and the hunt, disrupting the former peace of the forest. All this could not have failed to harm the species, now in rapid decline. Its numbers have already shrunk too much to be saved by protection laws, which in any case are ineffectual in the most remote areas. The Masoala and Betampona nature reserves where the indris is present are not large. The new reserve near Perinet has a few specimens, but the area has been made barren, so the habitat offered is not conducive to the indris settling and surviving. Britain and the United States have placed a restriction on importation of the indris. What is necessary is to improve conditions on the reserves where the indris exists, and to create one or more reserves specially designed for its needs. This would be both important and interesting from the scientific point of view, owing to the almost total lack of data on the ecology, zoogeography, psychology and morphology of this lemur. The indris, even in its own country, does not survive captivity outside its natural environment, although a specimen could be seen at the Paris Zoo for a short period in 1939. As it is not possible to rear them and make them reproduce in captivity, this truly unique animal can only be saved through a rigid and effective programme of protection.

Black Lemur

(Lemur macaco macaco)

Class: Mammals Subclass: Eutheria
Order: Primates Suborder: Prosimiac
Family: Lemuridae Genus: *Lemur*
French: *Lémur macaco* Italian: *Maki macaco*
German: *Mohrenmaki*

Description. This is the smallest of the *Lemur* genus, measuring 92cm (3ft), including the 50cm (20in) tail. The colour differs according to sex, the males being black and the females a reddish-brown. As this difference does not occur in the other sub-species, such as the *Lemur macaco fulvus*, the Black Lemur was considered by some authorities to be a species by itself. It lives in a group of about ten – usually with a prevalence of males – led by an adult female. Each group has its own territory which is marked out by a secretion that has a distinctive odour. Unlike most of the lemurs, which sleep in a sitting position, the Black Lemur sleeps on its belly along a branch, with its limbs hanging down. The species is nocturnal and vegetarian. Mating takes place within the territory between May and July. After a gestation period of about four-and-a-half months, the single offspring is born, though twins are not unknown. The young weigh 70–80g (2–3oz). They are suckled for six months and reach maturity at eighteen months. The length of life varies; some have lived in captivity for twenty-seven years. In Rome Zoo various examples have been long-lived, reaching well over the twenty-year mark.

Geographic distribution. The Black Lemur originally covered a vast area of Madagascar from the north-west coast to the Bay of Bombetoka in the south. Now it exists in a much smaller area, namely the Sambirona territory to the south of the Ampasindava Bay, and on the islands of the Nossi-Be and Nossi-Komba.

Habitat. The Black Lemur, a forest animal, frequents the woods where there is a high level of humidity. The Sambirona area, in which the species is now confined, offers exactly these conditions; so that, although largely given over to the production of cereals, cocoa and *ilang-ilang* and densely colonized, here the Black Lemur has adapted itself. The lemurs harvest the plantations themselves, finding in the fruit a basic food source. The local inhabitants, who formerly respected the animal according to taboos, now use every means from poison to lead-shot to kill the lemurs. On the island of Nossi-Be the Black Lemur lives on the Lokobe Reserve – 1,160h (2,866 acres) – where the natural forest vegetation has been preserved.

Population. Some decades ago, through the tolerance of the local inhabitants, the population of the Black Lemur reached a higher-than-average density. Now the numbers are falling all the time and the species is in danger. In the restricted areas, however, having adapted to the local conditions and making use of them – as with the plantation fruit – the lemurs are fairly numerous. Here, instead of being killed by every possible means, the lemurs may be captured so as to be introduced into other territories or to satisfy commercial demand, despite the fact that this encourages the illegal depredation of other populations of the species; thus they are more easily destroyed. The lemur is protected by law, but this is in effect almost impossible to enforce. The United States and Britain prohibit the importation of the species, except in specific cases. To safeguard the species for the future, protection measures must be reinforced. The Lokobe Reserve should be enlarged and zones designated where hunting is prohibited. In 1973 there were 38 males and 44 females in captivity, of which 20 males and 21 females were born in 14 different zoos. In given conditions, the species will reproduce fairly easily. It would be helpful, therefore, to breed them with the aim of repopulating and setting up colonies, without having to remove any from the original territory.

Aye-Aye

(Daubentonia madagascariensis)

Class: Mammals Subclass: Eutheria Order: Primates
Suborder: Prosimiae Infraorder: Lemuriformes
Family: Daubentoniidae Genus: *Daubentonia*
French: *Aye-aye* Italian: *Aye-aye* German: *Fingertier*

Description. Because of its bizarre looks which are quite different from those of any of the other lemur forms, the aye-aye constitutes the super-family Daubentonioidae, the family Daubentonidae and the genus *Daubentonia*. It is 1m (3ft) in length; a good three-fifths of this is the long, extremely hairy tail. Its murky blackish colour shows up the white colouring of the muzzle, cheeks, throat and two spots above the eye. The head is round, the auricles smooth, pendulous and membranous. The round eyes have a forward stare; the body is slight; the limbs are graceful, with long supple fingers. The aye-aye resembles some form of forest spectre, an image that especially suits its nocturnal habits. Other characteristics make the animal look strange and always a little puzzled. The incisors, although not long and crooked like a rodent's, are of similar structure and also grow continuously. The cranium is similar to that of a squirrel, the brain somewhat reminiscent of that of the insectivores. The aye-aye is a solitary animal travelling alone over its own hunting ground of around 6h (14 acres). It has only been sighted singly, though some authorities say the species lives in pairs. The food consists of various vegetables, bamboo shoots, sugar cane and, more importantly, birds' eggs and insects and their larvae are eaten, with a special predilection for the *Xilofaghe*. The aye-aye has a unique way of extracting the insects. It moves over the trunk or branch and then strikes the wood with its third digit (illustrated in the detail on this page). Next it listens to the noise caused by the movement of the insects inside. It then bites away the opening to the hole, puts in the third finger as a probe and, with its curved nail, hooks out the prey. Apart from catching insects, this middle finger is used to hit anything that attracts the animal's attention, to comb its coat, to remove parasites and as a means of scratching itself. The other fingers are meanwhile bent against the palm. The aye-aye in fact uses its fingers to scoop up water to drink. It always moves on four legs but can climb vertically. When it is on the ground, the tail is carried in the shape of an 'S' as with other lemurs. It has a short strident cry, sounding like two pieces of metal grating together. During the day it rests in a hole in a tree or in a hollow between branches. According to some authorities, it makes a spherical nest of leaves. The female certainly builds a nest for protection when she gives birth, but little is known of the aye-aye's sexual habits and reproductive cycle. Possibly the female gives birth to one offspring in February/March – biannually, not every year. The longest period of life is said to be three years in captivity; others say the aye-aye lives at least nine years.

Geographic distribution. The first zoo-geographic studies on this species indicated its presence in Madagascar's coastal forest and in all the low-altitude forests in the north, west and east of the island. Now, as far as it is possible to judge, there are only a few individuals scattered in the north-east and probably in the north-west coastal area.

Habitat. A forest-dweller, the aye-aye is tied to areas of vegetation with tall stems where the *Xilofaghe*, its principal food, can be found. Exploitation of the forest has created an anomalous situation to which the aye-aye has responded with two slight adaptations: moving from the low-lying forest to the high forest, and occupying the old mango plantations created by the first colonizers. The species' drop in numbers shows, however, that these adaptations have not checked its decline.

Population. If one can use the term for an animal that lives by itself, the aye-aye 'population' has been largely destroyed – in spite of legal protection. The species is prohibited from importation into the USA or Britain, except for research. A small reserve was set up at Mahambo where a few individual aye-aye settled in 1957. Eleven were introduced to the island of Nossy-Mangabe where the conditions are favourable for them. The rarity of the aye-aye, its infrequency of reproduction and our inadequate knowledge of the species make renewed efforts for its preservation imperative. Only rarely has it been held in captivity. One pair lived for two years at Maroansetra and in 1970 were transferred to Tananarive; they were known to be still alive in 1974. No cases of reproduction in captivity are known.

Red Uakari

(Cacajao rubicundus)

Class: Mammals Subclass: Eutheria Order: Primates
Suborder: Simiae Family: Cebidae
Subfamily: Pitheciinae Genus: *Cacajao* (*uakaris*)
French: *Ouakari rubicond* Italian: *Cacaiao rubicondo*
or *Uakari rosso* German: *Roter Uakari*

Description. The uakari has an overall length of 59–67cm
(23–26in), of which 43–48cm (17–19in) is the head and
trunk. It is characterized by a yellow coat of thick, long,
coarse hair and by its brilliant crimson-red face. Little is
known of the species' habits and social behaviour. It is
believed to live in small groups, perhaps based on the
family, although Lomberg observed large groups of
around 100. They move on four legs rather than two.
The hand is prehensile. Although the uakari was thought
to be lazy and apathetic, it has recently been seen – at
least in captivity – to be very active.

Geographic distribution. As recently as 1930 the Red
Uakari lived throughout an area extending from the
Amazon and Rio Yavari in eastern Peru to the south-
east of Brazil. Now it ranges from Rio della Amazzoni
to Putumayo, and this is reduced again to western
Brazil and eastern Peru where it seems to be confined to
the northern sectors of the Amazon region, limited to
low altitude areas – 300m (984ft) – along the banks of
the Rio Putumayo, Rio Napo and the lower reaches of
Rio Ucayali, and also along the Rio Madre de Dios.

Habitat. The uakari, a forest animal, is restricted to the
bands of the Amazon forest that are periodically flooded
along the river banks.

Population. The species remains rare throughout its
given area. Being tied to a certain environment restricts
any migration and prevents interchange between different populations, thus endangering the species. With
their natural habitat being destroyed and being unable
to transfer to another area, the groups are bound to
perish. The most serious threat comes from hunting;
despite being illegal, it is carried on clandestinely by
professional hunters and local settlers. Exploitation continues in spite of the loss of the important North
American market, import of the species now being prohibited. Between 1962 and 1968, 433 examples were
exported from Iquitos. Although protected by Brazilian
and Peruvian law, the uakari will not survive unless
reserves are immediately set up. In 1975 in 12 zoos there
were 13 males and 19 females – of these, 3 males and
2 females were born in captivity. There are possibly
9 more in other zoos.

Woolly Spider Monkey

(*Brachytelis qrachnoides*)

Class: Mammals Subclass: Eutheria Order: Primates
Suborder: Simiae Family: Cebidae
Subfamily: Atelinae Genus: *Brachyteles*
French: *Éroïde* Italian: *Brachitele* or *Atele ragno*
German: *Spinnenaffe*

Description. This monkey is 110–137cm (43–53in) in
length, of which 65–75cm (26–29in) is made up by the
tail. It has long limbs and a prehensile tail. The coat is
grey or brown; shades of yellow are more evident in the
male. The face is pink when the animal is young, and
turns dusky in adulthood. The hand has no thumb. The
movement is on all four limbs or by hanging from hand
to hand along tree branches. There are no records con-
cerning the biology of this species.
Geographic distribution. In Brazil, from the state of
Bahia to the state of São Paulo in the high forest areas
of the Sierra de Mar and the Sierra Mantiqueira and in
a few forest strips in the interior of the state of Minas
Gerais.
Habitat. Tropical coastal forest and mountainous rain
forest.
Population. The population is estimated at between
2,000 and 3,000. The habitat of the species is in a critical
situation because of the destruction of trees to clear the
land for cultivation and human population. Legal pro-

tection with regard to hunting is effective in limited
areas and there are restrictions on importation to the
USA and Britain. Small groups of spider monkeys live
in the parks of Itatiaia (Rio de Janeiro), Sierra dos
Orgaos (São Paulo), Rio Doce (Minas Gerais) and in
the Nova Lombardia Reserve (Espirito Santo). In 1975
the only Woolly Spider Monkey in captivity was a
single female in the São Paulo Zoo, in Brazil.

Douc Langur

(*Pygathrix nemaeus*)

Class: Mammals Subclass: Eutheria Order: Primates
Suborder: Simiae Family: Cercopithecidae
Genus: *Pygathrix*
French: *Douc* Italian: *Langur duca*
German: *Kleideraffe*

Description. It has an overall length of 117–152cm (44–
58in); 56–76cm (23–30in) of this is the tail. The species
is brightly coloured. Very little is known of their life and
behaviour.
Geographic distribution. Laos; Vietnam; Hawaii, between 8° and 23° latitude North and between 100° and
111° longitude East.
Habitat. Purely a forest animal – tropical rain forest up
to 2,000m (6,750ft) above sea level.
Population. There are no recent records. In Vietnam and
Laos the habitat has suffered for years from bombard-
ment, fires and devastation and by the disturbance
caused by troop movement, aircraft and shelling. Many
of the species have been killed for food. No conservation measures have been put in motion. In 1975 there
were 54 examples in 11 zoos (22 males, 32 females); 20
of them were born in captivity. There is no record of the
9 formerly in the zoo at Bangkok. It may perhaps be
possible to regenerate the species with those reared in zoos.

Lion-Tailed Macaque

(Macaca silensus)

Class: Mammals Subclass: Eutheria Order: Primates
Suborder: Simiae Family: Cercopithecidae
Genus: *Macaca*
French: *Macaque Ouanderou* Italian: *Sileno* or
Uanderú German: *Wanderu*

Description. Although not the largest representative of the *Macaca* genus, this monkey reaches a considerable size: the male is 1m (3¼ft) long and the female 78cm (2½ft); the tail takes up about two-fifths of this overall length. The coat is distinctive, being strongly marked in contrasting black and white. The whole appearance of the animal demands attention not only because of the luxuriant beard covering most of the face but also because of the alert and vivid expression of its bright brown eyes. The Lion-tailed Macaque's behaviour is similar to that of the majority of the tree-living species of the genus, as mentioned in modern text books. The old classic works based their descriptions on accounts obtained from the local Indian population and to a great extent derive from myth and religion.

Geographic distribution. In 1859 the species extended from Goa – to be more exact, from 14° latitude North – to Cape Comorin, occupying the entire region of western Ghats. Even then – according to contemporary accounts – it was limited to the remote forest zones, which were more widespread and numerous. Basically the area has not changed much. There is no precise data of the species being present north of 11° latitude North. Only one valid record gives a sighting on Anshi Ghat between Kadra and Kumbharwada (15° latitude North) at an altitude of around 300m (around 1,000ft) above sea-level.

Habitat. Evergreen forest up to an altitude of 600m (2,000ft) above sea-level. The species is strictly tied to a certain type of habitat and its existence relies on particular ecological conditions.

Population. A species seriously in danger. From data taken in a given section of their area (between 9°30′N and 11°30′N) and then applied proportionately to the whole area, it was estimated in 1968 that there were no more than 1,000. The numbers are still falling despite various measures taken to safeguard them. Several factors have contributed to the virtual destruction of the macaque: agricultural expansion of the tea and coffee plantations; the felling of trees to meet industrial demands for timber and for use by the local inhabitants as fuel; the replacement of native trees and shrubs by alien ones, such as the eucalyptus. Although the latter is perhaps a profitable exercise, it is foreign to the ecology of the Indian continent. Hunting, above all, has taken its toll – not only by catching the young macaques but also by killing the adults, especially the females. There was a commercial demand for the monkeys – charming as pets, they are especially endearing when young – but this has been stopped, mainly because their importation has been banned by the USA, formerly one of the most important markets. The hunting of all monkeys, including the Lion-tailed Macaque, has been banned in Madras, thus affording the species real protection. In the Periyar Wildlife Sanctuary too, it has found shelter and is said to be doing very well there. However, incidence of poaching by the natives is reportedly far too high. To ensure the survival of the species a comprehensive study of its ecology must be carried out to assess its tolerance to changes and environment, and consequently to calculate the effect of the introduction of exotic vegetation, and containing it accordingly. Current zoo-geographic studies will effectively chart the boundaries of the area inhabited by the species. The example of the United States in banning its importation must be followed by other countries. Surprisingly, Britain – usually in the forefront of wildlife preservation – has offered no direct protection to this species. Current legislation must be more rigidly observed; other more effective laws should be introduced. In 1975 there were in captivity 266 specimens (129 male, 136 female and 1 unknown) in 65 collections; of these, 155 were born in captivity. It might therefore be possible to save the species through intensive breeding and repopulation. However, a 1970 census on those in captivity in North America showed that the number of births hardly covered the total of deaths.

Golden Lion Marmoset

(Leontopithecus rosalia)

Class: Mammals Subclass: Eutheria Order: Primates
Suborder: Simiae Family: Callitricidae
Genus: *Leontopithecus*
French: *Petit singe-lion* Italian: *Leontocebo rosalia*
or *Scimmietta leonina*
German: *Goldgelbes Löwenäffchen*

Description. The Golden Lion Marmoset is 53–73cm
(21–29in) long, of which over half is the tail. In the
typical sub-species *Leontopithecus r. rosalia* (depicted
left) the long and silky coat is completely golden; in the
other sub-species, it is black with gold markings. The
face is a browny-black. The hand is prehensile, but the
tail, as with all the callitricidids, is not. The species live
in small groups. The period of gestation is not known.
It is fairly usual for twins to be born. The young are
suckled for three months and reach full size at one year.
Many modern authorities consider the three species
R. rosalia, *L. chrysonelas* and *L. chrysopyagus* to be sub-
species – classified as *L.r. rosalia*, *L.r. chrysonelas* and
L.r. chrysopyagus.

Geographic distribution. The species inhabited the forested coastal strip through the Brazilian states of Guanabara, Rio de Janeiro and (in the southern section)
Espirito Santo. Now it exists only in the 900sq km
(350sq miles) of forest remaining in the state of Rio de
Janeiro.

Habitat. Seasonal tropical forest with varied flora;
various combinations in different places. Throughout the
area the *Tapirira guianensis* is found; the marmoset is at
least partially dependent on this for food.

Population. In 1968 the number of lion marmosets in
the wild was estimated to be 600; in 1971 the estimate
was 400. The natural environment of the species has
been destroyed by the takeover of the plantations and
by urban encroachment. The most important home of
the lion marmoset – at Silva Jardim – is under sentence
of death; a bridge now connects the area with the city of
Rio de Janeiro, to turn it into a suburb. The protection
of the species by law and the ban on importation to the
USA and Britain, are not adequate measures to guarantee its survival. The Tijuca Bank of Lion Marmosets has
been set up; from this reserve the Tijuca National
Park in Rio de Janeiro will be repopulated. It will also
supervise the transfer of animals, whose former habitat
has been irrevocably destroyed, or which have been
confiscated after being caught illegally, to new areas
suited to the species. A reserve for the species has been
created at Poco das Antas (Silva Jardim) with an area of
3,000h (7,413 acres). In 1975 in 13 zoos, there were
45 males, 34 females and 1 whose sex was unknown;
55 of these were born in captivity. In the Bronx Zoo,
USA, a lion marmoset lived for 10 years and 4 months.

Pigmy Chimpanzee
(Pan paniscus)

Class: Mammals Subclass: Eutheria Order: Primates
Suborder: Simiae Family: Pongidae Genus: *Pan*
French: *Chimpansé nain* Italian: *Scimpanzé pigmeo*
or *Bonobo* German: *Zwergschimpanse*

Description. At one time all the *Pan* genus were subdivided into numerous species based on exterior characteristics that were highly variable and of negligible or non-existent systematic value. These species are now gathered into one: *Pan troglodytes*. However, it subsequently became clear that certain chimpanzees were set apart by their small size, their slim muzzle and the brownish-black coat with black face even in the young. Therefore, in 1929, a new species was recognized and called the Pigmy Chimpanzee. Its behaviour is very like that of the larger members of the species. As far as is known, the pigmy is social, living in groups of around thirty; these are in a state of continual change because as some leave the group others will join it.

Geographic distribution. West Central Africa, from the southern bank of the Congo river to the southern end of the Kasi river and Sankuru, along 8–9° latitude.

Habitat. In practical terms the species adapt themselves to prevailing conditions in their area: in the forest they are tree-living, but in the treeless savannah and scrubland with few plants they behave as if purely earthbound.

Population. There are no statistics on the population of the Pigmy Chimpanzee and the number in the wild has never been definitely recorded. As their habitat is increasingly occupied by man, the species' area is becoming very limited and it is easy to assume their numbers are dropping. The species is included in Class A of the African Convention of 1969 and is therefore protected from hunting. Effective control of the local population is impossible in the most remote sectors and inevitably killing continues. The USA and Britain have banned importation of the Pigmy Chimpanzee to their relative territories. Only with a fuller knowledge of the species will it be possible to give it sensible and valid protection. In 1975, in 7 zoos, there were 10 males and 18 females; 9 of these were born in captivity. It is probable that in case of necessity the species could be built up in this way.

Orang-Utan

(Pongo pygmaeus)

Class: Mammals Subclass: Eutheria Order: Primates
Suborder: Simiae Family: Pongidae Genus: *Pongo*
French: *Orang-outan* Italian: *Orang-utan*
German: *Orang-Utan*

Description. This is the only large anthropomorphic Asian monkey. Tree-living, the species adapted to the trees through a series of particular morphological characteristics of which they are the result. The front limbs are very long, with large hands and strong fingers. The finger-bones are curved to ensure a better grip on the branches. The hind limbs are short. Orang-utans can be 180cm (5ft 10in) in height. The average male stands about 137cm (4ft 5in) tall; the females are a little shorter. There is a marked difference in weight, however, the male being twice as heavy as the female. The male Sumatran orang-utan weighs around 70kg (155lb) and the female 37kg (83lb); the male from Borneo weighs up to 189kg (418lb) and the female 80kg (178lb). The hair is long; in the adult male it forms full side-whiskers together with a moustache and beard. The orang-utan is a variable yellow colour; the face is grey and has circular areas which are either naked or covered in short bristle. The adult male develops a large throat sac connected to the larynx, which aids voice projection. The orang-utan lives in families of two to four; sometimes an isolated male will live alone. They are tranquil animals, silent and usually shy. They move through the trees, mainly along branches by means of hand or foot. Their movements are agile but not acrobatic, the adults moving with slow assurance and without haste. On the ground the orang-utan goes along on the knuckles of the hand and the lateral edge of the feet, a most ponderous action as might be expected in a tree-living animal. Mating takes place at any time of the year. The gestation period is nine months. The new-born chimpanzee weighs a little under 1.5kg (3½lb). Maturity is reached at 7–10 years and the life-span may be 40 years or more. One pair in Philadelphia Zoo were 56 years old when they died in 1975! Two sub-species are recognized: *P.p. pygmaeus* (Borneon) and *P.p. abelii* (Sumatran) which differ in size and other minor morphological characteristics.

Geographic distribution. Sumatra (Atjeh, to the north of the Wampoe river, along the Simpang-Kanan and Peureulak rivers, the eastern coast between Menlaboh and Singkel) and Borneo (Sabah, Sandakan, Sarawak between the Sadong and the Butang Lupar rivers, to the south of the Rajang and Balek rivers, sources of the Balui and the Baram Kalimantan).

Habitat. Tree forest in the primary and secondary tropical rain forest.

Population. A very rough estimate puts the population of the species at 5,000–10,000. The density of population varies in different areas: on the plains the average is three animals per sq km; in the mountains, it is one per sq km. Over a large part of their area the density is more difficult to judge, so the population estimate is even less reliable. The species is in serious danger as a result of radical changes to its habitat and from hunting. The forest has been cleared for agricultural purposes and trees are being felled for timber. Mechanization has not only speeded these operations but has inflicted far more damage than the axe to the animals' habitat. Other activities linked to the timber industry have harmed the essential vegetation. The orang-utan is not a species which adapts to unsuitable conditions; in spite of the fact that it will perish in an area where the ecology is being changed, it cannot move elsewhere. To do so, the animals would have to pass over completely unsuitable territory and, in any case, could hardly find their way to a distant place of safety, whose existence or location is unknown to them. The orang-utan is protected by law. There are a small number of reserves in Sarawak, Sabah and Indonesia. Importation into the USA and Britain is prohibited. The International Union of Directors of Zoological Gardens has placed a voluntary control on the trading of orang-utans. The question of a sensible re-introduction on to reserves of those orang-utans confiscated from illegal hunters has been studied. But the capture of orang-utans – involving the crude killing of the mothers so as to take the young – continues in the remote areas. Besides this illegal trade, the slaughter of the animals for food has not been effectively prevented. In short, although conservation measures exist, they are inadequate. What is needed is not so much new schemes but the strengthening, widening and more efficient operation of the present ones. Above all, there must be rigid enforcement of the ban on trading and the severest penalties imposed for any contravention of the law. The number of reserves should be increased. In 1975, there were 307 males and 313 females in captivity, and possibly another 100 unconfirmed; 241 of these were born in captivity. Orang-utans will live in zoos quite contentedly with careful rearing based on exact feeding and controlled surroundings, without drawing on the natural environment of the species. Keeping them in captivity deprived of their basic needs should be prohibited.

Mountain Gorilla

(Gorilla gorilla beringei)

Class: Mammals Subclass: Eutheria Order: Primates Suborder: Simiae Family: Pongidae Genus: *Gorilla* French: *Gorille de montagne* Italian: *Gorilla di montagna* German: *Berggorilla*

Description. The Mountain Gorilla used to be considered a species by itself; but the characteristics on which this was based were hardly valid, and now it is thought by most authorities to be a simple sub-species. It has characteristics similar to the typical sub-species *Gorilla gorilla gorilla* (the Coastal Gorilla). The gorillas are the largest primates; on all fours, the male reaches a height of 1.75m (5ft 9in) – similar to, or even a little taller than, the average man. Standing erect, as it does very occasionally, the gorilla can be 2m (6ft 6½in) tall. The female is always smaller. She also weighs substantially less – 70–140kg (160–310lb) as against the male's 135–275kg (300–610lb). In captivity and in cases of obesity, a gorilla can turn the scales at 300kg (660lb) or even 350kg (770lb). Prolonged and accurate observation of gorillas in the wild has produced a lot of detailed information about their behaviour. They live in pairs, in families or even in quite large groups of up to thirty. Each community has its own territory but is not intolerant of others which cross into it. In the groups a third are males. Following a 9½-month pregnancy, the female gives birth to a single offspring which seems extraordinarily small beside its parents. It is suckled for 6 months, sometimes for a year, although from 2–3 months onwards it is taught to eat solid foods. In the wild, gorillas are vegetarian, preferring leaves, bark and shoots. Most of their food is bitter and fibrous. At night, the gorilla builds a nest out of branches roughly woven together. Unlike the chimpanzee, it does not know how to use wood or other objects as tools. The usual life-span of the species is 40 years but a gorilla in Philadelphia Zoo reached the age of 46 in 1977.

Geographic distribution. Burundi, Rwanda, Uganda, Zaïre. This vast area gives a false impression, however, as the sub-species is only present on the volcanic peaks of the Virunga range, and the massif of Mount Kahuzi; although these cover a number of states, the relevant territory is comparatively small.

Habitat. Mountain rain forest to a considerable height In some areas (Kahuzi-Biega National Park in Zaïre) Mountain Gorillas also live in secondary forests. The principal vegetation of their habitat is bamboo, *Hypericum*, *Hagenia*, giant seneci – altogether a rough, impoverished source of food.

Population. In 1971 the sub-species had an estimated population of 1,000 in the wild; 200–250 in the Kahuzi-Biega National Park and 375–400 in the Mount Virunga zone. While the Kahuzi-Biega population has remained much the same, by 1972 the Virunga count showed a drop in numbers to crisis point because of the interference of man, and in 1974 the estimate was down to 272. Obviously the animal is in great danger even though a large part of its territory was made into a national park. Man's occupation and exploitation of the species' habitat remains a problem. Those in search of grain, wood, coal and contraband interfere with the gorilla groups. The herds of animals kept by the Watussi on the woody pastures present direct competition. Poaching has caused buffalo and elephant to migrate to places where they consume the gorilla's food resources. In 1969 10,000h (24,700 acres) of the Parc des Volcans in Rwanda were given over to pyrethrum cultivation, thus altering the botanical environment and bringing in more human occupation than was compatible with the requirements of a nature reserve. The present Rwanda government is striving to make up for the errors of its predecessors. There are only four national parks and reserves that contain Mountain Gorillas: Virunga and Kahuzi-Biega (Zaïre), Parc des Volcans (Rwanda) and the Gorilla Game Reserve (Uganda). Those in Zaïre are satisfactorily administered, but elsewhere are conducted less efficiently. The laws must be enforced more rigidly, and additional protected areas, with conditions suitable to new populations of the species, should be designated. The ban on the hunting and import and export of the Mountain Gorilla must be firmly implemented, and all illegal trade wiped out. In 1975, 14 Mountain Gorillas – 5 males and 9 females – were registered in 5 zoos: at Antwerp, Chester, Cologne, Edmonton in Canada, and Oklahoma City, USA. Only one of these specimens was born in captivity – at Antwerp in 1968. It is thought, however, that they could be bred as successfully as the similar Coastal Gorilla, 136 of which had been born in captivity by 1975 – 100 of these were live births; the first was in Columbus Zoo in 1956.

Giant Armadillo
(Priodontes giganteus)

Class: Mammals Subclass: Eutheria Order: Edentata (Edentates) Suborder: Xenarthra
Family: Dasypodidae (Armadillos) Genus: *Priodontes*
French: *Tatou géant* Italian: *Armadillo gigante*
German: *Riesengürteltier*

Description. The Giant Armadillo is the largest and most rare of the twenty species of armadillo, reaching 1.5m (4ft 10in) in length, of which 50cm (19in) is the tail, and weighing 50kg (110lb). The upper part of the body is covered with curved armour-plating composed of buckler-like plates and movable transverse bands growing towards the stomach. Owing to the flexibility of this structure and the strong cutaneous muscles, the armadillo can curl up completely; when in danger, it rolls itself into a tight ball which not even a jaguar can open. The smooth rectangular armour plates are sparsely covered with hair. Their colour varies from yellow-beige to brown. The ears are large and rounded, and the skull heavy. The muzzle is larger than that of other armadillos. The hind legs are very large, with blunt nails on all five toes. The forelegs are specially adapted to digging and four of the digits have long curved claws; the fifth digit has a massive claw – larger than that of any other animal. This claw is used to break open termite nests; the armadillo extracts the insects, its principal food, by means of its long cylindrical sticky tongue. When attacking the termites' stronghold with its claws, the armadillo supports itself on its hind legs and muscular tail. The strong claws also provide it with an alternative means of defence – safer than that of rolling itself up into a ball. It can dig a hole in the ground with incredible speed and disappear inside it within a few seconds. The Giant Armadillo digs a hole large enough for a man to crawl into. It is a nocturnal animal, seldom entering areas inhabited by man and only rarely crossing his path. The Brazilian natives kill the animal not so much for food but because it damages cultivated land. The name 'armadillo', which is given to all the species of the Dasypodidae family, derives from the Spanish *armadillos*, meaning 'little armed ones'. In French they are called *tatou* after their local name *tatu*.

Geographic distribution. The Giant Armadillo has a very wide area of distribution – from Colombia and Venezuela to the south-east of the Andes as far as Amazonian areas of Peru and northern Argentina, including almost the whole of Brazil and the areas immediately to its west, north and south.

Habitat. The species is very rare within a vast territory. It likes the dense forest of the Amazon and the Mato Grosso, far from the vicinity of man. It passes the day hidden in a den dug between huge tree roots in terrain which is not liable to flood.

Population. The species is in a vulnerable situation. Its numbers have much diminished or been wiped out in almost the whole of its territory. Apart from persecution by the natives, it is now threatened by canal and irrigation projects. The principal causes of its decline are agriculture, sheep rearing and tree felling. Its population in the wild is not known. It is protected in Argentina by a 1928 law prohibiting its slaughter or capture. In Paraguay it can only be hunted between March and September. In the other countries there is no protection. The only reserve is the Macavena in Colombia. If the species is to survive, it must be protected by law in all the countries where it lives, and part of its already reduced habitat should be transformed into parks or reserves. It is rarely to be found in captivity, where it seldom survives longer than 3–4 years. One example in Berlin Zoo lived for 7 years. In 1975 there were only 10 specimens in 5 zoos – at Antwerp; Duisburg and Neuwied, in Germany; Chicago and Oklahoma City, USA.

Giant Anteater
(Mirmecophaga tridactyla)

Class: Mammals Subclass: Eutheria Order: Edentata
Family: Myrmecophagidae Genus: *Myrmecophaga*
French: *Grand fourmilier* Italian: *Formichiere gigante*
German: *Grösser Ameisenbär*

Description. The Giant Anteater, also known as the yurumi, is about the size of a large dog. Its overall length may exceed 2m (6ft 6in), including the tail of 80cm (2ft 6in). The male weighs 55kg (120lb). Its physical characteristics are extraordinary. The very long head leads to an equally long conical muzzle which gently curves towards the tip. At the extreme end of this is the mouth which is only 2cm ($\frac{3}{4}$in) in diameter, while the very flexible tongue is at least 1cm ($\frac{3}{8}$in) wide and 50cm (20in) long. There are no teeth and the mandible is hardly jointed. The thick, strong forelegs are relatively short. The hands have fingers armed with powerful nails, the nail on the third digit being of exceptional length – 7cm (nearly 3in). Because of the shape of the hand and the length of the nail, the anteater walks with its fist closed, the outer edge placed on the ground being protected by a callous growth. The coat, very rough and bristly, is short on the head, long on the neck, and forms a sort of mane along the line of the vertebrae. On the animal's sides, forelegs and tail the hair is long enough to hang like a fringe. The basic food is insects, particularly ants and termites; these are retrieved by means of the long sticky tongue after the nest has been broken down by the strong claws. The anteater hunts at night and spends the day in a hole in between shrubs, covered by its tail. It is a timid creature, but can defend itself by striking with its claws. The female gives birth to a single young in the spring.

Geographic distribution. Southern America, from Costarica al Gran Chaco to northern Argentina.

Habitat. The species lives in both the savannah and dense forest.

Population. The population is not known, but the species has undoubtedly disappeared from areas that have been developed – as has happened in Argentina, Brazil and Peru, where it is only surviving in places so far left untouched. Wherever it is present in national parks, the species is protected by special laws; nevertheless there remains the risk of extinction through the continuing advance of civilization and the difficulty of imposing the laws. In 1975 there were 166 examples in 77 zoos.

Chinchilla

(Chinchilla laniger)

Class: Mammals Subclass: Eutheria Order: Rodentia
(Rodents) Suborder: Caviomorpha (Cavies)
Family: Chinchillidae Genus: *Chinchilla*
French: *Chinchilla* Italian: *Cincillà lanigero*
German: *Chinchilla*

Description. The chinchilla is halfway between a mouse
and a rabbit. It measures 25–26cm (10in) and has a
17–18cm (7in) tail. The extreme thickness of the coat
makes the fur very valuable. With eighty hairs per
follicle, it is five hundred times finer than human hair.
Chinchillas reproduce three times a year, with one to six
young in each litter. They can live up to eighteen years.
Geographic distribution. At the time of the Spanish con-
quests the chinchilla was common in Bolivia, Peru,
Chile and the Argentine from the slopes of the Andes to
the coast. Now it exists only in Chile and Bolivia.
Habitat. The inaccessible and arid zones of the Andes,
at altitudes of 3,000–6,000m (9,800–19,500ft).
Population. Hunted by the Incas, who fashioned the
finest cloth from its fur, the chinchilla was nearly
exterminated between 1800 and 1900 because of the increasing value of its fur. There remain isolated colonies
whose population is unknown. It is possible they are
increasing in Chile.

Kaibab Squirrel

(Sciurus Raibabensis)

Class: Mammals Subclass: Eutheria Order: Rodentia
(Rodents) Suborder: Sciuromorpha (Sciurids)
Family: Sciuroidea Genus: *Sciurus* (Red Squirrels)
French: *Ecureuil di Kaibab* Italian: *Scoiattolo del
Kaibab* German: *Kaibab-Hörnchen*

Description. The Kaibab Squirrel is roughly the same
size as the North American Grey Squirrel, which is the
largest and strongest of the Euro-Asian squirrels. The
Kaibab Squirrel is grizzled grey-brown, with shades of
browny-red; its underside is black. The ears are adorned
with long tufts of dark hair. The tail, large and thick, is
white with an indistinct grey stripe along the top.
Geographic distribution. Exclusively inhabits the Kaibab
Plateau in Colorado, USA, on the northern side of the
Grand Canyon. Within an area covering 50 by 115km
(30 by 70 miles) inside a national park.
Habitat. Oak and yellow pine forest. They feed exclusively off the bark of the yellow pine.
Population. Isolated for a million years because of the
insurpassable Grand Canyon, the species is different
from any other squirrel – those on the other side of the
Canyon do not have the white tail. Today there are no
more than 1,000; they are in danger of extinction
because of the decline of the yellow pine which has been
cleared for fire-prevention measures.

European Beaver

(Castor fiber)

Class: Mammals Subclass: Eutheria Order: Rodentia (Rodents) Suborder: Sciuromorpha (Sciurids) Family: Castoridae Genus: *Castor* French: *Castor d'Europe* Italian: *Castoro europeo* German: *Europäischer Biber*

Description. The beaver, with its massive body, is one of the largest rodents. The European Beaver and the Canadian Beaver are so alike that the most recent classifications show them as one species with listed sub-species. The European Beaver measures up to 1.3m (4¼ft), including 30cm (1ft) for the tail, and can weigh up to 30kg (66lb). The hind legs have digits linked with membrane for swimming; the forelegs are like arms and have prehensile digits. The ears are semi-hidden in fur and can be closed hermetically, as can the nostrils, when the beaver swims under water. The coat consists of two different types of fur: one is dark, thick and downy, while the other is tough, long and bristle-like. The tail, which is 12–15cm (5–6in) wide and shaped like a spatula, is scaly and hairless. It is used basically as a rudder or for kneading the mud when building dams. The incisors are chisel-shaped, of continuous growth and covered in yellow enamel. The beaver moves clumsily on land, but is an agile swimmer. It feeds on meat, shrubs and water-lily roots in summer and fresh bark in winter. They have a lifespan of fifteen years; one example in a zoo reached the age of thirty.

Geographic distribution. Originally spread all over Europe East of the Pyrenees and a good part of central-northern Asia, today only a few survive in protected areas – at the base of the Roclanes in France, along the Elbe river in Germany, in Scandinavia, Poland and Russia.

Habitat. The beaver lives in the wooded flats along torrential rivers and lakes. Their burrows are dug through the banks with two openings under water. In dry periods, the beavers build dams – using logs gnawed by their teeth, stones and mud – to prevent the water falling below the level of their entrance holes.

Population. The European Beaver, although not in immediate danger of extinction, has been greatly reduced in numbers as a result of being hunted for its valuable fur. The populations of the various countries are numbered only in hundreds. European Beavers were recently reintroduced into Switzerland where they had been extinct since 1820. The Canadian Beaver is more often found in zoos, as the European Beaver does not reproduce easily in captivity.

Indus Dolphin
(Platanista indi)

Class: Mammals Subclass: Eutheria Order: Cetacea (Whales) Suborder: Odontoceti (Toothed Whales) Family: Platanistidae Genus: *Platanista* French: *Dauphin de l'Indus* Italian: *Platanista dell'Indo* German: *Indus-Delphin*

Description. The Indus Dolphin differs from the similar Ganges Dolphin only in some characteristics of the skull. The Indus Dolphin is only 2–3m (7–10ft) long, but there is a record of a female of 4m (13ft). The eyes are very small, the pectoral fins are short and fan-shaped, the dorsal fin is flattened. The beak-shaped muzzle is 18–20cm (7–8in) long and narrow. There are 28–29 teeth on each side of the jawbones. The forehead is almost vertical to the base of the beak. It is lead to blackish grey in colour, the underneath being slightly lighter. A freshwater dolphin, it comes up for air at thirty-second to two-minute intervals. Strange and inoffensive, it lives in groups of three to ten or even more Being blind, it searches for fish, crustaceans and other organisms on the river-bed by means of its sensitive muzzle. The female produces one offspring after a gestation period of eight or nine months. At birth the young is about 45cm (18in) long and weighs 7kg (15 lb).

Geographic distribution. Until the middle of the nineteenth century the dolphin was spread throughout the Indus and its principal tributaries as far as the river mouth. Now it exists only in certain limited parts of the Indus, especially between the Sukkure and Guddu dams and in the artificial basins created by dams in the tributary. They are sometimes also found in irrigation canals.

Habitat. The species prefers turbid water where the river current is rather slow. By day they stay in deep water but at night they go to the shallower water near the banks to search for fish and shrimps. Their habitat has been progressively reduced because of the increasing amount of water which is being drawn from the rivers for irrigation and hydroelectricity (there are already six hydroelectric plants on the Indus and ten on its tributaries).

Population. The number of surviving Indus Dolphins is not known, but is estimated at between 700 and 1,000. It has been protected in some zones since 1972 but is still occasionally hunted by fishermen, and is sometimes caught in their nets. In 1974 the World Wildlife Fund together with the Indian authorities organized an expedition to create a reserve of 75km (47 miles) of the Indus in the Sind province, downstream from the Guddu Dam, where the dolphin is most common.

Blue Whale

(Balaenoptera musculus)

Class: Mammals Subclass: Eutheria Order: Cetacea (Whales) Suborder: Mystacoceti (Baleen Whales) Family: Balaenopteridae (Fin Whales)
Genus: *Balaenoptera*
French: *Balénoptère bleu* Italian: *Balenottera azzurra*
German: *Blauwal*

Description. The Blue Whale is the largest animal on earth. It is larger than thirty elephants or three of the largest dinosaurs. It is heavier than 2,000 men; its heart weighs 550kg (1,200lb), its liver a ton, and its tongue 350kg (775lb). This whale (illustrated with Killer Whales) can measure 30m (100ft) in length and weigh 150 tons. The largest Blue Whale recorded, which measured 33.27m (109ft), was captured near Shetland, Australia. The heaviest, which weighed 200 tons, was a female killed in 1924 in Walvis Bay in south-west Africa. Its most salient characteristic are the folds of skin which run along the throat and chest which enable the whale to open its mouth very wide and swallow vast quantities of water rich with plankton. When the mouth is almost completely shut, the lower part of the mouth cavity contracts again, pushing the tongue against the palate and forcing the water to gush out sideways. Instead of teeth, specially laminated bones with fringed borders frame the upper jaw; these function as a sieve and trap the food – principally 'krill' (*Euphausia superba*) a form of shrimp. Hunters have found up to two tons of krill in the stomach of a dead whale. The Blue Whale has neither a sense of smell nor acute vision, but has excellent hearing. As all whales, it can identify objects by sending out precise cries and measuring the echoes. It breathes through its lungs and has two blow-holes for nostrils on the top of the head. It surfaces every ten to fifteen minutes for air and its warm breath forms spray on contact with the cold air, sending a jet up to 6m (20ft) high. After breathing three to eight times it submerges again. It is also named the 'winged whale' because its front fins, which are used to direct and stabilize, are one-seventh of the body-length. The powerful tail undulates from top to bottom and gives the whale a surface cruising speed of 8–21km (4–13 miles) per hour; when chased, the animal can travel at 33km (20 miles) per hour, and maintain that speed for twenty minutes. The name 'Blue Whale' comes from its blue back and sides. After ten or eleven months of gestation, the female produces one offspring measuring 7–8m (23–26ft) at birth and weighing up to 3 tons. The foetus increases by 7kg (15lb) a day from conception to birth. The young is suckled by its mother for six or seven months and drinks up to 490l (130gal) a day; the mother's udder muscles contract so that her milk can be pumped into the offspring's mouth. At this rate, the young increases at around 90kg (200lb) a day. In the first twenty-three months (of which 11 are the gestation period) the young whale grows to a weight of 26 tons. During the suckling

period the mother produces an amount of milk equal to her own weight and loses a third of her weight in order to do this. At six to seven months the young measures 16m (52ft). As the period from conception to weaning takes eighteen to nineteen months, the female only produces every two years. A sub-species called the Minor Blue Whale (*Balaenoptera musculus brevicauda*) measures 20m (66ft) in length (maximum 24m (79ft)).

Geographic distribution. Atlantic, Pacific and Indian Oceans; more abundant in the Southern than the Northern Hemisphere. It is principally found in the southern part of the Indian Ocean.

Habitat. Oceanic. The Blue Whale migrates from the summer feeding grounds in the polar waters which are rich in plankton and where the krill spread in bands of 10m (30ft), to their winter breeding grounds in temperate waters.

Population. The decline in numbers of the Blue Whale began in 1865 with the introduction of cannons which shot fire-charged harpoons and with the advent of steam whaling-ships. This has been accelerated by the development of the fishing ship which can hoist the whale on board and process it totally for its products in one hour. One Blue Whale constitutes 27 per cent fat, which can give from 140,000 to 150,000l (37,000–40,000gal) oil, 30 per cent meat and 18 per cent bone which is powdered and used as fertilizer. In 1934–5, 16,500 Blue Whales and 12,500 Fin Whales were killed in the Antarctic, compared with 1,800 other species. In 1960–1, however, only 1,744 Blue Whales were killed in the same area. Today, the species is rigidly protected by international law (in the Atlantic since 1960, in the Antarctic since 1965, in the Pacific since 1966 and throughout the world since 1967). Since 1969 importation of any types of product from any whale is prohibited in the USA. The world population of Blue Whales was probably between 200,000 and 300,000 of which 10,000 were the sub-species. In 1963 this was reduced to 4,000. Today, thanks to complete protection, it is possible that the species is increasing. There are possibly a few hundred in the North Atlantic; an uncertain number, around a few thousand, in the northern Pacific; and approximately 6,000, of which 2,000–3,000 are the sub-species, in the Antarctic.

Finback Whale
or Common Rorqual
(Balaenoptera physalus)

Class: Mammals Subclass: Eutheria Order: Cetacea
(Whales) Suborder: Mystacoceti (Baleen Whales)
Family: *Balaenopteridae* Genus: *Balaenoptera*
French: *Rorqual commun* Italian: *Balenottera comune*
German: *Finnwal*

Description. The Finback Whale is the second largest
animal after the Blue Whale. The average length is
18–24m (60–80ft) but some measure over 27m (90ft).
This species is slimmer than other whales and swims very
fast. The back part of the body is supple and streamlined. The pectoral fins are small and measure only
one-ninth of the body's length. The dorsal fin is large
and triangular. The colouring is strangely asymmetrical:
the dark colour on the back is more accentuated and
wider towards the abdomen on the left side than on the
right; the right mandible is a whitish colour on the
outside and dark on the inside, while the left mandible
is the opposite (detail below); the left half of the tongue
is white. The 'whale-bones' (the horny, elastic substance
hanging from the upper jaw) are blue-grey on the outside edge on the left, while on the right they are white in
front and blue-grey behind. The throat and chest have
the skin folds characteristic of all the Balaenopteridae.
It has the same reproductive cycle as the Blue Whale.
The life-span is supposedly twenty to thirty years. The
Finback Whale enjoys leaping entirely out of the water,
like Humpback Whales, rising over the waves and high
spray. Unlike other whales which live alone or in pairs,
the Finback Whale lives in groups of fifteen or sixteen,
or even more. Like the Blue Whale its principal food is
the krill (*Euphausia superba*) of which it prefers the
young shoals.

Geographic distribution. All oceans from the equatorial
to the polar waters. Larger Finback Whales tend to live
near the poles.

Habitat. Finback Whales generally keep to the deep
ocean waters, rarely approaching coastal waters.

Population. Intense hunting, particularly in the course
of this century, has notably reduced the numbers.
Hunting is still permitted, although the number legally
killed is such that the species can still survive and
increase. It is estimated that there are today around
7,000 in the north Atlantic, 15,000 in the northern
Pacific (there were 43,500) and 77,000 in the Southern
Hemisphere (where there were originally 380,000!).
Since 1935 hunting of mothers with young has been
prohibited.

Humpback Whale

(Megaptera novaeangliae)

Class: Mammal Subclass: Eutheria Order: Cetacea (Whales) Suborder: Mystacoceti (Baleen Whales) Family: Balaenopteridae (Fin Whales) Genus: *Megaptera* French: *Megaptère* Italian: *Megattera* German: *Buckelwal*

Description. The Humpback Whale is far more squat than the other balenopterids. Its length varies from 12–15m (45ft) (maximum 20m (65ft)) and its back is noticeably streamlined. The pectoral fins are very large, about 1m (3ft) wide and 4–5m (13–16ft) long. Numerous series of cutaneous tubercules, some with bristles, cover the top of the head and jawbone; 14–20 deep furrows – the cutaneous folds of all Balaenopteridae – run from the jaw to the navel. These enable the Humpback Whale to open its mouth very wide so that the water which is taken in can be expelled while the 'whale-bones' trap the food – molluscs, crustaceans and small fish. The adult Humpback Whale weighs 30–40 tons (maximum 64 tons). In spite of its weight and huge bulk it is most agile and fond of games, and leaps high out of the water like the dolphin, diving back with an enormous splash. When courting, the male and female swim side by side, knocking against each other with their long pectoral fins and leaping continuously. The young are 4–5m (12–16ft) at birth and are suckled for about six months. The humpbacks are the most sonorous of the Balaenoptera; when emitting air through the blow-holes they produce a siren-like sound. They are black on the back and sides, white on the belly and inside of the fins, and sometimes mottled black and white near the tail.

Geographic distribution. There are two populations of Humpback Whales throughout the oceans of the world – one in the Northern Hemisphere and the other in the Southern Hemisphere – and there is little exchange between them.

Habitat. Unlike other whales which always live in the deep sea, the Humpback Whales have a predeliction for coastal waters up to the entrances of bays and ports and sometimes the mouth of a large river. They migrate seasonally from cold waters in winter to warm waters in which they reproduce in summer. They travel in large groups.

Population. Agile and mobile, the Humpback was formerly the most difficult whale to hunt. It was not until this century, therefore, that their numbers rapidly declined. It is estimated that in 1930 there were still around 22,000, while in 1956 they had been reduced to less than 3,000. Today, they are totally protected by international laws (in the North Atlantic in 1955, in the Australian seas in 1960, and in the northern Pacific in 1966), and the number has risen to between 7,000 and 8,000. They seem to be increasing principally in the North Atlantic. Their coastal prevalence makes them prey to the dangers of pollution.

Greenland Right Whale
or Bowhead

(Balaena mysticetus)

Class: Mammals Subclass: Eutheria Order: Cetacae (Whales) Suborder: Mysticeti Family: Balaenidae Genus: *Balaena*
French: *Baleine boréale* Italian: *Balena boreale* or *Balena franca* German: *Grönlandwal*

Description. The Greenland Right Whale has an extraordinarily squat body. The head takes up one-third of its total length. The mouth is huge, measuring 5–6m (16–20ft) long and 3m (10ft) wide, with enormous lips which cover the jawbone and also completely cover the 'whale-bones'. There are 300–360 whale-bones on each side and a single one can be 4.5m (15ft) long, 25–30cm (10–12in) wide and weigh 3kg (6½lb). The upper lip is distinctly arched. The blow-holes are two narrow fissures measuring 45cm (18in) in length and are placed at the highest part of the head, about 3m (10ft) from the tip of the muzzle. The eyes, which see better underwater than above, are very small in proportion to the rest of the head and are directly over the corner of the jaw. The hearing pipes are directly behind the eyes and are no larger than a pencil's diameter. The edges of the jawbone are covered in short, rough, white hairs. The tail fin is 2m (6½ft) long and 6–8m (20–26ft) wide; there is no dorsal fin. The species grows up to 20m (66ft) in length and weighs up to 83 tons. In common with other whales, a strip measuring 20–45cm (8–18in) of fat (blubber) lies under the smooth skin. The basic colour of the body is blue-black but adults have a grey-white stain on the muzzle. The axillary region and the junction of the caudal fin is greyish. A similar species and equally rare is the Black, or Ice, Whale (*Eubalaena glacialis*) which is divided into three sub-species: the Basque, Japanese and Australian, which in some classifications rank a species by themselves. In the Japanese sub-species, the Black Whale is up to 20m (66ft) long. The head, which is a quarter of the total length, is smaller than the Greenland Right Whale's; the 'whale-bones' are no longer than 3.5m (11½ft). There are white areas on the skin housing parasites; on the jawbones is a horny excrescence, 20 by 30cm (8 by 12in), completely covered in small crustaceans. Correctly, these whales belong to the genera *Balaena* and *Eubalaena* which are called Right Whales because, due to their huge bulk and slowness compared with the balaenopterids, they were the 'right' whales to hunt when whalers pursued these great creatures in rowing boats.

Geographic distribution. The Greenland Right Whale is virtually confined to the Arctic Ocean in four isolated groups, though it has reappeared in the Sea of Japan where it was thought to be extinct. The Black Whale is found in the North Atlantic and northern Pacific as far as Formosa in the winter and in the Southern Hemisphere between 30° and 50° latitude south.

Habitat. The Greenland Right Whale lives in arctic waters between huge icebergs that sometimes directly block its passage from one feeding ground to another. The Black Whale lives in temperate waters.

Population. The Greenland Right Whale was almost exterminated in the nineteenth century and has been totally protected by international law since the end of 1935, apart from a small number which are legally killed by Eskimos. It seems that they are now increasing in the Pacific area and are slowly increasing in the Atlantic. The total population is put at a few thousand. The Black Whale has also been protected since 1935. This species was intensely hunted in the eighteenth and nineteenth centuries principally because of its presence in temperate waters, its large rendering of oil and the fact that, once killed, the carcass floated. It is now increasing slowly, both in the western part of the North Atlantic and in the Southern Hemisphere. Altogether there must be a few thousand. The importation into the USA of all products from whales has been prohibited since 1969. The International Whaling Commission is the organ of international control which fixes each year the number of captures allowed for all species. It established in 1972 a scheme of international control whereby both whaling fleets and whaling stations on land respect the prohibition on hunting the Greenland Right Whale and the Black Whale.

Wolf
(Canis lupus)

Class: Mammals Subclass: Eutheria Order: Carnivora
Suborder: Fissipedia (Terrestrial carnivores)
Family: Canidae Subfamily: Canid Genus: *Canis*
French: *Loup* Italian: *Lupo* German: *Wolf*

Description. The wolf looks very like the German Shepherd Dog (Alsatian) and its size varies from individual to individual. Some authorities divide the wolf into sub-species according to geographic distribution. The male can grow up to 85cm (34in) in height and 1.70m (5½ft) in length, of which 40–45cm (16–18in) belong to the tail. It weighs 80kg (175lb). It has an agile body with a broad chest and hollow sides. In profile, the back tends to slant towards the rear and the tail is usually carried low with a gentle curve. The large head is wide at the beginning of the jaw, diminishing to a point, and in profile almost in line with the head. The teeth, unlike those of most other Canidae, are extremely powerful; it is said they can shatter the femur of an elk in one bite. The colour varies (there are dark, almost black wolves found in the south, and grey, almost white ones in the north). The coat is fairly short but in cold regions it is thicker with a ruff around the neck and very thick on the belly and haunches. The wolf is generally gregarious and lives off prey which it hunts in packs. As it always takes as prey the oldest, most ill and debilitated, it can be argued that the wolf performs a purification of the species which it hunts. It seems from various studies that its social organization is similar to man's. According to W. Herre, it is likely that its dependence on a particular type of food signifies one of the most evolved forms of organization among mammals. The prey, in fact, consists of medium to large animals, roe-deer or elk, depending on the area of distribution. In order to pursue and kill their prey collectively, the individual wolves have concord, communication and a division of labour between them. The pack leader is usually an adult male, and his main function is to maintain order and respect for the various grades of the hierarchy – he does not necessarily lead the pack. The physical leading may be delegated to another, even a female. The mating season is between February and April, depending on the latitude. The hierarchy is respected with regard to mating and it is very difficult for a male wolf of a lower rank to find a mate if there are others of a higher rank around. The gestation period is nine weeks, at the end of which the female gives birth to between three and ten pups, blind, helpless and unable to move. The birth takes place in a sheltered, secure lair perhaps adapted by the female from a fox's or beaver's abandoned lair. After the first eight weeks of milk-feeding, rearing is also undertaken by the father and even by other young, usually female members of the pack. The young reach full size after one year and sexual maturity after three years. The wolf can live for up to ten years in the wild with difficulty, but in captivity, as with domestic dogs, they can live longer. There are frequent cases of reproduction in captivity.

Geographic distribution. The distribution of the wolf and all sub-species still covers a large part of North America, a number of European countries (it is extinct in England, Holland, Belgium, Denmark, France, Germany, Switzerland, Austria and Hungary), and Asia, particularly in the centre and north.

Habitat. The wolf lives in many different habitats and at different altitudes. It can be found in tundra, bush, evergreen or deciduous forest, open country or near towns in cultivated inhabited areas.

Population. The wolf has been reduced in numbers everywhere. It is, however, still quite common in Alaska, Canada and parts of Russia and Asia. The numbers vary according to the sub-species and species; *Canis lupus irremotus*, for example, seems to have only a few dozen left in a part of its original territory in North America. Another, *Canis lupus rufus*, the red wolf, again North American, has been reduced to about 200. A pack numbering between 80 and 120 of the species of *Canis lupus italicus* (a wolf from the Apennines) has been observed prowling the Roman countryside. The principal reason for the wolf's disappearance is the relentless hunting that man has continually waged against it with traps, guns, snares and poison. The disappearance of game – again destroyed by man – which was part of the wolf's diet, has also aided its decline. Today the wolf is rigidly protected in many countries; a number also live in national parks and zoos.

Maned Wolf

(Chrysocyon brachyurus)

Class: Mammals Subclass: Eutheria Order: Carnivora
Suborder: Fissipedia Family: Canidae
Subfamily: Canid Genus: *Chrysocyon*
French: *Loup à crinière* Italian: *Crisocione* or
Lupo dalla criniera German: *Mähnenwolf*

Description. The Maned Wolf is the largest and most beautiful of the numerous South American Canidae. It is 1.35–1.45m (4–5ft) long including the 40cm (16in) long tail, and is 85cm (33in) tall at the shoulders. It weighs 20–23kg (44–51lb). The name 'Maned Wolf' is strictly incorrect as it has no kindred link with the wolf. In proportion to the body the head is small, and has a long muzzle. The ears are straight and tent-shaped. The eyes are large and slanting, but their meek expression is unusual for a wild carnivore. The coat is thick and soft; on the nape of the neck and back it forms a visible black mane. It is red-brown to golden red on the back and sides, black around the mouth and base of the neck and limbs, and white on the throat. The tail ends in a white quiff, and is short and wide – hence the name *brachyurus*. The limbs are exceptionally long and thin which enable the Maned Wolf to successfully hunt its prey in the grass steppes. It eats guinea pigs and other small rodents, occasionally birds, and even fruit and nuts. The large molars demonstrate adaptation to a partly vegetarian diet. In marshy areas it also eats snails, lizards, locusts and toads. It never chases its prey because it does not have sufficient endurance. It has a rolling gait and does, in fact, 'pace', lifting two legs on one side and then two legs on the other. When this becomes a trot the head falls in line with the body. It is a solitary animal which seeks company only at the mating season and in order to bring up its young. The gestation period is just over two months after which two to five young are born. These weigh 500g (1lb) at birth and are covered in dark grey fur. Their life-span is roughly the same as that of a wolf or dog. One lived to be over ten years old in a Washington zoo.

Geographic distribution. The interior of Brazil from the state of Piaui to Rio Grande do Sul and Mato Grosso. It is also probably present in the extreme eastern zones of Bolivia, Paraguay and northern Argentina. Until the nineteenth century it also lived south of Rio de la Plata and in the interior of Uruguay.

Habitat. The steppe and semi-desert zones of Chaco in Paraguay and the forests of the Mato Grosso in Brazil.

Population. The position of the Maned Wolf is most vulnerable. It is very rare and its survival in Argentina is precarious. It is, however, moderately secure in the Paraguayan Chaco and in the Mato Grosso. It is protected only in a few parks and reserves. It is a very timid animal and retreats from the fronts of civilization and from the exploitation of the forests which protected its habitat. Basing the calculation on the number caught in 1964–7 it can be estimated that in a given area of 650,000 sq km (250,000 sq miles) in Brazil there are between 1,500 and 2,200. They are principally concentrated on the plateau of central Brazil or on the Mato Grosso. It is one of the animals most coveted by zoos. In 1974 there were only about 60 in 21 zoos; 20 were born in captivity. San Diego Zoo, California, first bred them successfully in captivity in (1963–4) but the young were abandoned by the mother and did not survive. The first successful rearing of young by the mother in captivity was in Frankfurt Zoo, 1967. There are now three or four births a year in zoos, but frequently the young do not survive.

Spectacled Bear

(Tremarctos ornatus)

Class: Mammals Subclass: Eutheria Order: Carnivora
Suborder: Fissipedia Family: Ursidae
Subfamily: Tremarctinae Genus: *Tremarctus*
French: *Ours à lunettes* Italian: *Orso dagli occhiali*
German: *Brillenbär*

Description. The Spectacled Bear is now the only representative of the subfamily Tremarctinae which was common in the Americas during the Ice Age. The male is larger than the female reaching 1.40m (4½ft) in length and 80cm (31in) in height. It weighs 130kg (287lb), the female 60–65kg (132–143lb). The principal characteristic that differentiates this bear from other black bears is the whitish or yellowish mask that adorns the muzzle. The mask starts at the base of the nose, turns in towards the eyes, almost covers the forehead, runs down the sides of the cheeks and meets again under the throat on the chest (illustrated below). The species can be either solitary or gregarious, but in the latter case generally only in family groups. Its diet consists mainly of vegetables and fruit. Its climbing ability is specially developed for picking the latter. However, it does not refrain entirely from eating meat and kills wild animals, cattle or llamas with blows from its strong legs. The gestation period is eight months after which the female produces three young. The first Spectacled Bear to be born in captivity was in Buenos Aires Zoo, July 1947; another was born in a zoo in 1953. Today, there are many zoos that can claim its reproduction.

Geographic distribution. The Spectacled Bear is sparsely distributed in the mountainous areas of western Venezuela, in Colombia, Ecuador, Peru and northern Bolivia.
Habitat. The species is moderately tolerant of the variations in altitude, climate and vegetation of its habitat. Although it is typically tree-living in the forest, it is equally adaptable to relatively arid environments: it moves from humid, rainy tropical forests to dry bush, and open areas deprived of vegetation, such as the alpine prairies on both sides of the Andes from 500–3,500m (1,000–1,500ft) (this includes the interior valleys but not the arid, deserted western slopes of Peru).
Population. The total number of the species is not known. It is estimated that in 1968 there may have been from 800 to 2,000 in Peru, while in Venezuela it has always been more rare. It is reckoned that the numbers in Columbia and parts of Peru have recently been significantly reduced. It is still common in Ecuador, however, because agriculture has not destroyed its environment; it has also survived in Bolivia. It is significant that in all the countries where the numbers have been greatly reduced, man is to blame. The search for meat as food for the workers building the railways, the trading of both the fur – very prized in Peru – and the fat, are all contributory factors. Moreover, much of its habitat has been taken over for cultivation. In order to preserve the species before the threat of extinction becomes a reality, hunting is prohibited in a few of the countries, for example in Peru and Colombia, although it is difficult to impose the ban in remoter areas. The species can be found in the national parks of Manu, Cutervo Park in Peru, in the Sierra de la Macarena Reserve, and in the Farallones de Cali and Perace Parks in Colombia, and the Sierra Nevada de Merida Park in Venezuela. There are 90 examples in 36 zoos.

Abruzzo Brown Bear

(Ursus arctos marsicanus)

Class: Mammals Subclass: Eutheria Order: Carnivora
Suborder: Fissipedia Family: Ursidae
Subfamily: Ursinae Genus: *Ursus*
French: *Ours bruns des Abruzzes* Italian: *Orso bruno
marsicano* German: *Abruzzo Braunbär*

Description. Recent research seems to indicate that the
largest of the European carnivores, the Brown Bear, is
one of the creatures most threatened with extinction in
Europe. The size of the animal varies considerably: it
measures 2–3m (3–6½ft) and weighs 150–780kg (330–
1,720lb). The Abruzzo Brown Bear tends to be on the
small side as compared to the other European creatures
of its species. This morphological characteristic may
well be a result of the long period of isolation endured by
the indigenes of the central Apennines after the gradual
dwindling of the population of the northern Apennines
had broken their link with the Alps and the rest of
Europe. Like others of the bear family, the Abbruzzo is
omnivorous: its diet varies with the seasons and it will
eat weeds, fruit, berries, root-plants, wild and domestic
animals – particularly chickens – as well as birds, eggs
and fledglings, and, occasionally, fish. Conception takes
place in the spring and summer: the gestation period of
the Brown Bear lasts from six to nine months and the
young, usually twins, are born between December and
January, by which time the female has usually retired to
her den for the winter. It seems that the young do not
leave the den before summer, unlike others of the family
which have left by spring. The Brown Bear lives for
about thirty years in the wild; in captivity some have
been known to live to over forty-five.

Geographic distribution. The sub-species is distributed
over the National Park of Abruzzo and beyond:
Abruzzo Brown Bears can be found from Bisegna in the
north to Piscino and Pizzone in the south, and from
Monte Corna in the west to Barrea and Alfedena in the
east.

Habitat. According to research carried out recently for
the Italian Association of the WWF, the regions inhabited by the Abruzzo Brown Bear can be divided,
according to their altitude and climate, into areas where
the bears seek refuge from the winter weather, and areas
of migration, where they spend the summer months.
Naturally, the areas of winter refuge tend to be at the
foot of the mountains, protected from the rigors of the
cold weather; those of migration stretch up the mountains toward the summits where the bears spend the
warm months. The boundaries of each area are strictly
dependent on the flora: forest trees, undergrowth and
weeds. Another interesting discovery made by the
researchers for the WWF relates to the bears' areas of
winter refuge: the researchers discovered that usually
these areas face south-east, and some extend due west.
Migration from one area to another – particularly in
autumn – becomes necessary as the natural resources
dwindle and force the animals to seek food in the
cultivated areas and pastureland.

Population. It is now thought that there are about a
hundred Brown Bears in Abruzzo, though this estimate
may not be accurate. Recent research has shown that
the natural resources essential to the survival of the sub-
species are not dwindling in the Abruzzo; furthermore,
the arrival at the National Park, in 1974, of a number of
deer and roe-bucks, may help to re-create a disappearing
environment in which wild herbivores necessary to the
natural biological balance take their place. To protect
and defend the sub-species in peril, the WWF provided
compensation from 1969 to 1973 for any damage done
by the bears in the park. In 1970, the WWF began an
enquiry to ascertain the numbers of the sub-species; this
enquiry makes up part of the international project
No 660 'Brown Bear in Abruzzo National Park, Italy'.
Today, any damage done by the bears is indemnified
directly by the local authority. The WWF continues to
research into damage done by poachers to the bears and
into the death of the bears caused by inconsiderate
drivers visiting the park. In Italy, another sub-species of
the Brown Bear was once common all over the Alps;
now it can only be found in the limited area of the
Tridentine Alps. According to research, subsidized by
the Italian Association of the WWF in 1972–73 *no more
than ten* Alpine Brown Bears survive. Their natural
habitat has gradually decreased with the growth of
tourism, the development of ski resorts and the construction of hydroelectric plants. Despite the fact that
the species is protected by law, the sub-species falls prey
also to poachers. In 1970, the first attempt to strengthen
the nucleus failed; a second attempt which began in
1974 has yet to be completed. To adequately protect the
Alpine Bears, otherwise certain of extinction, the WWF
has organized the control of poaching; and it is also
campaigning to have the area of Brenta, Adamello, Val
de Genova and Val di Torel made into a national park.

Polar Bear

(Ursus maritimus)

Class: Mammals Subclass: Eutheria Order: Carnivora
Suborder: Fissipedia Family: Ursidae
Subfamily: Ursinae Genus: *Ursus*
French: *Ours blanc* Italian: *Orso bianco*
German: *Eisbär*

Description. Recent reclassification has put the Polar Bear under the genus *Ursus*, subgenus *Thalarctos*. It was once considered to be the only species representing the genus *Thalarctos*. It is one of the largest living carnivores, second only in size to another bear, the kodiak, *Ursus arctos middendorfi*. The adult male reaches a length of 2.5m (8ft) and up to 1 ton in weight, particularly in the arctic Siberian region where the animal becomes especially rich in fat. The Polar Bear's coat is a typical example of adaptation as it is almost impermeable and permits long periods of immersion in the icy arctic waters. During the reproductive period, in autumn, the pregnant female abandons the ice floe and withdraws to a small hilly island where she hollows out a den in the shape of a tunnel with a large 'room' at the end; this den later becomes covered by snow falls. Here, in the warm protected refuge, she gives birth to one or two, or very rarely three, cubs which weigh 700–800g (25–28oz). Between March and April, after approximately five months of seclusion, the mother emerges with the cubs. The mating season, which in the wild takes place in April, is the only time when male and female cohabit; for the remaining months of the year, while the female attends to the rearing of the offspring, the male wanders in search of food, alone and independent. The cubs follow their mother on the hunting trips during their first summer. They are not yet self-sufficient, however, and feed mainly on milk which the mother provides in shelters or niches formed in the ice. In fact, during the rearing of the young, a female polar bear is unlikely to leave the ice flow and venture on land where wolves are a real threat to her cubs. As soon as winter arrives the mother again retires to a cave together with the cubs, which by now are the size of large dogs; here they spend the coldest months of the year and emerge the following spring. After this, the cubs grow a new set of teeth. At liberty once again, the young are now sufficiently large and strong to assist the mother in hunting; they follow her and rapidly learn by imitation the skills of ambushing and perseverance in the chase. The mother and her young may separate either during the second or third summer, and, once independent, the cubs lead a solitary and errant life. Although the Polar Bear is a carnivore, it may adapt itself to a partially vegetarian diet should game become scarce: lichen, berries and roots satisfy its appetite. In spring, when the coasts of the islands are free of snow and inhabited by colonies of breeding birds, eggs and fledglings also provide food. The Polar Bear may attack large mammals such as the reindeer and musk-ox, and also smaller ones such as the lemming, when abundant. Like many other Ursidae, this giant of the ice is an expert and patient fisher, capable of lying in wait in the water for hours ready to swipe a fish and send it flying on to the bank.

Geographic distribution. This species is limited to the Northern Hemisphere, particularly the arctic zone. Generally, they are most common near the southern edge of the ice-cap but they have also been recorded as far as 80°N latitude. Their distribution is related to the movement of the ice.

Habitat. The areas frequented by the Polar Bear include the permanent ices of the polar basin, the arctic islands and the northern shores of the most northerly land masses. The Polar Bear is an excellent swimmer and can cover great distances in the water.

Population. It is very difficult to estimate even approximate numbers. The areas of distribution are not very extensive for the Polar Bear inhabits only a small part of the Arctic Ocean, whose entire surface area is less than the size of Europe. Moreover the difficulty of carrying out research in such a hostile environment greatly limits the possibility of more exact knowledge. Today, the population is thought to number about 20,000. Since 1956, the species has been under absolute protection in the Soviet Union, and since 1960 there has been a progressive increase in protectionist measures throughout their habitat. These have helped to reduce pressure from hunting; to keep the reservation areas – particularly the polar bears' places of refuge – under more rigid control and to safeguard those predatory species and other environmental factors that are beneficial to the survival of the Polar Bear. Since 1973, a group of specialists of the UICN, composed of scientists from each of the five countries concerned – Canada, USA, Denmark, Norway, and the Soviet Union – have met frequently to decide on international provisions for the protection of this species. The agreements presage greater collaboration between these countries to research into the displacement of the bear across the frontiers. It is illegal to hunt in international waters and although the hunting rights of the indigenous (Eskimo) population are still recognized, this can only be practised by traditional methods. It is also strictly forbidden to hunt from the air (this 'sport', incidentally, is practised by some rich North Americans) and finally by any motorized means, including snowmobiles. In short, the female and her young enjoy complete protection. Polar Bears are frequently found in zoos, and in some cases they have even bred and reared young successfully.

Giant Panda

(Ailuropoda melanoleuca)

Class: Mammals Subclass: Eutheria Order: Carnivora
Suborder: Fissipedia Family: Procyonidae
Subfamily: Ailuridae Genus: *Ailuropoda*
French: *Panda géant* Italian: *Panda gigante*
German: *Bambusbär*

Description. The Giant Panda has been the object of more affection and publicity than any other wild animal despite the fact that it was unknown in the Western World until 1869. (It has been known in China for at least 4,000 years and is mentioned in ancient documents.) In 1869, the French Jesuit naturalist, Father Armand David, described the animal for the first time, having studied the skins of two pandas killed by Chinese hunters on Mu-ping Mountain. Forty-seven years were to pass before another European, J. H. Edgar, a missionary, found an animal which he identified as the panda asleep under an oak tree in the high valley of the Yang-tse. The attraction of the Giant Panda lies in its peculiar markings; the large black patches around the eyes, the black ears crowning its white face, the belly shaped like a large bear cub's, the white hair on the body, with black paws and shoulders – all these features give it the appearance of a teddy-bear. In addition, its habit of sitting or lying on its back while chewing the food it holds in its front paws makes its appeal irresistible – the reason the world has been assailed by thousands of different types of toy panda. The Chinese call the Giant Panda *bei-shung*, which means 'white bear'. They also call it 'Father David's Bear' and 'Bamboo Bear'. An adult panda grows to a length of 1.80m (6ft) and to a shoulder height of 75cm (30in); it weighs up to 135kg (300lb). For many years it was believed to belong to the family Ursidae because of its appearance and movement. Today, most scientists classify it with the family Procyonidae. It is sometimes also called Major Panda because its closest relative is the Lesser Panda or Golden Panda (*Ailurus fulgens*). Some modern classifications consider that it belongs to a family of its own, the Ailuridae. The Giant Panda is a plantigrade, that is, it walks on the soles of its feet like bears. It is a very agile tree-climber. It does not hibernate in winter and adapts itself to the very low temperatures of its habitat. An essentially solitary creature, the panda makes its lair in cavities beneath protruding rocks or in hollow tree-trunks, where it constructs a bed of bamboo. It spends almost its entire life roaming around the dense bamboo forest. Equipped with powerful jaws and long molar teeth typical of carnivores, the panda eats enormous quantities of fibrous bamboo shoots, although occasionally it hunts small mammals, birds and fish to complete its diet. The female normally gives birth to a single cub – rarely two – after a gestation period of about five months. At birth the cub weighs less than 450g (1lb), but it grows rapidly, reaching 30–35kg (66–77lb) at the end of the first year. The panda may live for up to fifteen years. An interesting characteristic are the very soft and fleshy small pads under each forepaw which are used like thumbs to grasp slender bamboo shoots and hold them tight while it chews the fibres. The first Giant Panda to reach the West alive was Su-lin, a female cub captured by Ruth Harkness of the USA in the course of an adventurous expedition in 1936, and purchased by Brookfield Zoo (Chicago) for $8,700. So far, a total of 29 Giant Pandas have come from China (11 to the USA, 8 to London, 2 to Moscow, 2 to Tokyo, 2 to Paris, 2 to Mexico City and 2 to North Korea) but the most famous are Chi-chi, the female from London Zoo, and An-an, the male from Moscow Zoo (both died at about fifteen years of age early in 1973). Two unsuccessful attempts were made to mate them; Chi-chi was sent to Moscow for three months in 1966 and two years later An-an went to London for six months.

Geographic distribution. Although in prehistoric times the Giant Panda was widely distributed over southern China, today it is found only in the mountains of western Szechwan, eastern Sinkiang and in the east Tibetan plateau.

Habitat. Inhabits bamboo and coniferous forest up to an altitude of between 2,500 and 4,000m (between 8,000 and 13,000ft) in a cold and humid climate. In summer it moves to higher mountain slopes.

Population. The Giant Panda is very rare. Its exact population and whether it is increasing or decreasing are unknown. The number is believed to be in the low hundreds. Its natural enemies are a species of wild dog and the leopard, but its survival is not apparently endangered. It has been strictly protected under Chinese law since 1939, and the restricted zone in which it lives has been proclaimed a nature reserve. Local people are instructed by the government to respect the panda and no Giant Pandas have been sold to the West since it became a protected species. The few that are found outside China today were all given by the government to important visitors or as pledges of peace to friendly countries. There are currently young Giant Panda couples (all given between 1972 and 1976) in the zoos in Washington, Tokyo, Mexico City and London, plus one female in Paris Zoo (the male died four months after arrival). In Chinese zoological gardens, mainly in Peking and Shanghai, there are only about twenty pandas. Peking and Shanghai zoos have successfully bred pandas a dozen times; in four of these cases (all at Peking) the young have survived and developed. The mother of the first two was Li-li who has lovingly reared the two cubs Ming-ming (born 9 September 1963) and Lin-lin (born 4 September 1964). Since 1961 the Giant Panda has been adopted as the symbol of the World Wildlife Fund and unites people from all over the world in the struggle for the conservation of nature.

Black Footed Ferret

(Mustela nigripes)

Class: Mammals Subclass: Eutheria Order: Carnivora
Suborder: Fissipedia Family Mustelidae (mustelids)
Subfamily: Mustelinae (mustelins) Genus: *Mustela*
French: *Putois à pieds noirs* Italian: *Furetto dai piedi neri* German: *Schwarzfussiltis*

Description. The Black-footed Ferret is probably the rarest mammal native to the United States. It is also the only North American representative of the pole-cat, sub-species *putorius*. Adult males are about 63–64cm (2ft) long, including the tail. Most of the body is covered in a pale yellowish-buff fur; the face, neck and belly are lighter and almost white. A black mask crosses its face from one eye to the other. The tip of the tail and the feet are also black or blackish-brown. Like other Mustelidae, the Black-footed Ferret is equipped with anal glands which secrete a particularly offensive liquid. Little is known about the biology and behaviour of this mustelid, nor are the reasons for its rarity well understood. Recent attempts to study the animal more deeply have been frustrated by the difficulty of locating specimens. It mainly hunts the prairie dog (a North American rodent resembling the marmot) whose lair it usurps; indeed the very existence of the ferret may be intimately connected with these rodents.

Geographic distribution. Previously inhabited the great plains of North America from Canada to Texas and Arizona, and the slopes of the Rocky Mountains (up to a height of 3,000m [10,000ft]), always in the same habitat as the prairie dog. At present, it is found in very reduced numbers in the western parts of North and South Dakota, in Montana, Alberta (Canada), and possibly in Texas and New Mexico.

Habitat. The favoured environment of the Black-footed Ferret is basically prairie grassland which has largely been transformed by agriculture or taken over for grazing.

Population. Not known, but since 1955, 55 confirmed sightings have been made in 26 counties of 6 states. Its numbers are probably low because of the massive poisoning campaign against the prairie dog which breeders saw as dangerous competition for their cattle's grazing lands. The Black-footed Ferret is protected by law in South Dakota and has been reintroduced into Wind Cave National Park and Devil's Tower National Monument where numerous colonies of prairie dogs exist. Any prairie-dog lairs that are destroyed are first checked for the presence of ferrets. US law also decrees that any Black-footed Ferrets caught on private land must be given to a reserve or suitable park. The only Black-footed Ferrets in captivity (in 1975) were three males and two females at the Endangered Species Research Station at Patuxent in Maryland.

Giant Otter

(Pteronura brasiliensis)

Class: Mammals Subclass: Eutheria Order: Carnivora
Suborder: Fissipedia Family: mustelidae (Mustelids)
Subfamily: Lutrinae Genus: *Pteronura*
French: *Loutre géant du Brésil* Italian: *Lontra gigante*
German: *Riesenotter*

Description. Easily distinguishable from other related species by its clearly larger dimensions, the Giant Otter grows to a length of 1.5m (5ft) and a weight of 25kg (55lb). Gregarious by nature, this mustelid usually hunts for prey in a group of about twenty along the banks and in the rivers which form its habitat, usually between dawn and sunset. Its diet is composed mainly of fish but occasionally it eats small mammals, birds and their young. The Giant Otter's large body and strong teeth are immensely useful in confrontations with even fairly large predators which it fearlessly attacks. Little is known of the Giant Otter's breeding habits and the rearing of its young. The mother gives birth to one or two young in dens made between tree roots and vegeta-tion along a river bank. This animal shows a distinct need for company which can even be satisfied by human presence.

Geographic distribution. Although its population has greatly diminished, the Giant Otter is still distributed over a vast area: this includes many waterways of the central and eastern Brazilian Amazon basin, and in Venezuela, Paraguay, Uruguay and Guyana. A small colony seems to be present in Peru, but the least disturbed population is in the basin of the River Manu, in the Rio Madre de Dios drainage system. In Colombia a number still survive in the southern part of the Macarena Reserve.

Habitat. Like all otters, it frequents damp environments, rivers, lakes and marshes, and is prevalent in the 'black water' of the Amazon basin.

Population. Given the wide area within which this mustelid is found, it is impossible to give even an approximate figure. Today, it is well known that despite protection in many countries – Brazil, Peru, Ecuador and Colombia – it is still easy for fur hunters to reap a harvest of Giant Otter victims from the increasingly sparse population because of the difficulty of keeping a strict watch in such a vast area. While it is not difficult to see the Giant Otter in South American zoos, it is very rare in European zoos (in 1975 there were only three in Hamburg and two in Madrid).

Sea Otter

(Enhydra lutris)

Class: Mammals Subclass: Eutheria Order: Carnivora
Suborder: Fissipedia Family: Mustelidae (mustelids)
Subfamily: Lutrinae Genus: *Enhydra*
French: *Loutre de mer* Italian *Lontra marina*
German: *Seeotter*

Description. Although smaller than the Giant Otter, the Sea Otter can, in fact, be heavier, as its body, excluding the tail, is longer and more sturdily built. A Sea Otter which is 150–180cm (5–6ft) in length will weigh as much as 30kg (66lb). Its forefeet, which are small in proportion to the rest of its body, are webbed with short nails; the sole is hard and smooth. Its hind feet, which are placed fairly well back, are similar in form to some seals' (Pinnipedia), and have short crooked nails; the soles of the hind feet are covered in hair. The fur varies in colour from reddish-chestnut brown to black. Like other species of this subfamily, it is a diurnal creature, and is most active at dawn and sunset. At night, it rests in natural shelters in the rocky coast, although in summer it often prefers floating seaweed away from the shore but in a safe position from sharks and whales – its natural enemies. The Sea Otter's character is similar to other Lutrinae and identical to other Mustelidae: it is gregarious, remaining in family groups while on land – although never wandering far from water. The care shown between parents and offspring is remarkable: both male and female are warm and gentle towards the young and 'effusive' exchanges of affection are common. There is no breeding season; copulation may occur at any time of the year and females may always be seen with suckling pups. A single pup is born (twins are rare) and is reared by the mother with great care. When travelling across land, the mother carries the pup in her mouth; in water, she swims on her back with the pup resting on her belly. The first swimming lessons are given attentively by the parents, and at any sign of danger, or tiredness on the pup's part, the mother carries her offspring to safety. The Sea Otter is mainly carnivorous and its diet is composed of sea urchins, molluscs, shellfish (which it opens by means of stones as it floats on its back); it also eats a small proportion of vegetable substances, such as seaweed.

Geographic distribution. This otter once occupied the whole of the Pacific coast from Japan to the Aleutian Islands and thence southwards to California. Today, there remains only a small restricted population in the whole of this area.

Habitat. Fairly steep and rocky sea coasts and reefs close to the shore.

Population. It is difficult to estimate the present population as it is spread over such an extensive coastal area. On the basis of a census taken in 1960 along the coast of the Aleutian Islands where the largest Sea Otter colony survives, the population was calculated at between 15,000 and 30,000. Thanks to strict protectionist laws currently operating in the countries concerned, the species is making a distinct recovery. The Sea Otter does not apparently enjoy living in captivity and attempts to rear them artificially are not generally successful. This accounts for its rarity in zoos: in 1975 there were only six in two North American aquaria.

Brown Hyena
(Hyaena brunnea)

Class: Mammals Subclass: Eutheria Order: Carnivora
Suborder: Fissipedia Family: Hyaenidae (hyenas)
Genus: *Hyaena*
French: *Hyène brune* Italian: *Iena bruna*
German: *Schabrackenhyäne*

Description. The Hyaenidae family includes three species of two genera. The two most common and best known species are the Spotted Hyena (*Crocuta crocuta*) which inhabits almost the whole of Africa as far as the Sahara, and the Striped Hyena (*Hyaena hyaena*) of northern, central and eastern Africa and south-west Asia. Closely related to the latter is the rare and less well known Brown Hyena (*Hyaena brunnea*) of southern Africa. Similar to the Striped Hyena in appearance (and size), it is 90–100cm (3ft) long, 60–63cm (2ft) tall and 27–32kg (60–70lb) in weight, but has longer hair (up to 25cm [10in] long) which is greyish coloured on the head and uniformly brown over the body. The dorsal mane, which hangs loosely down the side partly covering the animal's body, is pale grey. Its paws have light chestnut stripes. It has a massive head, huge slim ears and powerful jaws capable of crushing even large carrion. The Brown Hyena is the most timid of its species: it is active only at night, spending the day concealed among rocks or hidden in other animals' lairs. Sometimes it searches the coast for fish and crab washed ashore. Normally, however, it feeds on small prey, such as hares, eggs and insects. The female gives birth to between two and six young (normally three to four) after a gestation period of about three months. The cubs are born and reared in a cave or underground lair. The Brown Hyena may live for up to twenty-five years.

Geographic distribution. Formerly throughout southern Africa as far north as Rhodesia, Mozambique and Angola. Diminished numbers now survive in the Kruger National Park, South Africa; in reserves in Natal and Angola, and in limited areas of Cape Province, Transvaal, Mozambique, Rhodesia, Botswana and south-west Africa.

Habitat. Low, arid, savannah regions with sparse tree and bush growth; open plains and thinly forested areas. In general, the Brown Hyena never occupies the same territory as the Spotted Hyena which prefers a less arid habitat.

Population. The Red Data Book defines the status of the Brown Hyena as 'vulnerable'. The number of Brown Hyenas living in the wild is unknown apart from those groups living in parks and reserves. The Spotted and Striped Hyena are found more commonly than the Brown in zoos. In 1975 there were 53 Brown Hyenas in 22 zoos, 24 of which were born in captivity (3 or 4 are born annually).

Ocelot

(Felis pardalis)

Class: Mammals Sublcass: Eutheria Order: Carnivora
Suborder: Fissipedia Family: Felidae (felids)
Subfamily: Felinae Genus: *Felis*
French: *Ocelot* Italian: *Ocellotto* German: *Ocelot*

Description. The ocelot, also known as the American Leopard, is of modest dimensions: its overall length is 1–1.50m (3–5ft) of which the tail accounts for 35cm (2ft). In humid forest climates, its coat is ochre or orange, while in dry and more arid climates it is greyish. The chest, abdomen and inside of the paws are pale coloured. Unlike many other felines, the ocelot live and hunt in pairs: generally hunting at night, they call to each other to signal their positions or that of their prey – usually small- or medium-sized mammals, such as monkeys, rodents, forest deer, birds, reptiles and amphibians. This species does not have a fixed mating season and copulation may occur at any time of year. The gestation period lasts about seventy days and normally two to four cubs are born. In captivity, and particularly when artificially reared, the ocelot displays a mild and affectionate disposition towards its keepers.

Geographic distribution. Formerly distributed from North America (Arkansas, Louisiana, eastern and southern Texas, north-eastern Mexico) to South America (northern Argentina), it is now limited to the southern extremes of Texas and certain areas of Mexico; in South America its distribution has hardly changed.

Habitat. Compared with other endangered American felines, this species has adapted itself to a wide range of environments from humid tropical and sub-tropical forests to coastal forests and mangrove swamps, from marshy savannah to arid scrub.

Population. The present ocelot population is unknown. In North America there has been a sharp decline in local populations of the sub-species *Felis pardalis albescens* (Texas and Mexico). The typical South American sub-species *Felis pardalis pardalis* is more numerous. The ocelot is primarily killed for its fur, but also because it is considered harmful to domestic livestock. In many countries it is illegal to hunt the ocelot or to sell its fur. Britain and the United States have banned the importation of ocelots or any part of the animal except for the purposes of research or repopulation. However, examples of this species can be seen in numerous European and American zoos.

Spanish Lynx

(Felis lynx pardina)

Class: Mammals Subclass: Eutheria Order: Carnivora
Suborder: Fissipedia Family: Felidae (felids)
Subfamily: Feldinae Genus: *Felis*
French: *Lynx d'Espagne* Italian: *Lince pardina*
German: *Pardelluchs*

Description. The physical characteristics and habits of
this sub-species do not differ greatly from those of the
typical species, the Common or European Lynx. The
Spanish Lynx grows to a length of 1m (3ft) including the
tail, which is about 15cm (6in). The height at the withers
is about 70cm (2ft). The coat markings of the Spanish
Lynx are similar to the Caucasian Lynx (*Felis lynx
orientalis*) and are more prominent than on other members of the sub-species. The lynx takes its name from
Linceus who, according to Greek mythology, was gifted
with such acute sight that he could see through opaque
objects. Experiments have proved that a lynx can distinguish a mouse at 75m (250ft), a rabbit at 300m (980ft)
and a roe-buck at 500m (1,650ft). The tufts of hair
(about 5cm [2in] long) on its ears serve an important
function in helping the animal to detect sources of
sound, and without them its directional hearing capacity
is greatly reduced. These 'earpins' also repel insects while
the animal rests in the summer heat. The edges of its feet
are covered in long thick hair which facilitates movement through snow. This feline is generally solitary and
hunts alone in a territory which is defined by its urine,
droppings, and scratch marks made with its claws on the
bark of trees. Lynxes prefer to hunt their prey – small-
and medium-sized mammals, birds, reptiles and amphibians – at twilight. During the mating season, the
female leaves her territory in search of a male. The
gestation period lasts from sixty-five to seventy-five days,
after which between one and four cubs are born. In the
wild, the male reaches sexual maturity at about two and
a half to three years and the female before two years;
in captivity, sexual maturity is achieved at an earlier age.

Geographic distribution. Until recently, the Spanish Lynx
was common. It was present in Italy, Sicily, Sardinia,
France, the Caucasus mountains, the Balkans south of
the Carpathians, Greece, Macedonia, Albania and also
in many mountainous areas of the Albanian peninsula.
Today, although it may be found on rare occasions in
some of these areas (apart from France and Italy) it only
definitely exists in Spain. Its distribution there is limited
to the Sierra Morena, the Sierra de Guadalupe, the
Monte di Toledo and the 'Marismas de Guadalquivir',
which are the marshes at the mouth of the Homonymous
river. A small number may possibly live in Portugal.

Habitat. This feline, the largest of the western Mediterranean fauna, prefers mainly mountainous areas covered
in a combination of vegetation. Among the 'Mediterranean forest' composed of such trees as the home oak
and cork tree, and dense undergrowth formed by
arbutus, lentisk and juniper bushes, the Spanish Lynx
rules supreme. Various factors have contributed to the
decline of this animal: the sharp decrease in rabbits after
the 1960 myxomatosis epidemic in the south east and
the reafforestation of the mountain areas of Spain in
which the mainly high-level growth was replaced by
various types of vegetation. The animal has thus been
forced to live in more open and less protected regions,
thereby facilitating its capture by hunters and trappers.
Only on the flat lands of the Guadalquivir marshes has
the Spanish Lynx been able to find a safe refuge, and
the few that have escaped slow but constant persecution
are now carefully protected and studied by scientists at
the Doñana National Park.

Population. The total population is virtually unknown;
it is calculated that about thirty inhabit the Coto Doñana
National Park. It is believed that the animal is extinct
in most, if not all, of the areas it once inhabited. Hunted
until recently either for its skin or because it was considered harmful, the Spanish Lynx is today approaching
extinction and there is great concern for the fate of the
last survivors. In 1975 there were only seven Spanish
Lynxes in captivity in four zoos.

Clouded Leopard

(Neofelis nebulosa)

Class: Mammals Subclass: Eutheria Order: Carnivora
Suborder: Fissipedia Family: Felidae (felids)
Subfamily: Felinae Genus: *Neofelis*
French: *Panthère longibande* Italian: *Pantera nebulosa* German: *Nebelparder*

Description. The Clouded Leopard, also known as the Clouded Panther, is a unique species and can be seen as the bridge species between the feline and pantherine family. In fact, distinct similarities with representatives of the genus *Panthera* are to be seen in its skull and teeth, while the rest of its body is reminiscent of certain other Felidae, particularly those belonging to the genus *Felis*. When resting, the Clouded Leopard extends its forelegs forward and its tail almost straight behind in the manner of the lion, tiger and leopard – a cat in the same position usually bends its forelegs underneath the body and curls its tail around the flank. The Clouded Leopard is also closer to the panther than the cat as it is much less precise. On average, its size is smaller than most other leopards: it has an overall length of about 2m (6½ft), of which about 1m (3ft) is the tail, and weighs up to 23kg (50lb). Superbly arboreal, this carnivore is capable of climbing a tree at great speed and coming down again head first. Similarly, it can work its way along a horizontal branch while upside down. It hunts mainly at twilight and its prey are commonly squirrels, monkeys, birds and small terrestrial mammals. The gestation period lasts about ninety days at the end of which the female gives birth to two to four cubs. The young have dark markings on their coats which become lighter as the cubs grow into adulthood.

Geographic distribution. India, Burma, Indochina, Borneo, Sumatra and Formosa.

Habitat. In keeping with its tree-dwelling habits, the Clouded Leopard frequents evergreen forests which range from sea-level to an altitude of 2,000m (6,500ft).

Population. This species has noticeably declined as a result of the demand for its fur and the destruction of the forests with the advancement of agriculture. It is now a protected species and a small number live in parks or reserves. Britain and the United States have also banned its importation. The Clouded Leopard has been successfully bred in captivity – in the zoos in Chicago, Dublin, and Frankfurt. In 1975 there were about 115 of the species in 55 zoos.

Barbary Lion

(Panthera leo leo)

Class: Mammals Subclass: Eutheria Order: Carnivora
Suborder: Fissipedia Family: Felidae (felids)
Subfamily: Felinae Genus: *Panthera*
French: *Lion de l'Atlas* Italian: *Leone berbero*
German: *Berberlöwe*

Description. The lion was once widespread over the African continent apart from the central part of the Sahara and the humid tropical forest. It was also found across Asia, from the Arabian peninsula to India. Four of the numerous sub-species still live in Africa south of the Sahara (it is, incidentally, difficult to identify the sub-species because of the notable differences between *individuals* in the same area). One sub-species seriously threatened with extinction (the Asiatic Lion, *Panthera leo persica*, illustrated overleaf) inhabits the Indian forest of Gir; two are extinct – the Barbary Lion (*Panthera leo leo*) and the Cape Lion (*Panthera leo melanochaita*). The Barbary Lion was a sizeable animal over 1m (3ft) high at the shoulders. The principal characteristic of the male was the enormous thick mane which covered the head, neck, chest and belly; in the surviving sub-species, the mane is limited to around the neck and, in some cases, is almost non-existent. The Cape Lion was also an imposing sight with its well developed, almost black mane.

Geographic distribution. At the end of the nineteenth century the Barbary Lion was limited to Morocco, Algeria, Tunisia and Fezzan. The Cape Lion inhabited South Africa, Cape Province and Natal.

Habitat. The Barbary Lion lived principally in the coastal regions which were rich in vegetation, and near the oases. It also ventured as far as the slopes down to the Atlantic.

History and causes of extinction. The Barbary Lion was at one time fought by local tribesmen who, in the remoter areas, considered it a wicked creature. The Ancient Romans began a tradition of capturing large numbers of lions – North Africa was once under the domination of Rome – to take part in their cruel games in arenas. Moreover, when the area was occupied by Europeans and their troops, they hunted the lion both for circuses and food. Its decline was therefore effected, and the last Barbary Lion was killed in Morocco, its final refuge, in 1920. Apart from the famous collection of the King of Morocco, there are still lions in Rabat Zoo. Many generations of lions bred in captivity have maintained unaltered the basic characteristics. One lion and two lionesses are now in Washington Zoo. A programme is being set up with the help of the UICN to recreate the sub-species in captivity. The Cape Lion was exterminated by 1885 as a result of intense hunting by settlers.

Asiatic Lion

(Panthera leo persica)

Class: Mammals Subclass: Eutheria Order: Carnivora
Suborder: Fissipedia Family: Felidae (felids)
Subfamily: Felinae Genus: *Panthera*
French: *Lion de l'Inde* Italian: *Leone asiatico*
German: *Persischer Löwe*

Description. Of all sub-species of lion, the Asiatic or Indian Lion is the one most threatened with extinction. Contrary to popular opinion, the differences in appearance and size between the Asiatic and African Lions are not clear-cut. It was generally believed that the Asiatic Lion had a smaller mane than the African Lion, that its tail was thicker and longer, and that the tufts on the elbows were more prominent. However, recent scientific studies have shown that, while in any case these characteristics are not always present, they do not provide a system for differentiating between the lions of the two continents. This is even more apparent when considering the large differences between individual African lions – colouring, length of the mane and the other supposedly salient characteristics. The Asiatic Lion has a tawny coat; the mane varies in colour from tawny to black, but it is usually bright. The males are about 1.70m (5½ft) long; the tail measures 90–100cm (35–39in). The shoulder height is approximately 90cm (35in) and the weight is 180–200kg (400–440lb). Females are smaller. After a gestation period of three and a half months between two and four (sometimes five or six) dapple-coated cubs are born weighing 1,200–1,500g (2½–3lb). The young are suckled for six to seven months, and the lion's mane appears at about eighteen months. Lions usually live up to fifteen years in the wild, but in captivity they can live as long as twenty-five. One male African Lion in Cologne Zoo was twenty-nine years old. Lions live in groups of two or three males and five to ten females with their young. Contrary to popular belief, lionesses do not search for food for the males: in common with other carnivores, the male snatches part of the female's prey. The male lion, the true king of the plains, kills only 13 per cent of what he eats. The Asiatic Lion mainly preys upon the antelope; it also eats small mammals and domestic livestock.

Geographic distribution. Until recently, the Asiatic Lion was found over the major part of Asia Minor – in Mesopotamia, Arabia, Persia and India. It was common in Israel during biblical times, but has been extinct there since the thirteenth century. A hundred years ago it was still present in Iraq, Iran and the whole of eastern India. It disappeared from Iraq and Iran between World Wars I and II (recent claimed sightings of the animal in Iran are questionable). Today, the Asiatic Lion is limited to its reserve in the forest of Gir which covers an area of 1,200sq km (450sq miles) and is situated in western India, to the north-east of Bombay.

Habitat. The Asiatic Lion inhabits the tree forest (preferably of teak) with a dense vegetation of acacia and fringed by cultivated land. During the rainy season many lions leave the forest and follow domestic livestock across the grassland to open areas.

Population. The Asiatic Lion is a direct descendant of the lions of biblical times. Killed and hunted throughout the ages, it was reduced in the last century to no more than 100 individuals confined to the forest of Gir on the peninsula of Kathiawar, protected by the nabobs of Junagardh. The sub-species was legally protected in 1900 and this protection allowed the lions to increase from 100 in 1936 to 289. However, 7,000 people and 57,000 head of cattle moved into the forest, and before long the herds of cattle destroyed the vegetation and man cut down the trees for wood. This resulted in the disappearance of the herbivores on which the lion depended for food, and the destruction of its habitat. The lion was therefore forced to move nearer to civilization in search of food, and local tribes, seeing it as a threat to their livestock, began to kill it. The only way of protecting it – by transferring the local inhabitants to another area – proved impossible, and conservation laws were therefore extremely difficult to enforce. The lion population, which had remained almost constant between the years 1936 and 1955, numbered 290 but by 1968 it had declined to 177. Further protection laws were imposed and by 1973 the lion population had increased to 200. It was also noticeable that the number of deer, antelope and wild boar – the natural prey of this lion – had augmented. Nevertheless, the sub-species of the Asiatic Lion is still in grave danger of extinction. The forest of Gir has been vital for the survival of this animal since 1965, and there is a programme to transform part of the area (125sq km [50sq miles]) into a national park. This would necessitate the removal of all domestic animals and the prohibition of forestry operations. It would also prevent the pilfering of the meat and skins of deer already killed by the lions, and so would increase the chances of the lion's survival. The majority of Asiatic Lions in captivity are found in Indian zoos; eighty, of which half were born in captivity. Otherwise, Asiatic Lions are found only in the zoos of Katmandu, Kuala Lumpur and Sydney, one pair on the island of Jersey, and one male and two females in East Berlin (1973). Also Chicago Zoo managed to obtain two in 1974.

Tiger

(Panthera tigris)

Class: Mammals Subclass: Eutheria Order: Carnivora
Suborder: Fissipedia Family: Felidae (felids)
Subfamily: Felinae Genus: *Panthera*
French: *Tigre* Italian: *Tigre* German: *Tiger*

Description. The tiger is the national symbol of India and one of the best known animals in the world. It appears both in the literature and culture of the countries it inhabits as well as in the history and legend of the Western world. This great cat – the largest of all the Felidae – is lithe and strong with a muscular, weighty body. The limbs are strong, solidly built, and relatively long; the head of the male adult is powerful without the apparent heaviness of the lion's. The total length can be as much as 3m (10ft) in the male and 2.70m (9ft) in the female; the average weight is about 190kg (400lb), reaching a maximum of 272kg (600lb). The skeleton and musculature are perfectly adapted and functional; they are designed above all to aid the animal in leaping and attacking. It has massive cervical and jaw muscles combined with a dentition with excellent canines which permit the tiger to bite through the toughest skin and sinews of its prey. The coat is basically yellow, but varies in colour according to the sub-species; it has transversal stripes (also varying according to the sub-species) on the sides, neck, limbs and head. The tiger's underneath is almost pure white. The coat, except in a few of the sub-species, is short and smooth, but slightly longer on the sides of the head, especially in the male where it forms side-whiskers. Tigers are carnivorous and generally hunt alone. It leaps onto its prey and the impact powered by the tiger's front legs and jaw against the body causes the vertebral column near the neck to break; the victim is then immediately immobilized. Despite its capacity to overcome larger and stronger mammals (even adult buffalo) the tiger's prey generally consists of deer, wild boar and other medium-sized mammals which are not too difficult to attack; if necessary, it will also eat frogs, lizards, mice and other small animals. The female starts to reproduce at around four years and gives birth to between two and four cubs of which only a half, or less than half, will live to become adults. In the wild, the tigress will give birth two or three times a year. The usual age reached by tigers in the wild is around fifteen years but they frequently die much younger.

Geographic distribution. The tiger inhabits only the Indian sub-continent and its surrounding islands, Indonesia and the Orient.

Habitat. The preferred environment of the tiger is the scrubland, steppes, reed beds and tundra up to a height of 2,400m (7,900ft) above sea-level. They seek out places that are damp, humid and close to water in which they love to swim.

Population. In 1930 it was estimated that there were tens of thousands of tigers, 40,000 alone belonging to the Indian area. Today the species is reduced to a maximum of 5,000 (including all the sub-species) throughout its area of distribution; the number for the sub-continent of India is now put at only 1,850. The rapid decline of the species has been caused by hunting principally for commercial purposes – its exquisite skin is much in demand. It is also hunted to preserve local legend. Moreover, its habitat has been destroyed through deforestation for the valuable timber. The tiger is now a protected species. Various countries have prohibited both the exportation of living tigers and their skins, but this law is difficult to enforce due to the irresponsible attitude of speculators who are not concerned with the grave situation of the tiger's limited numbers. In co-operation with the World Wildlife Fund ('Operation Tiger') various new parks and reserves are being set up and there are also a number of countries involved in programmes for conservation operations. In 1975 there were 1,100 tigers in captivity but it is almost certain that, including all circuses and private collections, there are many more. The species is reasonably adaptable to an artificial environment and its ability to survive in captivity has notably improved. It also succeeds in reproducing fairly frequently. However, the mortality rate of the cubs is fairly high, although the number of births is larger than those recorded in the wild. There are eight sub-species: Bengal Tiger (*Panthera tigris tigris* – the female is illustrated opposite) which inhabits the Indian sub-continent (population, 1,850); Caspian Tiger (*P.t. virgata*) inhabiting Iran and possibly Afghanistan (population, 50–80); the Siberian Tiger (*P.t. altaica*) inhabiting south-eastern Siberia and the Amur Basin (population, 170–180); Java Tiger (*P.t. sondaica*) inhabiting Java (population, 12); Chinese Tiger (*P.t. amoyensis*) inhabiting China – it is very rare and not protected; Bali Tiger (*P.t. balica*) inhabited Bali but is probably extinct; Sumatran Tiger (*P.t. sumatrae*) inhabiting Sumatra; Indo-Chinese Tiger (*P.t. corbetti*) inhabiting Malaysia, Burma, Thailand, Laos, Cambodia and Vietnam, and when last studied in 1968 was fairly numerous.

Leopard

(Panthera pardus)

Class: Mammals Subclass: Eutheria Order: Carnivora
Suborder: Fissipedia Family: Felidae (felids)
Subfamily: Felinae Genus: *Panthera*
French: *Léopard* or *Panthère* Italian: *Leopardo* or *pantera* German: *Leopard*

Description. The leopard is the most widespread species of the genus *Panthera*. There are various sub-species throughout Africa and Asia (for example, *Panthera p.chui*, illustrated opposite, is from Uganda). The sub-species can be divided by a common guideline: if they are from Africa they are leopards and if from Asia, panthers. The size of the animal differs between sub-species, varying from a total length of 1.5–2.5m (5–8ft), of which at least one-third is the tail. The streamlined body, short legs and long weighty tail with the tip just curling upwards, give the animal an elegance rarely seen in any carnivore. They also accentuate the leopard's extreme power and agility. The coat has a base colour varying from grey to yellow and patterned with the famous 'spots' which are very dark, almost black. The colour and marking of the coat enable the leopard to conceal itself for indefinite periods; consequently throughout Asia and Africa it has gained the reputation with the natives of being a supernatural creature. It is a solitary hunter and will usually stay within a well defined territory assuming there is sufficient prey. It is not certain whether or not the female also hunts within and defends her own territory. Principally nocturnal, the leopard hunts from sunset through the night. Its prey will be ambushed beneath a tree, in a hollow, or killed after a very long slow chase. When the prey is too large to be eaten in one night, the leopard will pick the softest parts and then leave the remainder for the following night's feast. However, the likelihood of hyenas or jackals eating the corpse necessitates the leopard hoisting the carcass into the branches of a tree out of their reach. This is a remarkable feat as the leopard is no bigger than a large dog. The African Leopard principally eats baboons, mandrills, gnus and large herbivores and will kill either the youngest or the oldest, thus carrying out a rigid form of natural selection. If very hungry, the leopard will not refuse smaller animals, such as rodents, birds and fish. It also eats fruit. In Asia, the leopard (the panther) hunts monkeys, deer, buffalo, ibex, wild boar and also smaller mammals. In Africa, and even more so in Asia, the leopard is considered a dangerous hunter and eater of men; there are many stories and documented accounts regarding this. It is almost certain that in such cases the 'man-eating' leopard has been either severely wounded or so old that it no longer had the strength and speed to capture an animal in the wild. Leopards have a single mate for life but hunt together only in the mating season. The gestation period is 100 days after which two to four cubs are born (occasionally one or five). In the wild, the leopard will reach sexual maturity at around three years.

Geographic distribution. Africa and most of southern Asia from Turkey to China; Sri Lanka; Java, where the Black Panther in particular is found.

Habitat. This cat is found in very varied environments: the humid African rain forests, arid savannah, the high cold mountains, the Indian jungle or the rocky areas of scattered vegetation of Iran and Afghanistan.

Population. The current population of this species is unknown. Some of the sub-species belonging to specific areas are threatened with extinction. The prime threat is the uncontrolled hunting for its valuable fur. Current information in the Red Data Book states that the sub-species most in danger are: the Barbary Leopard (*P.p. panthera*) from Morocco, Algeria and Tunisia, of which there are probably no more than a few dozen; the South Arabian Leopard (*P.p. nimr*) from the mountains and hilly steppes of the most southern part of the Arabian peninsula; the Anatolian Leopard (*P.p. tulliana*) from Turkey; the Amur Leopard (*P.p. orientalis*) from eastern Siberia and northern Korea; the Sinai Leopard (*P.p. jarvisi*) perhaps still in Sinai. All these sub-species are protected by law and also many studies are under way to gain a more specific knowledge of their population. In some European countries efforts are being made to reproduce these sub-species with a view to repopulation. Leopards are very common in zoos and reproduce in captivity fairly easily.

Snow Leopard

(Panthera uncia)

Class: Mammals Subclass: Eutheria Order: Carnivora
Suborder: Fissipedia Family: Felidae (felids)
Subfamily: Felinae Genus: *Panthera*
French: *Léopard des neiges* Italian: *Leopardo delle nevi*
German: *Schneeleopard*

Description. The Snow Leopard is about the same size as the Common Leopard: its total length, including the tail, can be over 2m (6½ft). Some authorities believe that the Snow Leopard provides the link between the genus *Felis* and the genus *Panthera* due to the similarities in musculature and purring capacity. However, some zoologists attribute the animal with a genus of its own and have named it *Uncia*. The Snow Leopard is diurnal, hunting alone except in the mating season or while the cubs are reared. Two or more may hunt together when prey is scarce and their individual hunting territories have to be widened. Generally, they hunt ibex and other mountain herbivores but, if necessary, birds and small mammals. In winter, it hunts wild boar, deer, gazelle and hares on lower levels. The gestation period is 100 days and between two and five cubs are born. In captivity, the male also helps with the rearing of the young.

Geographic distribution. Limited mainly to the mountains of central Asia, the animal's former range is uncertain. It is also encountered in northern Iran, Tadzhikistan, north China, Mongolia and Russia as far south as northern India.

Habitat. Occurs between the tree line and the permanent snows between 3,000 and 6,000m (9,800 and 19,700ft). Descends into the upper valley bottoms (1,500–2,000m [4,900–6,500ft]) in winter.

Population. Exact numbers are unknown. There are still 100 in Pakistan although this number is disproportionately high compared to other areas. Although legally protected by the countries it inhabits, it is hunted both for its skin and because it is seen as a threat to domestic animals. In 1971 the International Fur Trade Federation agreed to a voluntary ban among its membership on the use of Snow Leopard furs. There are few in captivity. In 1973 there were around 150 in 50 zoos, a third of which were born in captivity.

Jaguar

(Panthera onca)

Class: Mammals Subclass: Eutheria Order: Carnivora
Suborder: Fissipedia Family: Felidae (felids)
Subfamily: Felinae Genus: *Panthera*
French: *Jaguar* Italian: *Giaguaro* German: *Jaguar*

Description. At first glance the jaguar is similar to the leopard but there are differences: the body is heavier, the head larger, and the tail shorter; the legs are short and compact; the claws are stronger, and the colouring is sandy-red with markings of large spots surrounded by smaller ones in contrast to the regular markings of the leopard. Its total length varies from 1.60 to 2.60m (5–8½ft), including a tail length of 45–75cm (18–30in). Like the leopard, the jaguar hunts within its own territory – an area ranging between about 5 and 30km (2 and 18 miles) in diameter. It is a solitary animal except during the mating season when it joins and hunts with its mate; the mating season is not restricted to a particular time of the year. The gestation period is 90–110 days; two to four cubs are born, weighing no more than 1kg (2lb) at birth.

Geographic distribution. Formerly ranged through forests from the south-west of the United States to Patagonia.

Habitat. Basically water-loving, it is found in tropical forest, sub-tropical forest and savannah, including mangrove swamps and scrub thickets around rivers and lagoons. Although its diet consists mainly of forest mammals, such as tapirs, deer, monkeys, and rodents, it will also eat smaller animals if necessary, as well as birds, reptiles and their eggs.

Population. Impossible to estimate as it is spread over a vast area. Some sub-species fairly common decades ago are now rare, if not already extinct. Among those practically extinct are *P. onca veracrucensis* and *P.o. hernandesi* from Mexico, and *P.o. ariconensis* from Arizona. The main cause of its decline – particularly during the 1960s – was the demand for jaguar skins by the fur trade. After 1970 this trade declined due to the strict protection laws and scarcity of jaguars. There are small populations in the large national parks in South America. In order to preserve the species there, it must be protected within its natural habitat. The jaguar can be seen in many European and American zoos and reproduces fairly easily in captivity.

Cheetah

(Acinonyx jubatus)

Class: Mammals Sublcass: Eutheria Order: Carnivora
Suborder: Fissipedia Family: Felidae (felids)
Subfamily: Acinonychinae Genus: *Acinonyx*
French: *Guépard* Italian: *Ghepardo* German: *Gepard*

Description. The cheetah was originally classified under the Latin name *Cynailurus* – 'dog-cat' – because it is more similar to the dog (greyhound) than it is to the cat (leopard). The cheetah is like a leopard, but smaller, slimmer and with long, supple legs. It is 2–2.30m (6–7½ft) long, of which 60–80cm (24–31in) is the tail. Its height at the withers is 70–90cm (28–33in). It weighs up to 60kg (130lb). The cheetah has thirty teeth, in common with other Felidae; the canines, however, press together like those of the Canidae. The eyes are yellow-brown; the pupils remain round even when contracted. The cheeks are marked with an oblique black stripe from under the eyes to the corners of the mouth. The slightly rough coat is yellow-ochre on the top and sides, white on the underneath and patterned with round black spots equally distributed on the head, limbs and tail. On the nape is a short mane (from which it takes the name *jubatus*). The tip of the tail is white preceded with black rings. The feet are supple and armed with non-retracting claws. The gestation period is 90–95 days and the female gives birth in a protected place, either in long grass or among shrubs. Between one and five young are born which weigh 250–280g (9–10oz). The cubs are born with a dull-yellow coat and also with a long bright-coloured mane extending from the top of the head, over the nape dull-yellow coat and also with a long bright-coloured weeks. The cheetah can live for up to fifteen years. It prefers to hunt in sunlight although also active at night. It hunts the antelope and gazelle in particular and, having skilfully brought itself close to the prey, it takes advantage of its own exceptional speed. This can easily reach 70–75km (approximately 42 miles) per hour and can reach speeds of 100km (62 miles) per hour in 7.5m (25ft) bounds for stretches of up to 500m (⅓ mile). The cheetah has gained the reputation of being the fastest animal in the world, notably faster than certain antelopes which can reach the speed of 80km (50 miles) per hour. In the wild, it avoids those areas inhabited by man but once captured it is adaptable and easily domesticated.

The cheetah was used for hunting by the Sumerians (3000 BC) and Ancient Egyptians. Marco Polo records the fact that at the Court of the Great Khan there were a thousand cheetahs which were taken out to hunt with leather caps over their heads similar to those used in training falcons today. The Asiatic sub-species of cheetah (*Acinonyx jubatus venaticus*) is similar to the African Cheetah although slightly smaller. In southern Rhodesia there is one particular sub-species, the Royal Cheetah (*A.j. rex*), which has a wonderful coat on which the spots on the flanks and back form almost equidistant stripes longitudinally. This sub-species is considered by many to be merely an accident of nature rather than a sub-species in its own right, and it is now almost certainly extinct.

Geographic distribution. The cheetah once inhabited Asia from India up to the Red Sea and extended across the whole African continent, with the exception of the humid tropical forest and the central part of the Sahara desert. Now it exists in Africa in a larger part of its original territory but in substantially diminished numbers, except where it is protected in parks and reserves. The Asiatic sub-species is almost extinct in all its original territory and can currently be found only in the arid zone on the frontiers of Afghanistan and Turkmenistan (USSR) and in a few of the zones of eastern Iran.

Habitat. Arid savannah is the most favourable environment for the cheetah but occasionally it is found in high grassland and on the edges of forests. The Asiatic species has found it easier to adapt to even drier regions. Agricultural development and the spread of civilization has reduced or spoiled much of the cheetah's natural habitat so that it has disappeared from many of these areas.

Population. The position of the African Cheetah is extremely vulnerable as it is extinct in many areas and notably reduced in others. The Asiatic Cheetah has also disappeared from the major part of its original territory and is considered to be in grave danger of extinction. However, it seems to be increasing in Iran where there are 200–300. None have been sighted in India since 1951. The population of the African species probably totals between 8,000 and 25,000 (there were probably 100,000 only a century ago.) The cheetah is protected by law in almost all Africa, with the exception of the South African Republic, and the USSR and Iran. However, its valuable coat for fur clothing has encouraged killing and illegal trade. The importation of cheetah skins has been prohibited in the United States and Great Britain. Although the International Federation of Fur Trading recommended that a limit be placed on this trade for three years (1971–74), this suggestion was ignored by the majority of fur traders, especially in France, Italy, Spain, Scandinavia and Japan. There are today around 600 African Cheetahs in captivity in 135 zoos; one Asiatic Cheetah is held in Teheran Zoo (1974). It is very difficult for them to reproduce in captivity; this was first achieved in 1956 in Philadelphia Zoo and again in 1966 in a private zoo in Rome, since when there have only been eight or nine cases of reproduction in captivity a year.

Mediterranean Monk Seal

(Monachus monachus)

Class: Mammals Subclass: Eutheria Order: Carnivora
Suborder: Pinnipedae (pinnipeds) Family: Phocoidea
Subfamily: Monachinae (Monk Seals)
Genus: *Monachus*
French: *Phoque moine* Italian: *Foca monaca*
German: *Mittelmeer-Mönchsrobbe*

Description. There are three species of Monk Seal which all live in sub-tropical waters in the Northern Hemisphere, although each live in separate areas: *Monachus monachus* lives in the Mediterranean; *Monachus tropicalis* in the Caribbean and *Monachus schauinslandis* on one of the Hawaiian Islands. The Monk Seal is the only pinniped which lives in a sub-tropical region. The name 'monk' derives from its unique colouring which is uniformly dark over the back and white on the chest, vaguely resembling a nun's wimple. This pinniped has long strong nails on the front flippers while there are few or no nails on the back flippers. The Mediterranean Monk Seal is a large animal, larger than the Common Seal, and the male adult can grow up to 3m (10ft) in length. It can weigh over 300kg (600lb). The female is smaller. This animal has a massive head with a short muzzle, large soft lips and long stiff whiskers. The nostrils are oblique and the eyes large, luminous and expressive. The limbs are short. The fore-limbs have graduated digits; the first and fifth digits of the hind-limbs being more developed than the others. The Mediterranean Monk Seal has a coat of short bristly hair, a yellowy-grey-brown colour on the back which contrasts with the white on the chest and belly. The Monk Seal lives in small groups, preferably inside marine caves. The female gives birth to one young which is jet black and weaned after six weeks.

Geographic distribution. The Monk Seal once lived along the Mediterranean coast, the Black Sea and north-western Africa as far as Cape Blanco and also around Madeira Island and the Canary Islands. Today, it exists only along the coast of Bulgaria, in the most remote Dodecanese Islands, the Mediterranean coast of Turkey, Cyrenaica, and the three Italian islands of Sardinia, Sicily and Montecristo (although it may have been extinct there since 1974). It can also be found around Cape Blanco and around the ex-Spanish Sahara coast and Mauretania.

Habitat. Sea-caves, particularly those with submarine entrances which it finds on isolated islands or rocky coasts of the continent. It is not known whether the Monk Seal prefers to live in caves through choice or as a result of man's encroachment on its natural habitat.

Population. The Mediterranean Monk Seal is considered in grave danger of extinction. Its total population is between 500 and 1,000. It has declined largely due to persecution by fishermen who see it as a competitive threat. Further, man now lives near the coasts it inhabits and this problem has increased with the introduction of pleasure boats and underwater swimming. The Monk Seal is protected in Italy, France, Yugoslavia, Greece and Bulgaria, but the law is difficult to enforce. In Africa it is protected by the African Convention of 1969. The most numerous group (200) live on Cape Blanco. In Italy, research carried out in 1974 by the Italian Association of the World Wildlife Fund found a dozen Monk Seals in Sardinia which had taken refuge in the caves on the east coast of the island, and a colony of four or five seals on the north-western coast of Sicily. One or two other Monk Seals have been seen on the island of Montecristo. The Caribbean Monk Seal is probably extinct (the last one was seen in 1952); the Hawaiian Monk Seal, although very much on the decline, is not in imminent danger. The only Mediterranean Monk Seal currently in captivity is a female. Captured near Cape Blanco it has been in an aquarium in Lisbon since 1954.

Walrus

(Odobenus rosmarus)

Class: Mammals Subclass: Eutheria Order: Carnivora
Suborder: Pinnipedae (pinnipeds) Family: Odobenidae
Genus: *Odobenus*
French: *Morse* Italian: *Tricheco* German: *Walross*

Description. The walrus can be divided into three sub-species: the Arctic Walrus (*Odobenus rosmarus*), the Laptev Walrus (*Odobenus rosmarus laptevi*), and the Pacific Walrus (*Odobenus rosmarus divergens*). It is the only species from the one genus of the family Odobenidae. The total length of the adult male can reach and occasionally exceed 4m (13ft); it can weigh up to 1½ tons. Females are generally smaller. Rootless upper canines, similar to long curved tusks, protrude; the premolars and molars are smaller. Walruses move along the ground in a similar manner to sea-lions; they lift themselves up on their long front limbs and move with their back feet turned inwards. On land they are awkward and clumsy; in the water they are agile and fast. They eat crustaceans, molluscs, echinoderms, and various worms, all of which they dig from the sand or scratch off the rocks with their long tusks. They are gregarious animals and live in large groups which are sub-divided into a family nucleus consisting of one adult male, two or three females and a number of young. The gestation period is one year with the single young being born in April/May.

Geographic distribution. The Arctic Walrus, which once inhabited the same area as the Arctic Seal, exists around Greenland and Hudson Bay. Today, it has disappeared from the more southern areas. The Laptev Walrus is found along the northern coast of Siberia. The Pacific Walrus can be found from the Bering Sea to the peninsula of Kamchatka and in the Alaskan strait of Delphin. This sub-species has also disappeared from the more southern region.

Habitat. Open sea for migration periods; sandy beaches of islands or continental coasts for reproduction periods.

Population. According to the Red Data Book all three sub-species of the walrus are fast declining, although the Laptev Walrus is in the greatest danger. In 1930 the total population was estimated at 6,000–10,000; now, its total number is unknown. Research carried out in 1953–54 on the island of Pestchanyi, the area where the Laptev Walrus was considered most numerous, revealed that there were only 2,500–3,000. All the sub-species of the walrus have declined due to the excessive numbers killed annually. In 1957 they were placed under protection, which permitted only the local population and Arctic expeditions in need of sustenance to hunt them. In 1975 there were 28 walruses in 12 zoos, with one Arctic Walrus in St Louis Zoo. There are no Laptev Walruses in captivity.

Steller's Sea Cow

(Hydrodamalis stelleri)

Class: Mammals Subclass: Eutheria
Order: Sirenidae Family: Dugongidae (dugongs)
Genus: *Hydrodamalis* (=*Rhytina*)
French: *Rhytine de Steller* Italian: *Ritina di Steller*
German: *Stellersche Seekuh*

Description. Steller's Sea Cow was the largest of the Sirenidae, the order of aquatic mammals placed between the Cetaceae and the Pinnipedae which have horizontal tails in the form of a spatula. They could grow up to 8m (26ft) in length and they weighed up to 4 tons. The circumference of the massive body measured 6.20m (20ft). This species had no teeth and a skin which was profusely coated with crustaceous parasites. The animal's colouring was grey-brown and it had the appearance of an oak-tree trunk. The front legs were very small and in the form of flippers; there were no back legs and there is no trace of a pelvic bond. The period of gestation was one year after which one young was born.

Geographic distribution. Steller's Sea Cow lived exclusively on Bering Island and on the other islands of the small group of Commodore in the Bering Sea.

Habitat. This sea cow, which grazed on algae and submarine grasses, passed the day in shallow water, preferably around river mouths. It ate constantly and kept its head continually under water, only lifting it high enough for the nostrils to breathe every four or five minutes. In this way, it was able to remain hidden from passing ships.

History and causes of extinction. Steller's Sea Cow was discovered in 1741 by George Wilhelm Steller, a doctor on an expedition organized by the Dane, Vitus Bering. As the result of a storm, they landed at Bering Island and were forced to stay there for a few months. During this time, Steller observed their habits and later made the species public knowledge. Shortly afterwards, hunters descended on the island in search of walruses and silver foxes whose skins were valuable to the fur traders. The hunters soon realized that Steller's Sea Cow was an easily captured animal with strong, resistant skin. The massacre began at once and wiped out the entire species consisting of 1,500–2,000 animals within a few years. The last one was killed in 1768. Today, nothing remains of them except bones and some skins left in several Russian and German museums (there is a complete skeleton in Leningrad). In 1960, the crew of a Soviet fishing boat believed that they had found a small nucleus of Steller's Sea Cow. However, this was never proved and is disputable. Twenty-seven years after their discovery, man had rendered the animal extinct. This is one of the saddest stories in nature.

Sea Cow
(Dugong dugon)

Class: Mammals Subclass: Eutheria
Order: Sirenidae Family: Dugongidae
Genus: *Dugong*
French: *Dugong* Italian: *Dugongo* German: *Dugong*

Description. The Sea Cow has a spindle-shaped body which is approximately 2.50–3.20m (8 to 10ft) long. It weighs between 140–200kg (310–440lb) but the adult male can reach up to 300kg (660lb). The head is large and rounded but indistinguishable from the neck. The mouth is very large and the fleshy lips are enormous with small bristly hairs. It has two types of teeth: two corrugated plates for chewing and five or six pairs of molars. The male also has two incisors which, as the animal gets older, become very long and may even protrude beyond the lips. The eyes are small, without eyelids, and covered in membrane. The front legs have developed, for the purpose of swimming, into two short spatula-shaped flippers without nails. The skin varies in colour from brown to grey and is lighter on the belly; it is very thick, tough and completely hairless. The Sea Cow lives alone or in couples and very occasionally in small family groups. After a gestation period of a year the female produces one young. The young is 1·5m (5ft) in length and is suckled while the mother holds it with her flippers. It is possible that, centuries ago, sailors observed from a distance the female suckling her young in this way and, believing that it was a vast human form, originated the legend of the Sirens. (This name is now used in the animal's classification.)

Geographic distribution. Although enormously diminished in number, the Sea Cow still lives along the coast of the Red Sea and throughout the Indian Ocean from Africa, including Madagascar, to Arabia, India and as far as Malaysia, Indonesia, the Philippines and the northern coast of Australia.

Habitat. The Sea Cow is a typical marine-living mammal with a preference for coastal waters where the sea is not too deep. It lives on algae and submarine grasses, only lifting its head at one- to two-minute intervals in order to breathe. Occasionally, it ventures for a short expedition to river mouths.

Population. Although not in immediate danger of extinction, the position of the Sea Cow is vulnerable: it is hunted throughout the entire area of its distribution, and its numbers have diminished noticeably; it has even completely disappeared from many zones. The species is most numerous along the Australian coast and in New Guinea. It is hunted principally for its fat and also its meat. The Sea Cow is now protected in Australian waters (where a century ago it was relentlessly hunted) and in several other countries, but it is still the object of indiscriminate killing in many more. Only three or four Sea Cows have ever been held in captivity; today (1975) there is only one couple in captivity, in the aquarium at Mandapan, southern India.

Manatee

(Trichechus manatus)

Class: Mammals Subclass: Eutheria
Order: Sirenidae Family: Trichechidae
Genus: *Trichechus*
French: *Lamantin* Italian: *Manato* or *Lamantino*
German: *Manati*

Description. The genus *Trichechus* covers three species of manatee: the Northern Manatee (*Trichechus manatus*), the Brazilian Manatee (*Trichechus inunguis*) and the African Manatee (*Trichechus senegalensis*). This animal has a spindle-shaped body, a smaller head than the Sea Cow, and a square muzzle. The upper lip is thick and each half can move independently of the other. It is sparsely covered with bristles which grow 1.5cm ($\frac{1}{2}$in) apart. The front legs, which have been transformed into small fins, have vestiges of nails but these are missing in the species *inunguis*. The tail is very large and flat and not forked as the Sea Cow's. The skin is 5cm (2in) thick and varies in colour from grey to brown. It grows up to 4.50m (15ft) in length and weighs about 680kg (7cwt). Normally, however, sizes vary between 2.5 and 4m (8 and 13ft) and the weight between 140–360kg (300–800lb). After a gestation period of five to six months one young is born (sometimes two) which is about 1m (3ft) long. The birth takes place underwater, but the mother immediately brings the new born pup to the surface. The pup stays with its mother for around two years and is suckled for eighteen months.

Geographic distribution. The Northern Manatee used to inhabit all of the coastal waters of the Americas from the Atlantic coast of Carolina and Mexico, through Central America as far as the Guianas, also around the Bahamas and the Greater Antilles. Now it is limited to Florida, the West Indies, the Atlantic coast adjacent to Mexico, and the northern coast of South America. A small number of the Brazilian Manatee inhabits the Amazon and Orinoco rivers around the upper basins. The African Manatee inhabits the rivers and creeks along the west coast of Africa from Senegal to Angola, in Lake Chad and occasionally along the Gulf of Guinea.

Habitat. The shallow coastal waters of bays and estuaries, occasionally lagoons and rivers where the current flows slowly: the manatee graze in these areas on submarine grasses and algae.

Population. The manatee has been intensively hunted throughout its area of distribution because of its good-quality meat, the abundance of fat and its tough skin. It has also suffered as a result of the polluted coastal waters of America. Although it is protected legally in the United States and several other countries, the species continues to diminish. In Florida, a large number are killed every year by motor-boat propellers. There are about 1,000 manatees in the United States and several thousand more throughout the other countries it inhabits. The American national appeal for the World Wildlife Fund has set up a project for their conservation. The Brazilian Manatee, although protected in Brazil and Peru, is in imminent danger of extinction. The African Manatee, which is protected by the African Convention of 1969, is also intensely hunted and its numbers are declining.

Przewalski's Wild Horse

(Equus przewalskii)

Class: Mammals Subclass: eutheria
Order Perissodactyla = Odd-toed ungulates
Suborder: Hippomorpha Family Equidae (equines)
Genus: *Equus*
French: *Cheval de Przewalski* Italian: *Cavallo di Przewalski* German: *Przewalski Wildpferd*

Description. Przewalski's Wild Horse is the only un-domesticated species of horse today. It is 1.20–1.45m (4–4¾ft) high at the withers and 2.20–2.80m (7–9ft) long. It weighs 200–300kg (4–6cwt). The long hairy tail is approximately 1m (3ft) in length. It is different from all other horses because its mane is stiff and almost erect – about 15–20cm (6–8in) long and without a forelock. The body is golden-red or golden-brown on the upper parts and whitish on the underneath and muzzle; the mane, tail and legs are a browny-black. The dark stripe on its back is hardly noticeable. In winter the colour deepens slightly and the coat becomes longer and thicker. Its head is large with a short stumpy neck. In common with the domestic horse, the female gives birth to one foal after a gestation period of about 330 days, and the foal is suckled for six or seven months. The species can live in the wild for up to twenty-eight years, although some in captivity have lived longer – one female born in Philadelphia Zoo and transferred to Washington Zoo reached the age of thirty-three. It can be crossed with the domestic horse and produce fertile hybrids. It has also been crossed with the zebra, but sterile hybrids were produced. Attempts at crossing it with the ass have been unsuccessful. Little is recorded of the species' behaviour in the wild: it passes the day in desert territory and at dusk moves to pasture to graze; returning to the desert after dawn. The small herds that have been observed consist of a maximum of twenty, led by an adult male who puts himself at the back of the herd when danger arises to defend their flank. The species eats tough grasses which the domestic horse would reject. The foals are born between April and May. There have been a few cases of Przewalski's Horses which have been trained and ridden, but generally it is not possible to domesticate them.

Geographic distribution. It is thought that in prehistoric times Przewalski's Horse inhabited a vast area. At the time of its discovery in 1879, it was already very rare and only inhabited the steppes on the frontiers of Mongolia and China (Zungaria and the Gobi Desert). Now it only inhabits an area of 650 sq km (250 sq miles) in the desert hollows on the Takhin Sharnuru and Baitag-Bogdo.

Habitat. Southern slopes of high mountains and their northern valleys in autumn and winter; moves to semi-desert areas in spring and summer. The species depends on natural water sources but it is in competition with nomads who require the water for themselves and their domestic animals. The timid horses are thus driven away into more and more remote areas.

Population. Przewalski's Horse was discovered in 1879 in the Gobi Desert by the famous Russian scholar, Nikolaj Przewalski. The animal was then studied by the Russian zoologist I. S. Poljakov, who established it as a new species and gave it the name of its discoverer. The size of its population, which was not very large at the time of its discovery (although in this century some people have stated that there are many thousands in Mongolia) was reduced radically between 1930 and 1950 as a result of the poor pasture land and the frozen terrain. It was further diminished by political disturbances and frequent border conflicts (1948–56). It is not known how many of these horses live in the wild, but it is definitely in grave danger of extinction. The most recent sightings have been of only one or two horses at a time (there have also been claims from shepherds in the area of sightings of herds of seven to eleven horses): it can thus be guaranteed that at least a small group does still exist in Mongolia. The species has been legally protected by the People's Republic of Mongolia since 1926, but it is essential that reserves are set up where the species would be protected from other animals – particularly the domestic horse – and where those reared in captivity could be reintroduced into the wild to help with reproduction. The continuation of the species can be assured by the breeding in zoos: between 1897 and 1902 (the year when importation was ceased) 53 were imported into Europe and now their descendants are kept in zoos and parks. The number has increased from 36 in 1956, to 153 in 1968, and 254 in 1976, held in 60 collections and all reared in captivity, with the exception of one female born in the wild. The two main herds in captivity are at Prague, and at Catskill in the USA. Prague Zoo keeps a 'stud book', in which births and deaths are recorded of Przewalski's Wild Horses in captivity. Between twenty and thirty are born in captivity each year; the majority survive and are successfully reared.

Tarpan

(Equus gmelini)

Class: Mammals Subclass: Eutheria
Order: Perissodactyla Suborder: Hippomorpha
Family: Equidae (equines) Genus: *Equus*
French: *Tarpan* Italian: *Tarpan* German: *Tarpan*

Description. The tarpan, the extinct forefather of the Indo-germanic domestic horse, had a grey coat with a large dark stripe the length of the vertebrate column. The coat was long and thick and became denser during the winter months. It was the size of a medium to small horse.

Geographic distribution. The southern Russian plains along the course of the river Don and Dnieper and the scrubland of central and eastern Europe.

Habitat. Steppes and scrubland.

History and causes of extinction. The species became extinct between the eighteenth and nineteenth centuries due to the transformation of its habitat, slaughter by domestic horse-breeders who found the male tarpans polluted their stock, and in its hybridization through this cross-breeding with domestic stock. The last one died in the Ukraine on 25 December 1879. Various strains of basic domestic horse have been found in Germany and Poland which, being very similar to the tarpan, give us an idea of its appearance.

Mountain Zebra

(Equus zebra)

Class: Mammals Subclass: Eutheria
Order: Perissodactyla Suborder: Hippomorpha
Family: Equidae (equines) Genus: *Equus*
French: *Zèbre de montagne* Italian: *Zebra di montagna*
German: *Bergzebra*

Description. This species of zebra is characterized by the grid-shaped markings on the rump; the body is covered with thin parallel stripes which are finer at the hooves. The Mountain Zebra is up to 1.30m (4ft 3in) tall. There are two sub-species: the Cape Mountain Zebra (*Equus zebra zebra*) which is slightly smaller (no taller than 1.25m [4ft 1in]) and the Hartmann Zebra (*Equus zebra hartmannae*, illustrated above) which is a little larger and has finer stripes.

Geographic distribution. The Cape Mountain Zebra inhabits only two reserves on the mountains in the southern part of Cape Province; the Hartmann Zebra inhabits the mountainous part of south-west Africa and southern Angola.

Habitat. The Cape Mountain Zebra has been forced from grassland to unsuitable scrubland. The Hartmann Zebra inhabits arid semi-desert areas.

Population. The Cape Zebra was reduced in 1913 to only 27 examples which were transferred to a reserve. Now its number has increased to about 200. The Hartmann Zebra numbers about 7,000; there are 150 of the species in 47 zoos (1975).

Quagga

(Equus quagga)

Class: Mammals Subclass: Eutheria
Order: Perissodactyla Suborder: Hippomorpha
Family: Equidae (equines) Genus: *Equus*
French: *Couagga* Italian: *Quagga*
German: *Steppenzebra*

Description. The quagga is a species of Plains Zebra which interbred with the Burchel Zebra (*Equus burchelli*). The latter have been extinct since 1910, but three surviving sub-species are descended from it. Of these, the Chapman Zebra (*Equus b. antiquorum*) and the Grant Zebra (*Equus b. bohemi*) are the two most commonly found in zoos today. The quagga was 1.30m (4ft 3in) high at the withers and 2.60m (8½ft) long, including the tail which measured 60cm (2ft). In common with the Plains Zebra the ears were short and the tail well developed. The coat was glossy and smooth, with brown and white stripes only on the head, neck and upper part of the back; the belly, legs and tail were white. Along the back as far as the tail ran a brown-black stripe, edged with grey-brown. Its characteristic cry had no similarity either to the bray of an ass or the neigh of a horse, but sounded a 'qua-ha' from which it received the name of quagga from the Hottentots.

Geographic distribution. The quagga once inhabited South Africa, principally in the eastern regions, and extended from Cape Province to the Kalahari Desert, and to the interior of the Transvaal.

Habitat. The plains of South Africa where the species roamed in great herds.

History and causes of extinction. Even at the beginning of the nineteenth century the quagga was numerous throughout its area of distribution. The species fell victim to slaughter by the Boer settlers who killed thousands for their meat and hides. The last quagga in the wild was killed in 1878. Until that date many lived in various European zoos, but the last one, a female, died in Amsterdam Zoo, in 1883. If there had been any notion of wild-life conservation at that time, and if the zoos operated under present-day standards, the species would probably have survived. All that remains of the quagga for posterity are about twenty embalmed examples and a few photographs. An attempt in the 1930s to reconstruct this zebra at Munich Zoo through cross-breeding of other Plains Zebras (a similar experiment had been tried with the tarpan and uro) was unsuccessful as the animals under experiment were killed in an air-raid.

Asiatic Wild Ass

(Equus hemionus)

Class: Mammals Subclass: Eutheria
Order: Perissodactyla Suborder: Hippomorpha
Family: Equidae Genus: *Equus*
French: *Hémione* Italian: *Asino selvatico asiatico*
German: *Asiatischer Wildesel*

Description. According to the Red Data Book this entire species is vulnerable. Two of the five sub-species are in danger of extinction; the Syrian Wild Ass (*Equus hemionus hemippus*) and the Indian Wild Ass (the khur) (*E.h. khur*). The three other sub-species are the kulan (*E.h. hemionus*), the onager (*E.h. onager*) and the kiang (*E.h. kiang*, illustrated opposite). These wild Asian Equidae are similar to both the ass and horse. The two differences are that only the tip of the tail is covered with hair and the ears are similar to those of the African Wild Ass. Of the five sub-species, the kiang is the largest, reaching 1·50m (5ft) at the withers, and weighing 350–400kg (775–880lb). The behaviour of the Asiatic Wild Ass is virtually the same in all the sub-species: they are gregarious and graze in herds led by a female; by day it searches for food, eating plants and salty grasses in the hill country, and by night it shelters beneath shrubs. When resting or grazing the herd is well spaced for maximum security, so that it covers as large an area as possible while remaining a group. It can reach a galloping speed of 70km (45 miles) per hour but its normal speed, which it can maintain for long distances, is about 40–50km (25–30 miles) per hour. Unlike the African Wild Ass, the Asiatic Wild Ass is very dependent on water: it visits a watering place once or twice a day, preferably at dawn and sunset. There is no mating season as this depends on the environmental and seasonal conditions of each of the many areas it inhabits. The gestation period is eleven months. The foal is protected and cared for by its mother for the first fifteen days, after which it joins the herd.

Geographic distribution. The Asiatic Wild Ass was once found from Arabia to Tibet. The distribution of the two sub-species of greatest interest because of their rarity can be traced as follows: the Syrian Wild Ass found its way through Syria, Palestine, Arabia and Iraq. It may still survive in a small area immediately south of the Syrian-Turkish border, half way between Aleppo and Mosul but there is no definite information to substantiate this. The Indian Wild Ass, the khur, was numerous throughout north-west India and west Pakistan. Now the major area of distribution is a small desert zone of about 2,590 sq km (1,000 sq miles) along the Pakistan/Gujaret border. One small herd of about thirty has been sighted in Pakistan near Nagar Parkar.

Habitat. Desert and sub-desert areas with sparse shrub vegetation; the khur also inhabits areas richly encrusted with salt.

Population. The Syrian Wild Ass is now believed to be extinct. Those that inhabited the greater Syrian desert have probably been extinct for twenty to thirty years. It was wiped out in northern Syria by the local Anazeh and Shamnar tribesmen. The khur numbered between 3,000 and 5,000 in 1946; 870 in 1962; 400 in October 1969 and by December 1969 the number had decreased to a total of 368. The principal cause of this sub-species' rapid decline is a disease which has been killing it since 1940. The government started a programme in 1961 to inoculate horses and asses but it has not had the desired effect of preserving this species. In 1975 there were 330 onagers and kulans, 17 kiangs, and 10 khurs in 75 zoos and parks; no Syrian Wild Asses are held in captivity.

African Wild Ass

(Equus asinus)

Class: Mammals Subclass: Eutheria
Order: Perissodactyla Suborder: Hippomorpha
Family: Equidae Genus: *Equus*
French: *Ane sauvage de l'Afrique* Italian: *Asino selvatico africano* German: *Afrikanischer Wildesel*

Description. According to some authorities, the African Wild Ass is represented by one species divided into three sub-species: the Nubian Wild Ass (*Equus [Asinus] asinus africanus*, illustrated opposite, above left), the North African Wild ass (*Equus [Asinus] asinus atlanticus*) and the Somalian Wild Ass (*Equus [Asinus] asinus somalicus* illustrated in the foreground). The North African Wild Ass has been extinct for some time. The African Wild Ass is of medium size – the Nubian is smaller than the Somalian – reaching between 1.10 and 1.40m (3½–4½ft) at the withers. It is very elegant and well proportioned; the legs are long and slim, and the ears, although long, are in proportion to the head. The mane is short and the coat varies in colour from pure grey to yellowish or reddish grey. The Nubian Wild Ass has the shape of a cross on its back; this is formed by a longitudinal black stripe intersected at the shoulders. The longitudinal stripe is occasionally found on the Somalian Wild Ass, but never the stripe across the shoulders. The legs of the Somalian Ass are always ringed to a certain extent. Like all other Equidae, the African Wild Ass is gregarious and, before it became very rare, moved in large herds, usually led by stallions. They were constantly in search of food but rarely left their original territory. The African Wild Ass' diet consists of dry shrubs and acacia fronds. Hearing is its sharpest sense and acts as security against surprise from its enemies. At the first sign of danger they gallop at high speed, directed by the leading stallion or occasionally a female. Only when they meet at waterholes is the African Wild Ass likely to fall prey to one of the great cats or to man, who is always on the look-out for the ass for its highly appreciated meat and hide. Fortunately, nature has helped the African Wild Ass to avoid these threats: it has an exceptional resistance to thirst which permits it to water irregularly – certainly not daily – therefore reducing the number of times it encounters its enemies. According to authorities, the domestic strain derives from this ass.

Geographic distribution. The North African Wild Ass was widely distributed over the South Atlantic regions and it is possible to reconstruct some of its physical characteristics through the domestic strains re-released in that area. The present distribution of the Nubian variety covers the hill region around the Red Sea to south of the Suakin and as far south as the Eritrean border towards the river Atbara. In 1971 two examples were seen in Eritrea on the border with the Sudan. It is also said to have inhabited the area north of Tibesti in Chad. According to the Red Data Book, a small group was seen in the salt marshes of Hatiyet and Melva east of Giarabub, at the extreme northern point of the Libyan desert. The Somalian variety inhabited the area from Massawa in north Eritrea, to Uebiscebeli towards the south, and westward to the Auasc Valley across the Danakil Plains. The most numerous population of this variety has been noted on the east bank of the River Auasc from the north at Gewani to Tendaho.

Habitat. The original and/or current area inhabited by all three sub-species is semi-desert, arid, without water, and with poor shrub vegetation.

Population. The Nubian variety may possibly be extinct; otherwise, it has disappeared due to cross-breeding with the local domestic ass. A relatively recent census on the Somalian Wild Ass estimated it at 2,000–3,000 for the area including Gewani, Lake Abbe and Sardo in Ethiopia. There are only 250 in Somalia around Las Anod and Gebidebo. The causes for the decline of the species can be traced to its persecution by man, particularly during periods of war or civil disruption which always preclude any attempt at control or applied legal protection. Both the Somalian and the Nubian varieties are under complete protection now in Ethiopia and Somalia and have been included in Class 'A' of the African Convention of 1969, which means they can only be killed or captured with authorization for relevant scientific reasons. However, it is not possible to make protection effective in such a difficult area to watch. There are programmes to research the population of the Nubian Wild Ass and to create reserves. There is a plan to protect the Somalian Wild Ass by setting up a reserve in the Teo area, approximately 2,000 sq km (775 sq miles) to the south of the Auasc river and another in the Tendaho-Sardo area. In 1975 there were forty African Wild Asses in six zoos and parks, almost all descended from the first group imported in 1930 which constituted the famous herd at the Hellabrunn Park in Munich. In 1970, five were brought directly from Somalia and by 1 January 1973 two foals had been born. These are the only African Wild Asses in captivity which have come from the wild and from their original country.

Malayan Tapir

(Tapirus indicus)

Class: Mammals Subclass: Eutheria
Order: Perissodactyla Suborder: Ceratomorpha
Family: Tapiridae Genus: *Tapirus*
French: *Tapir de l'Inde* Italian: *Tapiro dalla
gualdrappa* German: *Schabrackentapir*

Description. The Malayan Tapir, also known as the
Indian Tapir, differs from the three American species as
follows: the coat has the characteristic dark colouring,
almost black, on the front of the body (head, neck,
shoulders, forelegs) and on the hind legs, including the
thighs, while the back and abdomen are a light grey –
like a saddle-cloth. Up to the age of two months, the
young retain the family colouring: a brown base striped
longitudinally with white, alternating with lines of white
spots; this colouring disappears after five months. This
species is larger than the American species, reaching up
to a total length of 2.50m (8ft) (the tail is a mere few
centimetres [1in]). The tapir's diet is very varied:
although it prefers young shoots, leaves and tender
branches of certain shrubby plants, it will also eat fruit
and water or field grasses. Unsociable by nature, tapirs
keep to the same area, making tracks in the landscape
through constant use of the same routes.

Geographic distribution. This area of distribution covers
the island of Sumatra across the Molucca Peninsula as
far as the south eastern tip of Thailand.

Habitat. This tapir, like the other species, inhabits humid
tropical forest, particularly the areas near rivers, lakes
and swamps. The Malayan Tapir, unlike others of its
family, is a first-rate swimmer and will walk along the
bottom of a river like a hippopotamus.

Population. In spite of the worrying reduction of this
species' numbers in recent years, its area of distribution
has not appreciably reduced. It is still present in protected areas in Thailand, although in much smaller
numbers. It was hunted there mainly for its meat which
was highly valued and until recently sold in markets.
Hunting is less of a problem in Sumatra and Malaysia as
the local Muslim population consider the meat impure.
However, the species is in serious danger of extinction in
these areas as the agricultural transformations, particularly the destruction of the forests, have limited the area
where the tapir can live. It is now illegal to hunt it in all
the countries it inhabits, and it is protected in sanctuaries. In 1975 there were 120 in 50 zoos and a few
instances of reproduction.

Mountain Tapir

(Tapirus pinchaque)

Class: Mammals Subclass: Eutheria
Order: Perissodactyla Suborder: Ceratomorpha
Family: Tapiridae Genus: *Tapirus*
French: *Tapir des Andes* Italian: *Tapiro di montagna*
German: *Bergtapir*

Description. There are four species belonging to the genus *Tapirus*, three American and one Asian. Although all four are in danger of extinction, the most serious threat is to the Mountain Tapir (also known as the Andes Tapir, and illustrated below). This species is smaller than the others: its maximum length is 1.80m (6ft) and it weighs no more than 250kg (550lb). The coat is characteristic of this species; it is soft and woolly, particularly on the belly, and the back has almost hairless patches. The Baird Tapir (*Tapirus bairdi*) (the largest of the American tapirs) is also thought by the UICN to be near extinction. It grows to a length of 2.20m (7ft) and its weight can be over 300kg (660lb). The tapir's diet consists of fruit, grasses and shoots of trees and bushes which are wrenched off with the short trunk. Apart from its prehensile function, the trunk has a tactile function as the tip is covered with sensory hairs.

Geographic distribution. The Mountain Tapir is found only in the Andes in an area including Venezuela, Ecuador, Colombia and Peru. The Baird Tapir is found from Vera Cruz in southern Mexico, across the central American countries as far as the Colombian and Ecuadorian Andes.

Habitat. The Mountain Tapir inhabits mountain areas up to the line of eternal snow, at around 4,500m (14,800ft), but it prefers the region between 2,000 and 3,500m (6,500 and 11,500ft) with its shrubby and low tree-covered vegetation. The Baird Tapir inhabits humid tropical forest and low-lying swamps, although it also inhabits mountain shrubland up to 3,000m (10,000ft).

Population. The total population of the Mountain Tapir is not known. It is estimated that there are between 200–300 in Peru and only a few dozen in the eastern areas of Cordigliera in the Andes. Between 1966 and 1970 a considerable number were captured and sold to zoos. The Baird Tapir's population is unknown. Both species are now legally protected in their countries of habitation and capture is only authorized for scientific reasons. In 1975 there were in 16 zoos, 5 male and 5 female Mountain Tapirs and 21 Baird Tapirs.

Indian Rhinoceros

(Rhinoceros unicornis)

Class: Mammals Subclass: Eutheria
Order: Perissodactyla Suborder: Ceratomorpha
Family: Rhinocerotidae (rhinoceroses)
Genus: *Rhinoceros*
French: *Rhinocéros unicorne des Indes*
Italian: *Rinoceronte indiano* German: *Panzernashorn*

Description. Both the Indian Rhinoceros and the Javan Rhinoceros are distinguished from the African Rhinoceros by the folds of skin which for centuries have been its most notable characteristic. The skin of the Indian Rhinoceros is hairless apart from the ears and tip of the tail, and the folds of skin on the shoulders fall backwards covering the shoulder blades. The tough skin is covered with horny patches and is as thick as an elephant's. The total length of the adult can reach up to 4m (13ft) of which 60cm (24in) is the tail. Its shoulder height is 1.60m (5ft) and its weight can be over 2 tons. The body is absolutely massive but, nevertheless, this does not prevent this powerfully-built giant from trotting lightly. It can gallop at a speed of up to 35–40km (25–28 miles) per hour. The feet have three toes covered with very large nails; they are separated by cushions of connecting tissue. The two incisors function as weapons. The Indian Rhinoceros, like all rhinoceroses, is vegetarian and eat shoots of shrubs and reeds which are torn from the branches with the upper lip which has developed specifically for this purpose into a kind of trunk. In captivity they are fed fruit, carrots, pellets composed of compressed grains, vegetables, meat and vitamins, as well as fresh grasses and hay. According to statistics gathered by some zoos, the adult Indian Rhinoceros will consume 20–25kg (44–55lb) of dry foodstuffs a day and drink up to 100l (26gal) of water. From observations made of the animal in the wild, it seems that this rhinoceros is not particularly solitary, nor does it stay in one place. It does, however, keep within the bounds of its habitat, wandering over a vast area in search of food and safety. Occasionally, two rhinoceroses will fight over territory, and scars from their battles can be found on the skins. One cannot say whether the species has natural enemies: none of the animals in the area will attack one, nor is the rhinoceros frightened of any except the elephant – in which case the rhino will usually retreat hastily, except when a mother sees that her young is threatened. The mating season falls between February and April and the gestation period is sixteen months. The newborn rhinoceros weighs around 65kg (143lb) and has no horn.

Geographic distribution. The species once inhabited a large area of northern India and Nepal, from the base of the mountains in the Hindu Kush to the west of Peshawar, and to the southern bush area of the River Indus to the south of Kashmir, and all along the Himalayan foothills as far as the borders of Burma through the Terai. Today it is limited to the Brahmaputra Valley in Assam, Jaldapara and Gorumara in West Bengal and the Rapti Valley region of Nepal Terai.

Habitat. The Indian Rhinoceros prefers plains covered with tall grasses and leaves, and swampy areas with small lakes and interconnecting streams. Today, however, particularly in Nepal, many rhinoceroses live in the forest and graze in the areas which are now cultivated for agricultural foodcrops.

Population. In 1973 the total population of this species was over 900; according to a census in March 1972, 658 are confined within the Kaziranga Wildlife Sanctuary. It was estimated that, in May 1973, the Jaldapara Reserve in West Bengal had 45. In Nepal there were at least 200 living within the confines of the Royal Chitawan National Park, and this number seems to be increasing. In some areas, poachers in search of the rhinoceros' horn – highly prized in the East as a powerful aphrodisiac – pose a serious threat to the animal's survival. In Jaldapara 29 of the 60 were killed between 1971 and 1972. Eight sanctuaries have been set up in India and one in Nepal specifically to protect this species. There are strict laws prohibiting poaching and a number of protective measures aimed at safeguarding the rhinoceros' habitat. Several countries have prohibited importation of the species, except for scientific purposes, with the aim of repopulation. In 1975 there were 60 rhinoceroses in 30 collections – most of them zoos: 33 males, 27 females and 3 of unknown sex; about 30 were born in captivity. They have been imported into Europe since the Middle Ages, but there is only one recorded case (1956) of its reproduction there in captivity.

Javan Rhinoceros

(Rhinoceros sondaicus)

Class: Mammals Subclass: Eutheria
Order: Perissodactyla Suborder: Ceratomorpha
Family: Rhinocerotidae (rhinoceroses)
Genus: *Rhinoceros*
French: *Rhinocéros de la Sonde* Italian: *Rinoceronte di Giava* German: *Javanashorn*

Description. The Javan Rhinoceros differs from the Indian Rhinoceros in the following ways: it is slightly smaller and has folds of skin across the back which meet at the shoulders; the horn is very small in the male and almost non-existent in the female; the head is slimmer but longer, and the digital upper lip is longer. It grows to a total length of 3m (10ft), including the tail. Shoulder height is 1.40m (4½ft). There is little information regarding the physique or habits of this species. We do know that its diet is similar to the Indian Rhinoceros – shoots and leaves of shrubs which it tears off branches with the developed upper lip. The species reaches maturity very quickly and the adults are not gregarious.

Geographic distribution. The species was once distributed over a large part of India, Bangladesh, Burma, Thailand, Cambodia, Laos, Vietnam, the Malaysian Peninsula and the islands of Java and Sumatra. It is certain that it is present in the Udjung-Kulon Reserve (360 sq km [140 sq miles]) at the extreme western tip of Java and it is probably present in the Leuser Reserve (6,000 sq km [2,300 sq miles]) in the northern part of Sumatra.

Habitat. The species prefers areas of dense vegetation as found in the Udjung-Kulon Reserve; forests and high mountains; marshy areas, coastal zones and even where there are human settlements.

Population. In 1967 the population of the Javan Rhinoceros in the Udjung-Kulon Reserve was estimated at between 21 and 28. However, by 1975 the species had increased to an estimated number of between 41 and 52. The number in the Leuser Reserve is not known but is estimated at about 25. Poaching to obtain the rhinoceros' horn, considered to be a powerful aphrodisiac and medicine in the East, still constitutes the major cause of this species' disappearance. The following projects have been mounted since 1921 to protect this rhinoceros: in 1967, R. Schenkel, from Basle, was invited to Java by the World Wildlife Fund, and in 1968 the World Wildlife Fund and the University of Basle co-founded the 'Basle Patronage Committee for the Udjung-Kulon'. There are no Javan Rhinoceroses in captivity.

Sumatran Rhinoceros

(Dicerorhinus sumatrensis)

Class: Mammals Subclass: Eutheria
Order: Perrisodactyla Suborder: Ceratomorpha
Family: Rhinocerotidae (rhinoceroses)
Genus: *Dicerorhinus*
French: *Rhinocéros de Sumatra* Italian: *Rinoceronte di Sumatra* German: *Sumatranashorn*

Description. The Sumatran Rhinoceros, the only species of its genus, is the smallest living rhinoceros. It is the least developed and the only one whose body is partly covered in hair. Its total length hardly measures 3m (10ft), its height is 1.40m (4½ft), and its weight just 1 ton. While all the other Asian rhinoceroses have a single horn, the Sumatran Rhinoceros has two. In the male, the first horn measures up to 60cm (23½in) and the second 20cm (8in); the female's horns are much smaller, the first being no more than 15cm (6in) and the second a mere outline. The hair, which is long and rough, grows all over the body. There is a fringe around the ears although it is less thick in the adult. Furthermore, the folds of skin on the back are less long and deep; those on the flanks, which start at the thighs, do not meet at the shoulder, and the coat has small regular lumps, not large, irregularly placed lumps. The Sumatran Rhinoceros is basically nocturnal and lives alone or in small groups, wandering in search of bamboo shoots and leaves to eat. According to some authorities, the mainland Sumatran Rhinoceros can be set apart as a sub-species, *Dicerorhinus sumatrensis lasiotis*, and is given the common name of Rough-eared Rhinoceros.

Geographic distribution. It was once found equally distributed throughout south-eastern Asia from Assam to Vietnam; throughout the Malaccan peninsula, and on the islands of Borneo and Sumatra. Today, the species is limited to a small population in Assam down to the Malaccan peninsula, across Burma and Thailand, and on the islands of Borneo and Sumatra.

Habitat. This species prefers the huge tropical forest, bush, swamps and reed beds which are rich in vegetation, from low plains to a height of 2,000m (6,500ft).

Population. This species is in grave danger of extinction due to its very small population which is widely distributed. It is more or less officially protected throughout its area of distribution. In 1972, the UICN and the World Wildlife Fund prepared an International Protection, No 884, which proposed a programme in two phases for the conservation of the species. Only one Sumatran Rhinoceros has been held for certain in captivity, in a zoo in Copenhagen; it died in February 1972. However, there is record of a Sumatran Rhinoceros held in a zoo in Calcutta, India, in 1889.

Black Rhinoceros
(Diceros bicornis)

Class: Mammals Subclass: Eutheria
Order: Perrisodactyla Suborder: Ceratomorpha
Family: Rhinocerotidae Genus: *Diceros*
French: *Rhinocéros noir* Italian: *Rhinoceronte nero*
German: *Spitzmaulnashorn*

Description. The Black, or Two Horned African Rhinoceros is the only one of its genus. The adult can grow to a length of 3.75m (12ft), excluding the tail, and a shoulder height of 1.60m (5ft). It weighs about 3 tons. It feeds mainly on shoots and leaves which it tears away using the specifically developed upper lip.
Geographic distribution. The species was once distributed in large numbers from Cape Province to Southern Angola in the west and to Ethiopia in the east. Today, it is found only in some defined territories within its original territory.
Habitat. Savannah with trees or bushes; open areas in forests; lowland grassy areas, such as mountainous regions up to 3,000m (10,000ft).
Population. According to the Red Data Book, the Black Rhinoceros' position is 'vulnerable'. Although legally protected throughout almost its entire habitation, it is persecuted by poachers; it is further seriously threatened by the transformation of its grazing grounds into cultivated areas. There are approximately 160 in 75 zoos.

White or Square-lipped Rhinoceros
(Ceràtotherium simum cottoni)

Class: Mammals Subclass: Eutheria
Order: Perrisodactyla Suborder: Ceratomorpha
Family: Rhinocerotidae Genus: *Ceratotherium*
French: *Rhinocéros blanc* Italian: *Rhinoceronte bianco*
German: *Breitmaulnashorn*

Description. The White, or Square-lipped Rhinoceros has two sub-species: the *Ceratotherium simum cottoni* in the north and the *Ceratotherium simum simum* in the south which is much less rare. The differences between these two sub-species are difficult to find. The White Rhinoceros is the largest of all the rhinoceroses, growing to 4m (13ft) in length, excluding the tail, and 2m (6½ft) in height at the shoulders. It weighs at least 3 tons.
Geographic distribution. The northern sub-species was once almost equally distributed in an area of Africa between 13° and 9° North. Today, those that survive live in the original territory in small, scattered groups insufficient to guarantee the survival of the species.
Habitat. Savannah and arid forests.
Population. According to the Red Data Book in 1972, the northern sub-species, which is in grave danger of extinction, had no more than 250 examples. The southern sub-species can virtually be considered out of danger. There are about 400 White Rhinoceroses in 100 zoos; 9 are from the north in 6 zoos (1975). About 30 have been born in captivity, the first of which was in Pretoria Zoo, 1967.

Pigmy Hippopotamus

(Choeropsis liberiensis)

Class: Mammals Subclass: Eutheria
Order: Artiodactyla Suborder: Nonruminantia
Family: Hippopotamidae Genus: *Choeropsis*
French: *Hippopotame nain* Italian: *Ippopotamo nano*
German: *Zwergflusspferd*

Description. At first glance, the Pigmy Hippo could be mistaken for the Common Hippopotamus, but in reality the differences are so significant that it has been classified under a different genus. It grows to a length of up to 1.75m (5½ft) and a height of about 80cm (31in). It weighs 180–260kg (400–575lb). Proportionately, the head is smaller and more round than that of the Common Hippopotamus. The mouth is very large; there is only one pair of lower incisors and the canines are developed into tusks. The coat is a blackish brown, sleek, hairless and kept constantly moist and oiled by the secretion of mucus. After a gestation period of about 100 days, the female gives birth to one young, weighing 4–6kg (9–13lb). The Pigmy Hippopotamus lives for thirty-five to forty years. Very little is known of the habits of this species. It is possible to travel for days within its area of distribution without sighting one of them. They are very shy and will flee from the presence of man. It has been thought for the last few years that, unlike the Common Hippopotamus which hides in water, the Pigmy Hippopotamus will take to the forest when threatened. It is also believed that, at the approach of danger, the species seeks out hollow paths that lead directly to a nearby river or swamp and hide there undetected. The species feeds off water plants, leaves, algae, grasses and fallen fruit.

Geographic distribution. The species is distributed irregularly throughout a restricted zone in West Africa–Sierra Leone, Guinea, Liberia and the Ivory Coast. It is believed that it is no longer present in Nigeria.

Habitat. The Pigmy Hippopotamus is less acquatic than the Common Hippopotamus. It inhabits inaccessible tropical forest and thick vegetation on river banks; at night it searches for food in forests.

Population. The species is very rare. Its decline has been caused by the destruction of its habitat and by the intense hunting by natives for its meat. It has been protected since the African Convention of 1969 but reserves should be created in the region it inhabits. The species adapts very well to captivity and reproduces normally in zoos. In 1975, there were about 190 in 60 zoos; more than half of these were born in captivity (there are records from various zoos that about 20 are born in captivity a year). One couple in particular, in Basle Zoo, have produced 38 young (10 males and 28 females), making it possible to place the animal in various zoos without withdrawing any from the wild.

Vicuña

(Vicugna vicugna)

Class: Mammals Subclass: Eutheria
Order: Artiodattili Suborder: Tylopoda
Family: Camelidae Genus: *Vicugna* (llama)
French: *Vigogne* Italian: *Vigogna* German: *Vikunja*

Description. It is difficult to believe that the vicuña is descended from the camel, or rather from a species crossed between the camel and dromedary. However, despite its characteristic appearance, the vicuña is not so different from its African and Asian cousins: outwardly, it is similar to the South American Llama or alpaca – many scientists, in fact, classify all these species under one genus, *Llama*. The vicuña is, however, much smaller than the llama, measuring between 70 and 90cm (28 and 30in) at the withers and weighing no more than 50kg (110lb). Its body structure is slim and elegant: it has long fragile legs, a long mobile neck and a small head with large, luminous eyes and great pointed ears. The lips are less pronounced than the camel's. The vicuña has two unique characteristics: the lower incisors are long, straight and grow continually, like a rodent's, in order to withstand their constant use cropping the very short grasses of the terrain it inhabits; it has long soft hair, more highly prized than that of any of the Camelidae. The coat is muted brown on the upper part of the body and whitish underneath; a white mane up to 35cm (14in) covers the neck and chest. Vicunas live in small groups composed of between five and ten families with their young under the leadership of one male. When danger arises, the male raises the alarm by a high-pitched cry, rather like a whistle, and places himself between the cause of danger and the females while they escape. Like the llama, the vicuña defends itself by spitting rapidly and hard, expelling air and saliva. It is a very graceful species, more so than any other hoofed mammal. It feeds by nibbling the sporadic tufts of short grass; it also eats mallow and similar plants found in sandy regions. One offspring (very occasionally two) is born in February or March after an eleven-month period of gestation. The young is able to stand up and move within a quarter of an hour after birth; it is suckled for six months and remains with the mother for its first year. The species usually lives up to twenty years, but in captivity can reach twenty-four. It is possible for the vicuña to cross with all the species of llama and this produces fertile hybrids. It has been crossed with the alpaca in particular, giving what is known as the 'paco-vicuña', a cross which is appreciated for its fine and very valuable wool.

Geographic distribution. The species was once distributed over a large area in the highest part of the Andes from 3,000 to 5,000m (10,000 to 17,000ft) in Chile, Argentina, Bolivia, Peru and Ecuador. There are still small herds in the first four of these countries, while in Ecuador the species is extinct.

Habitat. The higher plains of the Andes. In summer, it prefers the zone below the snow line, feeding off the succulent vegetation there; during the other seasons it frequents the 'puna', the high, very arid plain.

Population. The value of the vicuña's fleece is by no means a modern discovery and was exploited by ancient civilizations. During the period of the Inca Empire, the vicuña was held in the highest respect and hunting it was rigorously prohibited. Only in ancient times, and under the direction of the authorities, were groups of this species brought into enclosures, sheared and then released. It was only killed for the use of the skin when there was an abundance of males. The fleeces were then presented to the Inca and his family who were the only people permitted to wear such a precious cloth. However, during the domination by Spain, the vicuña was effectively massacred – as many as 80,000 were killed a year – and this so reduced the population that in 1825 Simon Bolivar (who obtained independence for his country) instigated a law to protect the species in Peru and Bolivia. Although this law was strengthened and imposed in Chile and Argentina, vicuña wool is so valuable and the territory that the species inhabits is so difficult to watch, that indiscriminate killing has always continued, even today. The species was attacked most heavily during the years 1950–60 when the number was reduced from 400,000 to less than 19,000 – a reduction of 98 per cent. Thanks to the efforts of Felipe Bonavides, President of the Peruvian World Wildlife Fund and a councillor for the International World Wildlife Fund, Peru created the first reserve, at Pampa Galeras, in 1966 after he had battled for some twenty years for the conservation of this species. In only a few years the numbers of the vicuña have risen from 640 to about 30,000. Other reserves have since been created in Peru, Chile and Bolivia. The USA and Great Britain have recently prohibited the importation of vicuña wool – an essential measure bearing in mind that 95 per cent of the wool was worked in Britain before exportation to the rest of the world. Nevertheless, it is still very difficult to protect this animal in its country of origin due to the value of its wool – poaching and illegal exportation are therefore irresistible. The measures imposed for its protection have enabled the vicuña to increase sixfold in ten years: there are now 45,000 in Peru, 2,000 in Bolivia and several hundred both in Chile and Argentina. The species is still considered to be in a vulnerable position but it is not in immediate danger. In 1975 there were 70 in 20 zoos, of which 59 had been born in captivity (10 being born each year).

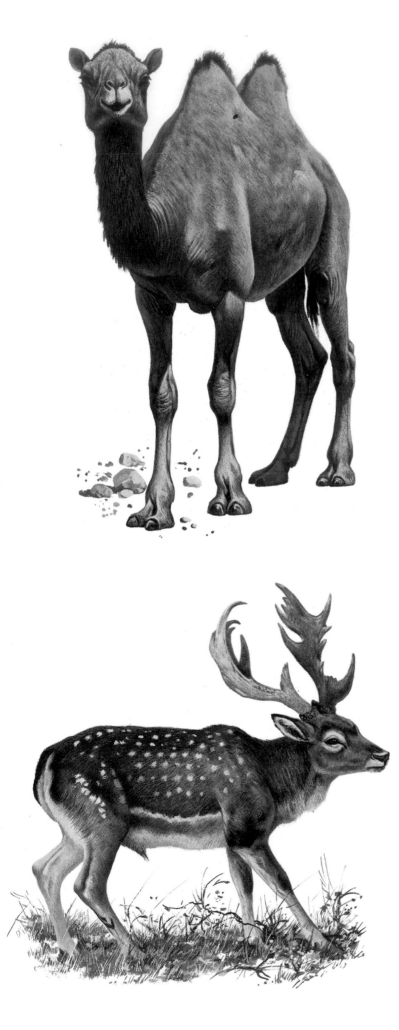

Wild Camel

(Camelus bactrianus ferus)

Class: Mammals Subclass: Eutheria
Order: Artiodactyla Suborder Tylopoda
Family: Camelidae Genus: *Camelus*
French: *Chameau sauvage* Italian: *Cammello selvatico* German: *Wild-Kamel*

Description. Compared to the domestic camel, the Wild, or Bactrian Camel is slimmer and less hairy, has a shorter muzzle and ears, smaller feet and smaller, upright humps. During the heat of the summer, the herds go up to the mountain zones as far as 3,000m (10,000ft); in winter they return to the desert. The young are born in March after a gestation period of thirteen months.

Geographic distribution. Up to 1920 the species was numerous in the Gobi Desert, in Mongolia and Turkestan. After this, the herd was divided into two main areas: south-western Mongolia and north-east China between Lake Lob Nor and Lake Bagrach Kol.

Habitat. The Gobi Desert, semi-desert and steppes.

Population. Enormously diminished because of intense hunting and its competition with domestic livestock, the species was considered to be extinct after World War II. As a result of research carried out in 1973 the population is estimated at about 900.

Persian Fallow Deer

(Dama mesopotamica)

Class: Mammals Subclass: Eutheria
Order: Artiodactyla Suborder: Ruminantia
Family: Cervidae Subfamily: Cervinae Genus: *Dama*
French: *Daim de Mesopotamie* Italian: *Daino della Mesopotamia* German: *Persischer Damhirsch*

Description. The Persian Fallow deer is notably larger than the Common Fallow Deer (*Dama dama*) from Europe. It can reach up to 105cm (41in) in height at the withers and a weight of 200kg (440lb). It is of brighter colour than its European counterpart but has the same white spotting on the upper part of the body.

Geographic distribution. Previously distributed from Syria and Palestine as far as Iraq and Iran. Now it is only found in two restricted zones in Iran on the banks of the Dez and Karkheh rivers.

Habitat. Thickest areas of vegetation along river banks.

Population. The species was held to be extinct in 1917 and then rediscovered in 1955. It is considered to be in great danger of extinction; according to an investigation in 1968 there are less than thirty on the banks of the River Dez and only five on the banks of the River Karkheh. The species is now protected by Iranian law and the two zones it inhabits have been national parks since 1968. A herd has been raised in captivity at Dasht-e-Naz which contains some twenty animals. Found only in two zoos in Germany: Kronberg and Munich.

Brow-antlered Deer

(Cervus eldi)

Class: Mammals Subclass: Eutheria
Order: Artiodactyla Suborder: Ruminantia
Family: Cervidae Subfamily: Cervinae Genus: *Cervus*
French: *Cerf d'Eld* Italian: *Tameng* or *Cervo di Eld*
German: *Leierhirsch*

Description. This south-east Asian deer can be divided
into three sub-species: Burmese Eld's Deer (*C.e.
thamin*), Manipur Eld's Deer (*C.e. eldi*) and Siamese
Eld's Deer (*C.e. siamensis*). The species is about 110–
115cm (43–45in) high, 108cm (43in) long and weighs up
to 150kg (330lb). The males have a dark brown winter
coat with a whitish belly; in summer, the dark brown
colour lightens and the belly becomes darker. The
females always keep the same yellow-brown colouring.
Geographic distribution. The sub-species inhabit the
countries from which they get their names. The Siamese
Eld's Deer also lives in Indo-China and on Hainan Island.
Habitat. Copses and plains with plenty of water.
Population. Having been slaughtered through hunting,
this deer is in great danger of extinction: the Manipur
sub-species, which is the rarest, has only 50 examples in
a reserve of 35sq km (14sq miles). Only the Burmese
Eld's Deer does not cause much concern with its population of 3,500. While the latter sub-species can be found
in 6 zoos, Paris Zoo has the only Siamese Eld's Deer in
captivity and the Manipur Eld's Deer is only found in
the zoos of Calcutta and New Delhi.

Sika

(Cervus nippon)

Class: Mammals Subclass: Eutheria
Order: Artiodactyla Suborder: Ruminantia
Family: Cervidae Subfamily: Cervinae Genus: *Cervus*
French: *Sika* Italian: *Sika* German: *Sikahirsch*

Description. The sika is a deer of medium size and compact build with a slender head and dappled coat. Its
height at the withers varies between 75 and 110cm (30
and 43in) and it is 105–115cm (41–45in) long. It weighs
about 110kg (243lb). There are seven sub-species, five
of which are in danger of extinction: the Formosa Sika
(*C.n. taioanus*, illustrated right), the Ryukyu Sika
(*C.n. keramae*), and those from north China, the North
China Sika (*C.n. mandarinus*), the Shansi Sika (*C.n.
grassianus*) and the South China Sika (*C.n. kopschi*).
Geographic distribution. From Siberia across Manchuria
and eastern China to Indochina; Japan and Formosa.
Habitat. Scrubland and forest of the mountain zones.
Population. The Formosa Sika: probably less than 300;
the Ryukyu Sika: probably less than ten; the North
China Sika: probably near to extinction in the wild; the
Shansi Sika: virtually extinct; the South China Sika:
also probably extinct.

Corsican Red Deer

(Cervus elaphus corsicanus)

Class: Mammals Subclass: Eutheria
Order: Artiodactyla Suborder: Ruminantia
Family: Cervidae Subfamily: Cervinae Genus: *Cervus*
French: *Cerf de Corse* Italian: *Cervo sardo*
German: *Tyrrenischer Rothirsch* or *Korsischer Rothirsch*

Description. The species *Cervus elaphus* comprises twenty-three sub-species six of which are in danger of extinction. Among these, the Corsican Red Deer is the most highly threatened. The species is similar to the Barbary Stag (*Cervus elaphus berberus*) from Algeria and Tunisia, which is also in serious danger; the similarity with North African deer is also found in several species on Sardinia – showing how the island was once a part of the African mainland. According to scientists, the Corsican Red Deer is a link between the Barbary Stag and the Central European Red Deer (*Cervus elaphus hippelaphus*), although it is smaller than the latter, measuring 1m (3ft) at the shoulder (the Central European Red Deer measures 1.20m (4ft). The Corsican Red Deer is considered to be one of the smallest of the twenty-three sub-species. Its antlers rarely measure over 75cm (30in) in length and 70cm (28in) in width. The coat is usually darker than that of any of the other small forms of deer: it is brown in summer and becomes almost black in winter. Deer are gregarious animals and each group remains within a defined territory from which it rarely wanders. For the majority of the year the two sexes live in separate herds; the male herds break up half way through July when the antlers have completed their growth. From this moment, battles are waged between the males. Sometimes they are just skirmishes but they become more serious as the mating season approaches. This is in August or September when the antlers have burst the covering skin (known as 'velvet'). After the battles, the males emit a raucous cry and gather a 'harem' around them. In the first half of October, having satisfied their sexual appetite, the males become disenchanted with the females and go alone in search of richer food to recover their strength. They join up to form herds again as winter approaches. A single fawn is born in May/June after a gestation period of 230–240 days. The year-old fawns are then made to leave the mother. Deer generally feed in the morning or late afternoon; they are grazing animals and their food consists of grasses and tree leaves. The species usually lives for 15–18 years but one example in Washington Zoo died in 1941 at the age of 26½.

Geographic distribution. The Corsican Red Deer was once distributed equally throughout Sardinia and Corsica. Now it is probably extinct in Corsica and exists in only two regions in Sardinia – Settefratelli and Capoterra, east and west of Cagliari respectively. It is possible that a third small group exists on the Costa Verde.

Habitat. The preferred habitat of this deer are Mediterranean copses, meadows and conifer woods.

Population. The Corsican Red Deer was decimated by uncontrolled hunting, particularly during World War II. It is protected by French law in Corsica and by the regional law in Sardinia, but these laws are difficult to enforce. Records show that poaching continues. This deer is considered in grave danger of extinction; in Corsica there were six in 1965 but by January 1970 none were observed and it may be extinct there. Two investigations carried out by the Italian World Wildlife Fund in 1968 and in 1972 have found that there are still between 100 and 150 in Sardinia. The World Wildlife Fund has recommended reinforced efforts to eliminate poaching and the establishment of a protected area. There are no Corsican Red Deer in captivity. There is one embalmed example in the Civic Museum of Natural History in Milan. However, the Barbary Stag, which is similar to the Corsican Red Deer, is in captivity in Tunis Zoo.

Père David's Deer

(Elaphurus davidianus)

Class: Mammals Subclass: Eutheria
Order: Artiodactyla Suborder: Ruminantia
Family: Cervidae Subfamily: Cervinae
Genus: *Elapharus*
French: *Cerf de Père David* Italian: *Cervo di padre David* German: *Davidshirsch*

Description. Père David's Deer is the only representative of the genus *Elaphurus*. This is a large deer: it is 1.5m (5ft) long and 1.20m (4ft) high at the withers; the tail is 50cm (20in), it weighs about 200kg (440lb). Its particular characteristics are the long tail – more like a horse's than a deer's – and the antlers, which divide just above the head into two branches – one branches almost parallel to the back and the other turns upwards and forms another branch. The history of this deer's salvation (it was only recently discovered) is an example of the work man can do to preserve an endangered species. In 1865 a French missionary, Father Armand David, was en route for Peking and heard about a wonderful nature park belonging to the emperor at Na-Hai-Tzu, only a short distance from Peking. A passionate zoologist, Father David desperately wanted to see this park and the marvels within it in spite of a protective wall 72km (45 miles) long and the Mongolian guards stationed along it. He escaped the surveillance of these guards, climbed on top of the wall and was able to admire all the things he had heard about. His attention was immediately attracted by a deer whose behaviour and physical appearance were unknown to him. On returning to Peking, he tried to find out from the local experts the deer's race and whether it was on record. He only discovered that the Mongolian guards occasionally killed them to eat the meat or very rarely to sell the antlers. After many unsuccessful attempts Father David obtained two skins of the animal and two living specimens were sent to Paris, but they did not survive the journey. The naturalist, Milne-Hedwards, studied the skins of these examples, gave a scientific description of the deer and, in honour of Father David, named it *Elaphurus davidianus*. At this time, the only examples existing lived in the park near Peking as the species was already extinct in the wild. In 1869 and 1883 four deer in all were sent to the Royal Zoological Society in London; one was also sent to Berlin. The Duke of Bedford, a passionate zoologist, obtained eighteen for the park at Woburn Abbey and this was the salvation of the species: a few years later, in 1895, the River Hun Hoo flooded its banks causing the protective wall surrounding the park to collapse. Most of the deer that escaped were killed by a starving population; a small number survived inside the park but were killed by the troops occupying Peking after the famous Boxer Revolt. Only one female survived; it died in Peking in 1920. The only surviving examples of the species are at Woburn Abbey, England.

Geographic distribution. The original distribution of Père David's Deer is still in dispute, but it is believed that it was the central and northern regions of China. Similar fossils have been discovered in Manchuria and in Japan.

Habitat. Of necessity, a humid or marshy area for which the feet are specially adapted.

Population. It is not certain what the population of this species was in the eighteenth century in Peking Park, but it is estimated that there were only a few hundred examples. In 1932, the herd was already 182 at Woburn Abbey; a few years later there were 320 and 220 of them were distributed throughout 100 parks and zoological gardens in the world. Recently, a couple have been sent to Peking to take over from the one survivor of the preceding couple which was sent from England in 1956. It is hoped that this will constitute the start of a new herd to repopulate the ex-Imperial park. The total number of Père David's Deer amounted to 726 in 1975, of which 153 were born in 1974.

Tamaraw

(Bubalus [Anoa] mindorensis)

Class: Mammals Subclass: Eutheria
Order: Artiodactyla Suborder: Ruminantia
Family: Bovidae (horned ungulates)
Subfamily: Bovinae Genus: *Bubalus*
French: *Tamarou* Italian *Tamarú* German: *Tamarau*

Description. According to some authorities, the tamaraw (illustrated below) belongs to the subgenus *Bubalus;* according to others it belongs to the subgenus *Anoa*. However, it mainly differs from the anoa (*Ano depressicornis*) because it is smaller; it is similar because the coat has the same light stripes running from the head to the base of the neck, and on the limbs. It is probable that these two species have developed their own characteristics inhabiting, as they do, two separate islands; the tamaraw is found on Mindoro and the anoa on Celebes.

Geographic distribution. The species was once equally distributed over Mindoro Island. Today it is found only in areas on Mount Iglit and Mount Baco, the Calavita mountains and the Sablayon region.

Habitat. As a result of research carried out in 1966, it seems that the species prefers primary forest, which once covered the entire island. Today, it is found in mountain forests up to a height of 1,800m (5,900ft).

Population. According to data given at the Tamaraw Conservation Programme in 1971, there were 148 examples on Mindoro. The only female in captivity up to 1972 was in Manila Zoo. It is hoped that this animal will be reared in several of the more qualified zoos.

Aurochs

(Bos primigenius)

Class: Mammals Subclass: Eutheria
Order: Artiodactyla Suborder: Ruminantia
Family: Bovidae (horned ungulates)
Subfamily: Bovinae Genus: *Bos*
French: *Aurochs* Italian: *Uro* German: *Ur*

Description. This wild bovine, the forefather of various domestic cows, has been extinct since the seventeenth century. The male was about 3m (10ft) in length and 1.85m (6ft) in height. It weighed up to 1 ton. Females were smaller. The horns could be 80cm (32in) long. The coat was brown in the male and a rust colour in the female and young.

Geographic distribution. In prehistoric times, throughout almost all the temperate zones of the Old World, from Europe to North Africa, Asia Minor, northern India and China. The last were seen in central Europe.

Habitat. Open scrubland, river valleys and the edges of forest.

History and causes of extinction. In Asia and North Africa the aurochs became extinct many ages ago, but it has only gradually disappeared from Europe in the course of the last millennium, probably due to the gradual disappearance of wooded areas and the subsequent loss of its food source. The last were gathered in the sixteenth century in the forest of Jaktorow about 50km (35 miles) from Warsaw. In 1599 there were twenty-four examples; in 1602 there were six and the last female died in 1627, rendering the species extinct. A herd was 'reconstructed' by cross-breeding selected strains of domestic cow in Munich Zoo in order to give an approximate idea of the species. The experiment was successful but it also served to demonstrate that man was unable to recreate a species that has become extinct.

Banteng

(Bos javanicus)

Class: Mammals Subclass: Eutheria
Order: Artiodactyla Suborder: Ruminantia
Family: Bovidae Subfamily: Bovinae Genus: *Bos*
French: *Banting* Italian: *Banteng* German: *Banteng*

Description. The banteng can be divided into three sub-species; the Javan Banteng (*Bos j. javanicus*), the Borneo Banteng (*B.j. lowi*) and the Burmese Banteng (*B.j. birmanicus*). The former does not appear as heavy and clumsy as the other two, and the legs are longer and more slender. The species can grow to a length of 2m (6½ft) and a height of 1.70m (5½ft). It weighs a maximum of 900kg (1,980lb). The males differ substantially from the females in both their bulk and colouring, which in the male is usually brown varying towards black or very dark blue, and in the female is a browny-red. The banteng live in herds composed of a few males and about thirty or forty females. They are active in the morning and at dusk; during the heat of the day and at night they retire to the protection of woody areas. The species' natural enemy is primarily the tiger and also the gregarious Canidae which are found in the higher regions of the species' distribution.

Geographic distribution. At one time the species was distributed throughout Burma and Thailand across the Malaccan Peninsula to the islands of Java and Borneo; only a few fossils have been found on Sumatra. The species currently inhabits its original territories but in limited areas and in greatly reduced numbers.

Habitat. The banteng prefers woody areas, forests, hills, and mountains up to a height of 2,000m (6,500ft). It passes the monsoon season on the hills; in the dry season it descends into the valleys which are rich in herbaceous vegetation.

Population. Today, the species is greatly reduced in number due to poaching and the transformation of its natural habitat into agricultural land. The banteng has been domesticated in Bali and Java although the domestic strain is slightly different from the wild variety. It has reproduced successfully in zoos in Berlin, Frankfurt and Rotterdam. In 1975 there were over 180 in 30 zoos.

European Bison

(Bison bonasus)

Class: Mammals Subclass: Eutheria
Order: Artiodactyla Suborder: Ruminantia
Family: Bovidae Subfamily: Bovinae Genus: *Bison*
French: *Bison d'Europe* Italian: *Bisonte europeo*
German: *Wisent*

Description. The European Bison is the only European representative of the genus *Bison*, the same genus represented in America by the American Bison (*Bison bison*). Until 1920, there were two sub-species of the European Bison: the Caucasian Bison (*Bison b. caucasicus*), which inhabited mountains and became extinct around 1925, and the Wood Bison (*Bison b. bonasus*, illustrated opposite), which inhabited the plains and still exists. The European Bison can reach very large proportions, with a length, excluding the tail, of over 3.5m (11½ft), a height of 2m (6½ft) and a weight of 1 ton. It is a gregarious animal like all bovines. In 1956, some European Bison were released into the Bialowieska Forest in Poland and have reproduced there since 1956. They live in large herds which, during the mating season, split up into small groups of about a dozen, led by an old female. In winter and spring, the animals join up again into large herds except for the most elderly males who live in a separate group. Both male and female reach sexual maturity at about two years, but the male is six or seven years old before it is fully grown. Its life-span is up to twenty-three years but in captivity may live for twenty-seven years. The gestation period is about nine months and the newborn calf weighs about 40kg (88lb). It is suckled for six to seven months but begins to graze after only one month.

Geographic distribution. Once inhabited almost all of Europe from the most western and northern parts as far as the Caucasian Mountains to the east, and up to the Lena river in Siberia to the north. There are now herds in captivity, but otherwise it is found in the Bialowieska Forest in Poland and in several parks in Russia.

Habitat. The European Bison inhabits tree-covered plains where it is able to find its preferred food, such as grasses, ferns, leaves, tree-bark and acorns.

Population. The population of the European Bison in 1975 was officially put at 1,514 head, of which 683 were male and 831 female. The herds existing in the wild are 3 in Poland and 11 in Russia, with a total of 652 head. The largest herd is found in the Bialowieska Forest which is 350 animals strong, the majority of which were born in the wild. All the other European Bisons are either in reserves established especially for the reproduction of the species, or in one of the 85 zoos covering 28 states of Europe, Asia and North America. Its near-extinction was brought about both by excessive hunting and the destruction of many forests. In 1914 there were 737 wild European Bison in Bialowieska Forest, but none survived World War I. The last one found in the wild was killed in 1921 by an ex-forestry guard. The current population has been created as a result of the fifty which were in zoos and private collections. The 'International Association for the Conservation of Bisons' was founded in 1923 at Berlin Zoo to protect the species, and the first small herd was released into Bialowieska Forest. There were 57 inhabiting Bialowieska Forest in 1963; 34 had been born in the wild. In 1967 the number of European Bison had rapidly increased to 860. This shows the most practical way to attempt to save a species in danger of extinction.

Wild Yak

(Bos grunniens)

Class: Mammals Subclass: Eutheria
Order: Artiodactyla Suborder: Ruminantia
Family: Bovidae Subfamily: Bovinae Genus: *Bos*
French: *Yack sauvage* Italian: *Yack selvatico*
German: *Wildyak*

Description. The Wild Yak has existed since ancient times. The male can reach a height at the withers of 1.90m (6ft) and weigh over 700kg (1,540lb). The female is smaller. Its most typical characteristic is the soft wavy coat which is of medium length on the flanks and back, and extremely long on the limbs and tail.
Geographic distribution. The species once inhabited a vast area of the Himalayas up to 4,500m (14,800ft). Today, its presence is limited to the high plains of Tibet and their neighbouring areas, from Ladakh in the east to Kuen-lun and Kansu.
Habitat. Alpine tundra; ice and desert regions of the high mountains, beyond man's habitation.
Population. The numbers of the Wild Yak are subject to vast fluctuations due to uncontrolled hunting by the armed forces in the area and by the local population. The species is officially protected by the Chinese government and partially protected by the Indian government.

Giant Eland

(Taurotragus derbianus derbianus)

Class: Mammals Subclass: Eutheria
Order: Artiodactyla Suborder: Ruminantia
Family: Bovidae Subfamily: Tragelaphinae
(Spiral-horned Antelopes) Genus: *Taurotragus*
French: *Eland de Derby* Italian: *Antilope derbiana*
German: *Westsuden Riesenelen*

Description. The Giant Eland is, according to some authorities, a sub-species of the antelope *Taurotragus oryx* and distinguishable from it by its large size – it can be 3.50m (14ft) long, including the tail, and 1.80m (6ft) high. The horns are close together and grow directly upwards; they are furled for the first third or half of their length. The long beard which grows on the chest is frequently dragged along the ground through mud or urine and then rubbed on to the branches of trees or shrubs to mark out the animal's territory.
Geographic distribution. Very limited numbers throughout an area from Senegal to the Ivory Coast, covering Gambia, Mali and Guinea.
Habitat. Shrub-covered or preferably tree-covered savannah.
Population. Exact population unknown. It is completely protected in the national park of Niokolo-Koba in Senegal and theoretically it is also protected by law throughout its area of distribution. In 1975 there were fourteen examples in three zoos: Antwerp, East Berlin, and Paris.

Bluebuck

(Hippotragus leucophaeus)

Class: Mammals Subclass: Eutheria
Order: Artiodactyla Suborder: Ruminantia
Family: Bovidae Subfamily: Hippotraginae
Genus: *Hippotragus*
French: *Hippotrague bleu* Italian: *Antilope azzurra*
German: *Blaubock*

Description. All we know of the bluebuck is the description left to us by nineteenth-century explorers and settlers. According to some authorities, it was a subspecies of the Roan Antelope (*Hippotragus equinus*) and should be classified as *H.e. leucophaeus;* others, on the other hand, believe that it was a species in its own right. The bluebuck was smaller than the other species of its genus; the male was probably no more than 1.20m (4ft) high at the withers; the female was considerably smaller. The overall colour was a bluish-grey with a brown chest; the areas above the lips and under the eyes were brighter than the rest of the body. Unlike the Roan Antelope, it did not have black-and-white patches on the front of the head; its ears were shorter and less pointed and without black tips. The horns were similar to the Roan Antelope's, but slightly smaller and slimmer. The skull and body-structure were smaller than those of the rest of its genus. There was a slight, dark vertical line on the lower half of its limbs. Although the bluebuck had been noted by pioneers and explorers in Africa for a long time and called by a local name, it was only officially described for the first time in 1766 by a Russian naturalist, called Pallas, who based his description on an example in Leiden Museum, Holland. He gave it the name of *Antelope leucophaea;* in 1844 the generic name *Antelope* was changed to *Hippotragus*, a name coined from the Sundevali.

Geographic distribution. The bluebuck was distributed over a restricted area in the extremity of South Africa.

Habitat. The species shared its territory of typical African scrubland with similar species, the Roan Antelope and the Black Antelope (*H. niger*).

History and causes of extinction. The bluebuck was the first antelope to be exterminated through the recklessness of African settlers. The Boers would not have considered that their hunting was equal to uncontrolled massacre, but it was indeed, as today's naturalists confirm. The people now inhabiting the country are in the forefront of nature conservation as if atoning for the past. The last bluebuck was killed in 1799. Today, there are only five embalmed specimens in the museums of Paris, Leiden, Vienna, Stockholm and Uppsala.

Arabian Oryx

(Oryx leucoryx)

Class: Mammals Subclass: Eutheria
Order: Artiodactyla Suborder: Ruminantia
Family: Bovidae Subfamily: Hippotraginae
Genus: *Oryx*
French: *Oryx béatrix* Italian: *Orice bianco o d'Arabia*
German: *Arabische Spiessbock*

Description. The Arabian Oryx is the smallest and rarest of the four species of antelope belonging to the genus *Oryx*. It measures up to 1m (3ft) at the withers whereas the other species grow up to 1.50m (5ft). It weighs about 100kg (220lb). The coat is almost pure white over the body; the legs are a blackish-brown colour, darker at the front than the back, with white pasterns; the hooves are larger and more rounded than those of the other species of oryx. There is a small hump on the withers. There are black patches on the forehead, nose and cheeks. The tail is white with a black quiff. There are some examples with a thin, dark horizontal stripe on the flank. The fine horns can measure up to 75cm (2½ft) in length and are very pointed; they grow almost vertically, diverging gradually from the base and curving slightly backwards; they are ringed for almost the entire length. The horns constitute a formidable weapon: when attacked, the Arabian Oryx will lower its head until the forehead is parallel to the ground and the horns pointing directly forward. In this way, it succeeds in putting the largest predator to flight. One young is born after a gestation period of about 260 days. The species lives up to a maximum of twenty years.

Geographic distribution. The Arabian Oryx was once distributed over almost the entire Arabian peninsula in the areas where it could adapt to the environment; from Mesopotamia to Sinai and as far north as Syria. Today, it is reduced to a part of the Sultanate of Oman, a quadrilateral area of about 400 x 160km (249 x 99 miles). It is believed that there may also be small isolated groups outside this region.

Habitat. Rocky or sandy desert areas, up to the edges of the sand desert, where it finds the type of vegetation on which it feeds. The species can go without water for considerable periods and covers long distances in search of pasture. It uses its hooves and horns in order to dig underneath shrubs and at the base of sand dunes to hide or shelter from the sun.

Population. This species is considered in grave danger of extinction in the wild but almost certainly it can be preserved in captivity. Its decline was brought about by excessive hunting, especially during the last decade when there was a sharp rise in the number of inhabitants in the area due to the exploitation of oil. The oryx was killed through organized hunting when the herds were followed by jeeps and other forms of motor vehicle and shot with automatic machine guns, a form of hunting equally used by Arabs, soldiers and oil-field workers. The affluent also found it amusing to hunt the oryx from the air, chasing it in private planes and helicopters. It was estimated in 1969 that there were less than 200 left, and by now the number is most likely even smaller; the species is therefore condemned to almost certain extinction in the wild. However, in 1962 the Fauna Preservation Society of London and the World Wildlife Fund launched 'Operation Oryx' in order to save the species. Their aim was to capture a number in order to form a nucleus from which to reproduce the species in captivity. They would then reintroduce it to its native habitat when local conditions were secure. Three animals were captured, one was donated by London Zoo, one was donated by the Sultanate of Kuwait, and four were given to the World Wildlife Fund by the King of Saudi Arabia. This nucleus of nine animals was then called the World Herd and was placed in Phoenix Zoo, Arizona, which has a similar climate to Arabia. The animals have reproduced with success and their number has risen annually. In 1972, in order to avoid the risk of disease, the antelopes were transferred to the wild animal park at San Diego, California. In 1976 the World Herd had 68 Arabian Oryx, 33 at Phoenix and 25 at San Diego. The zoo at Los Angeles now possesses 20 from an original group of 3 animals acquired in 1966. A few of these have been mated with those in Phoenix in order to avoid the dangers of inter-breeding. There is a herd of at least 25 in Qatar, Arabia; 5 in the zoo at Riad, and 5 in the zoo at Abu Dhabi. In all, there are 120 Arabian Oryx in captivity and the future of the species seems to be secure. This is one instance where man has saved an animal from extinction which he was responsible for almost exterminating.

Scimitar-Horned Oryx

(Oryx tao - Oryx dammah)

Class: Mammals Subclass: Eutheria
Order: Artiodactyla Suborder: Ruminantia
Family: Bovidae Subfamily: Hippotraginae
Genus: *Oryx*
French: *Oryx algazelle* Italian: *Orice dalle corna a scimitarra* German: *Sabelantilope*

Description. This species is similar in looks and size to the more common Gazelle Oryx except for the long horns which curve distinctly backwards (they are almost vertical in the other species). The adult male reaches over 1.25m (4ft) at the shoulders and weighs over 200kg (440lb). The coat is off-white with brown shading on the muzzle, neck, flanks and upper part of the legs. It is a desert species which can exist for weeks or months without water.

Geographic distribution. Once inhabited almost all Sahel to the north and south of the Sahara, from West Africa to the Red Sea. Today, it is found only on the southern areas of this territory, particularly in Chad and Nigeria.

Habitat. Semi-desert border of the Sahara.

Population. The numbers have diminished enormously due to uncontrolled hunting and the destruction of their fragile habitat by domestic livestock. The largest group is found in Chad where there are still about 5,000. In 1975, there were about 350 in captivity in 39 zoos where they have reproduced fairly successfully.

Addax

(Addax nasomaculatus)

Class: Mammals Subclass: Eutheria
Order: Artiodactyla Suborder: Ruminantia
Family: Bovidae Subfamily: Hippotraginae
Genus: *Addax*
French: *Addax au nez tacheté* Italian: *Addax*
German: *Mendesantilope*

Description. The addax is similar to the oryx species. Its length, excluding the tail, is just under 2m (6½ft), it has a height of 1.20m (4ft), and a weight of up to 125kg (275lb). The species was reared in captivity by the Ancient Egyptians who used the animal as a beast of burden and as a sacrificial victim.

Geographic distribution. At one time distributed throughout the Sahara desert. Today it is found in greatly reduced numbers in Algeria, Niger, the Sudan; the largest groups inhabit Chad, Mauritania and Mali.

Habitat. Areas without water, desert or sand-dunes.

Population. No more than several dozen in Algeria, Niger and the Sudan. An investigation in 1970 of the area in northern Chad revealed that there were about 1,500. The largest number is found in the Mauritania-Mali at Majabat-al-Kubra, where 5,363 were recorded in 1960. The species is protected by law. In 1975 there were 260 examples in 38 zoos and parks.

White-tailed Gnu

(Connochaetes gnou)

Class: Mammals Subclass: Eutheria
Order: Artiodactyla Suborder: Ruminantia
Family: Bovidae Subfamily: Alcelaphinae
Genus: *Connochaetes*
French: *Gnou à queue blanche* Italian: *Gnu dalla coda bianca* German: *Weissschwanzgnu*

Description. The gnu would undoubtedly win a prize for being the strangest of all antelopes: its body, which is similar to a horse's, is very high at the shoulders and dips right down at the back; the legs and the tail are also similar to that of a horse. Its head has a number of remarkable characteristics: it is similar to a bison's although smaller and slightly more delicate; both sexes have horns (the female's are smaller) which are very close together at the top of the head; from the base, the horns diverge upwards and then fold back down, close to the head, before making an upward curve to the tips. The coat also has notable characteristics; odd tufts of hair grow in varying lengths around the eyes, the side of the head and the chin; there is a mane from the nape of the neck down to the withers and a large beard across the chest down to the front legs. The male adult reaches just over 2m (6½ft) in length, excluding the tail, and 1.20m (4ft) in height. It weighs 180kg (400lb). The coat is a chocolate-brown colour. The young gnu develops a mane and beard, but not horns, and its head is more thick and square than the adult's. Very little is known about the behaviour of the White-tailed Gnu because it has been extinct in the wild since the beginning of this century. It is thought, however, that its habits are similar to those of the other species of its genus which are present in large numbers in the African savannah. The species is gregarious; it would have lived in large herds of about fifty alongside other representatives of the antelope genus and beside zebras and ostriches. The gnu's behaviour is also remarkable; though usually very calm and tranquil, the animal will suddenly, for no apparent reason, leap into the air and show off, race around and then stop and return quietly to its usual placid grazing.

Geographic distribution. The species once inhabited a large part of South Africa; Karoo Cape Province, southern Transvaal and Natal. Today, it is present only in zoos, parks and private reserves.

Habitat. Inhabited grassland and semi-desert scrubland.

Population. The species was saved from extinction due to private effort. In 1847 there were around 1,048 in the wild but the whole species was wiped out during the Boer War. Research carried out in 1970 found that there are now over 3,000 in captivity. There is a plan to reintroduce the animal into reserves set up in its native territory.

Slender-horned Gazelle
(Gazella leptoceros)

Class: Mammals Subclass: Eutheria
Order: Artiodactyla Suborder: Ruminantia
Family: Bovidae Subfamily: Antilopinae
Genus: *Gazella*
French: *Gazelle a cornes grêles* Italian: *Gazella bianca*
German: *Dünengazelle*

Description. The genus *Gazella* includes a dozen species with a large number of sub-species: among these, the Slender-horned Gazelle is one of the rarest. It is a medium-sized gazelle with a height at the withers of 72cm (28in) and a weight of about 28kg (68lb). It can easily be distinguished from the other species of its genus by its pale sand-coloured, almost white coat, which has a few, hardly distinguishable, darker patches. The tail is a darker colour with an almost black tip. This gazelle can also be distinguished by its horns which are long, slim and almost vertical. The hooves are long and slender, and slightly splayed to facilitate the animal's movement over sandy areas. Generally, a single offspring is born (occasionally two) which, after a few days, is able to follow its mother and, after only one week, can move almost as fast as its parents. The species can live for up to twelve years.

Geographic distribution. The Slender-horned Gazelle once inhabited all the desert regions of North Africa; from southern Algeria to the Nile; south as far as the central Sahara and the Sudan; north into Tunisia, and the Atlas Mountains. Today, it is found – in very reduced numbers – in only the northern part of its original territory: the desert regions of Algeria, Tunisia, Libya, Egypt, the Sudan and Chad.

Habitat. A truly desert-living species which prefers to inhabit sand dunes where few other mammals manage to survive. During periods of severe drought, it leaves the dunes in search of food elsewhere. It eats the desert vegetation and has little need of water.

Population. The species was once numerous wherever the desert provided sufficient vegetation to feed it. To-day, it is greatly reduced due to intense hunting and the decline of its habitat. It is considered in grave danger of extinction but the impossibility of studying it in its natural habitat means that we have no knowledge of numbers. There are no serious provisions for the conservation of this species, although it is theoretically protected by the African Convention of 1969. Protection measures and the creation of reserves in its habitation are required. It would also be wise to rear the species in captivity in the hope of later repopulating the areas from which it has already been exterminated. In captivity, there are only about 25 in 3 zoos, all in the USA – San Diego, San Pasquall in California, and Tampa in Florida. The only example in Europe was a female in Rome Zoo which died in October 1976 while awaiting the arrival of a male from San Diego to join her.

Chamois of Abruzzo

(Rupicapra rupicapra ornata)

Class: Mammals Subclass: Eutheria
Order: Artiodactyla Suborder: Ruminantia
Family: Bovidae Subfamily: Caprinae
Genus: *Rupicapra*
French: *Chamois des Abruzzes* Italian: *Camoscio
d'Abruzzo* German: *Abruzzo Gemse*

Description. The Chamois of Abruzzo is one of the main
sub-species of the genus *Rupicapra* of which the typical
strain is the Alpine Chamois (*Rupicapra rupicapra*). The
chamois is 70cm (28in) high at the withers and can
weigh up to 50kg (110lb). Both sexes have horns which
are initially vertical and then curve sharply backwards,
forming a hook. The Abruzzo Chamois is easily
distinguishable from the Alpine Chamois, especially in
winter when around the neck it has a band of white
bordered with two dark stripes which meet on the chest.
This characteristic, from which it derives the name
ornata (some scientists consider it to be a distinct species,
Capra ornata) disappears in summer. However, it is still
distinguishable from the Alpine Chamois by its horns,
which are larger and more definitely turned backwards.
One young (sometimes two, rarely three) is born in
May/June after a gestation period of about six months.
The chamois usually lives for up to twenty-two years.

Geographic distribution. Unlike the nineteenth century,
the Abruzzo Chamois inhabited the various high
mountains of the Apennine Chain; the last individual
was killed on the Gran Sasso in 1890. Today, the sub-
species is reduced and confined within a few of the most
accessible parts of the Abruzzo National Park and in the
adjacent mountains.

Habitat. In summer, the Abruzzo Chamois prefers the
northern sides of the highest peaks where it can find
fresh grasses; during the rest of the year, the herds –
consisting of fifteen to thirty females and young, the
male adults living apart except at the mating period –
descend to the sunny slopes and, in the winter, go down
to woods and valleys where they eat lichen, mosses, pine
kernels, seeds and bark.

Population. The Abruzzo Chamois is considered to be
virtually safe in the Abruzzo National Park, which was
established in 1922. The numbers were drastically
reduced due to intense hunting; in 1913 there were only
between 15 and 20 left. Today, it is rigorously protected
by law. In 1969 it was estimated that there were 150–
200; in 1976 the count was put at no less than 350–400.
It is now essential to transfer small groups of the
Abruzzo Chamois to other suitable regions in the
Apennines (Gran Sasso, Maiella, Monti della Laga) in
order to guarantee its survival in case of epidemic or
any other natural or artificial disasters which may befall
the original nucleus.

Takin
(Budorcas taxicolor)

Class: Mammals Subclass: Eutheria
Order: Artiodactyla Suborder: Ruminantia
Family: Bovidae Subfamily: Caprinae
Genus: *Budorcas*
French: *Takin* Italian: *Takin* or *Budorca*
German: *Takin*

Description. The takin is a strange animal that has distant affiliations with the musk-ox; it is considered by some scientists to be a link between the Antilopinae and the Caprinae. It looks much like one of the bovines with its large head, great muzzle; shoulder-height of up to 1.20m (4ft) and a weight of up to 320kg (705lb). The legs are short and tough with large rounded hooves. Both sexes have horns which draw out laterally initially and then turn back in an arc-shape; they are thick and ridged at the base, narrowing to a fine tip. The thick tough coat varies in colour according to the three sub-species: the Assam Takin (*Budorcas taxicolor taxicolor*, illustrated left) is golden-yellow to reddy-brown, with patches of black; the Szechwan Takin (*Budocas taxicolor tibetanus*) is shades of yellow to reddy- or silvery-grey with spots of black; the Shansi Takin (*Budorcas taxicolor bedfordi*) is whitish-yellow shading to gold, with little black. All three sub-species have their mating season in July or August and, after a seven- to eight-month gestation period, one young is born which can follow its mother a few days after. Dwarf bamboo and grasses are its staple diet.

Geographic distribution. The typical sub-species, the Assam Takin, lives on the mountains of Nepal, Assam and Bhutan; the Szechwan inhabits the Chinese province of that name, and the Shansi Takin lives on the Great White Mountain which is a sacred Chinese mountain in the southern part of the Shan-si Province.

Habitat. Mountain regions that are inaccessible from a height of 2,500–4,500m (8,200–14,760ft) between patches of rhododendrons, dwarf bamboo and grasses. The takin lives in small groups which, in winter, descend to the more protected valleys; in summer it lives on high grassland, making tracks through the thick undergrowth as it migrates.

Population. The Szechwan and the Shansi sub-species are particularly rare having been intensively hunted in the past for their meat. It is estimated that they number about 200. The Shansi Takin is considered to be so rare that it might well be extinct. The sub-species are strongly protected by Chinese law but in order to ensure their survival it has been necessary to set up reserves in the regions they inhabit. Above all, it would be advantageous to set up a national park on the Great White Mountain. In 1975, there were 12 in captivity: 3 in the Bronx Zoo of New York, 4 in Peking Zoo and 2 in Rangoon Zoo; 1 was born in captivity in East Berlin Zoo.

Nilgiri Tahr

(Hemitragus hylocrius)

Class: Mammals Subclass: Eutheria
Order: Artiodactyla Suborder: Ruminantia
Family: Bovidae Subfamily: Caprinae
Genus: *Hemitragus*
French: *Tahr du Nilgiri* Italian: *Tar del Nilgiri* or
Uarriato German: *Nilgiri-Tahr*

Description. The scientific name of *Hemitragus* means 'half goat' – the tahr is, in fact, half way between goat and sheep. The genus has three species: the Himalayan Tahr (*Hemitragus jemlahicus*), the Arabian Tahr (*H. jayakari*) and the Nilgiri Tahr (*H. hylocrius*). The last two are in danger of extinction. The Nilgiri Tahr is the largest of the three species, reaching a height at the withers of 1m (3ft) and weighing 105kg (230lb). The female weighs about 80kg (190lb). The horns are 40cm (16in) long in the male and just over 30m (12in) long in the female; they are close together at the base, arched and with a sharp fore-edge. The tail is short and similar to a goat's. The soft thick hair of its whole coat is long and dense; in the male it is a dark yellowy colour, in the females and young more grey-ish; in both sexes the underparts are lighter. The characteristic of the adult male is an off-white, saddle-like patch on the back. One young is born after a gestation period of six to eight months; the Nilgiri Tahr gives birth to twins fairly often. The young are suckled for six months and reach maturity at around eighteen months. The tahr can live up to sixteen years; a few examples in captivity have reached twenty years.

Geographic distribution. The Nilgiri Tahr once inhabited a large part of the mountainous regions of southern India. Today, it is limited to a very restricted area in the extreme south and a few of the peaks of the western Ghat mountains among the Nilgiri foothills from which it takes its name. The Arabian Tahr, whose original habitat was throughout the mountains and hills of Oman, is now limited to the mountains of Jobal Hafit and Jalan Shar Keeyeh at the extreme eastern tip of the Arabian peninsula.

Habitat. Monsoon region: the Nilgiri Tahr inhabits scrubland and grassy woody areas between 1,200 and 1,600m (4,000 and 5,000ft) where it lives in herds of between thirty and forty. The males form a separate group, only joining the females during the mating season.

Population. Both the Nilgiri Tahr and the Arabian Tahr are in serious danger and have greatly diminished due to excessive hunting and the destruction of their habitat. There are no more than 1,500 Nilgiri Tahrs, of which 300 live in the Nilgiri foothills. The species is protected by Indian law and four reserves have been set up. The Arabian Tahr is not protected; its population is unknown but it is certainly greatly reduced. There are only about a dozen Nilgiri Tahr in captivity in Memphis (USA) and in two Indian zoos. There are no Arabian Tahrs in captivity (1975).

Abyssinian Ibex

(Capra ibex walie)

Class: Mammals Subclass: Eutheria
Order: Artiodactyla Suborder: Ruminantia
Family: Bovidae Subfamily: Caprinae Genus: *Capra*
French: *Bouquetin d'Abyssinie* Italian: *Stambecco abissino* German: *Abissinischer Steinbock*

Description. Of the nine or ten types of ibex, two are in grave danger of extinction, namely the Abyssinian Ibex (*Capra ibex walie*) and the Pyrennean ibex (*Capra pyrenaica pyrenaica*). One other, the Portuguese Ibex (*Capra pyrenaica lusitanica*), has been extinct since 1892. The Abyssinian Ibex is similar to the Alpine Ibex (*Capra ibex ibex*). It measures 1m (3ft) at the shoulders and the adult male has horns 1.15m (3½ft) long. There is also a characteristic bone protruberance on the forehead. The coat is brown, redder on the upper parts of the body and paler underneath; the female is lighter in colour and smaller in size with slender, slightly arched horns measuring about 30cm (12in). One young (occasionally two) is born between May and June after a gestation period of 150–180 days. The Pyrennean Ibex can be distinguished by the shape of its horns which are outspread and curve backwards. The males live in separate groups only joining the females for the mating season in December and January. The species lives for up to fifteen years but it can live for over 20 years in captivity.

Geographic distribution. The Abyssinian Ibex lives exclusively on Mount Simien (4,500m [14,800ft]), situated to the north-east of Gondar in Ethiopia. It is probable that it has never lived outside this area. Until a few centuries ago, the Pyrennean Ibex lived on both sides of the Pyrennean range, but is now limited to the extreme north of Huesca province, around Mount Perdido.

Habitat. Mountainous. Ibex prefer high peaks in summer, descending to the lower slopes in autumn and winter.

Population. The Abyssinian Ibex has declined primarily due to the destruction of its habitat; hunting has also played a considerable part. The sub-species is considered in grave danger of extinction. It is estimated that the population is no more than 200. After many requests by the World Wildlife Fund, the Ethiopian government made the area on Mount Simien into a national park in 1969. The sub-species is now legally protected although this is difficult to enforce. The sub-species has never been held in captivity. The Pyrennean Ibex was almost exterminated by hunting by the end of the Middle Ages; there are now no more than twenty left. In 1975, there was only one couple in Barcelona Zoo and a female in Madrid Zoo.

Markhor

(Capra falconeri)

Class: Mammals Subclass: Eutheria
Order: Artiodactyla Suborder: Ruminantia
Family: Bovidae Subfamily: Caprinae Genus: *Capra*
French: *Markhor* Italian: *Markor* or *Capra di Falconer* German: *Schraubenziege*

Description. The markhor is subdivided into six sub-species which are distinguished by the shape of their horns; these vary from the wide and heavily spiralled ones of the typical sub-species, the Astor Markhor (*Capra falconeri falconeri*, illustrated below), to the V-shaped, finely spiralled ones of the Suleman Markhor (*C.f. jerdoni*). The markhor is the largest and heaviest of the wild goats: the male adult can grow to a height of 1.15m (3½ft) at the shoulders and a weight of 110kg (243lb). The horns of the male are about 1.50m (5ft) long; the female's are the same shape but short (a maximum of 25cm (10in). The old males are distinguished by the long thick beard which grows down to the chest. The coat is thick and silky, shorter and a yellowy-brown in summer, becoming longer and greyish in winter. The markhor is similar in behaviour to the ibex. The mating season is in the winter. One or two kids are born between the end of April and the beginning of June after a gestation period of six months. The animal has lived to an age of eleven years in captivity.

Geographic distribution. Once inhabited the mountains from eastern Iran along the Afghanistan/Turkestan/Pakistan frontiers to Soviet Turkestan and Indian Kashmir. Today, it is only found in restricted and isolated areas from the north-west Himalayas to the Beluchistan mountains, and the mountains of Kashmir and north Pakistan.

Habitat. Steppes, forests and grasslands, rocky slopes between 1,800 and 3,000m (5,900 and 9,800ft). In summer they go up to the higher meadows in groups of four or five; in winter they descend to the lower slopes and gather in herds of twenty to forty. In these areas, the markhor has to share its food with domestic animals, so it has adapted to eating tough oak leaves, sometimes going 7–8m (23–26ft) up into the trees to find more tender ones.

Population. The markhor has been drastically reduced in number through uncontrolled hunting and the rivalry of domestic stock in the meadows. With the total population of all six sub-species estimated at between 2,000 and 2,500, they are considered in a vulnerable position. Three of the sub-species are in danger of extinction: *Capra falconeri chiltanensis*, with 200 examples; *C.f. jerdoni*, with 700 examples, and *C.f. magaceros*, with only 50–80 examples. The protection measures are few and completely insufficient except in the Soviet Union. The markhor adapts well to living in captivity. In 1975 there were 157 in 39 different zoos, the majority of which were born in captivity.

BIRDS

Giant Moa
(Dinornis maximus)

Class: Aves Subclass: Neornithes
Order: Dinornitiformes Family: Dinornithidae
Genus: *Dinornis*
French: *Moa géant* Italian: *Moa gigante*
German: *Riesenmoa*

Description. The Giant Moa, the largest of the extinct order of Dinornitiformes, grew to a height of up to 3m (10ft) and a weight of 250kg (550lb). Vaguely similar to the ostrich, the moa had a small head with a long neck which was curve-shaped like an emu's. The massive legs had four toes with the undeveloped big toe at the back. It had no wings and there is no trace of them on the skeleton. The eggs were white with a very soft shell and weighed up to 7kg (15lb).
Geographic distribution. Exclusive to New Zealand.
Habitat. Probably lived in a similar habitat to the ostrich, and used rock hollows for nesting. The species fed off grasses, berries and seeds.
History and causes of extinction. The extinction of the various species of moa was caused by the Maoris who hunted it for the meat, bones and eggs; also by the transformation of the birds' habitat. The species became extinct between the tenth and seventeenth centuries; the last Pigmy Moa (*Megalopteryx didinus*) died in 1773.

Elephant Bird
(Aepyornis maximus)

Class: Aves Subclass: Neornithes
Order: Aepyornitiformes Family: Aepyornithidae
Genus: *Aepyornis*
French: *Aepyornis géant* Italian: *Epiornite* or
Occello elefante German: *Madagaskar-Riesenstrauss*

Description. Similar to the ostrich, the Elephant Bird was possibly the largest bird on earth: it could be 3.50m (11ft) in height and 500kg (1,100lb) in weight. It had a long neck, powerful body, small atrophied wings, and massive legs with three strong toes. Its enormous eggs, with a paper-thin shell, were over 30cm (1ft) long and had a capacity of 8l (2gal).
Geographic distribution. Exclusive to Madagascar.
Habitat. It finally retreated to the inaccessible forest of southern Madagascar.
History and causes of extinction. Possibly known to the Carthaginians, they were hunted for their meat. The first French Governor of Madagascar (1648–55) recorded their presence at the extreme southern end of the colony. The species probably became extinct in the second half of the seventeenth century. There is a skeleton in a museum in Paris.

Galapagos Penguin
(Spheniscus mendiculus)

Class: Aves Subclass: Neornithes
Order: Sphenisciformes Family: Spheniscadae
Genus: *Spheniscus*
French: *Manchot des Galapagos* Italian: *Pinguino delle Galápagos* or *Sfenisco mendiculo*
German: *Galapagospinguin*

Description. The Galapagos Penguin measures only 53cm (21in) in length and weighs around 2.2kg (5lb). The featherless wings are adapted to swimming and measure 23cm (9in). It is the customary black and white colour of penguins with blue shading. The head is decorated with the characteristic facial patterns; the beak is slender, pointed and hooked at the tip. The Galapagos Penguin lays two white eggs which hatch after forty days.

Geographic distribution. Limited to Fernandina and Isabella Islands in the Galapagos Archipelago.

Habitat. This is the only species of penguin to live in an equatorial zone along the coasts of the above-mentioned islands where it nests in rock hollows near the sea.

Population. The species has been reduced to a few thousand, probably no more than 2,000, due to hunting by the local population. The Galapagos Penguins are protected but the law is hardly enforced. There are none in captivity (1976).

Short-tailed Albatross
(Diomedea albatrus)

Class: Aves Subclass: Neornithes
Order: Procellariformes Family: Diomedeidae
Genus: Diomedea
French: *Albatros de Steller* Italian: *Albatro comune*
German: *Kurzschwanzalbatros*

Description. The Short-tailed Albatross is characterized by its colouring: the young are dark-brown and the adults are white (apart from a few dark feathers). Typical birds of the sea, albatrosses only go to ground for the period when they hatch the single egg and rear the fledgling.

Geographic distribution. Once present in large numbers throughout the islands of the Bonin group to the south-Islandeast of Japan, they are now seen only on Torishima.

Habitat. The environment of the high seas.

Population. Of the one million examples existing in the nineteenth century, only a small number survives today. Its decline can be seen as follows: 1930, 2,000 examples; 1953 (due to the demand for their feathers) 23 adults; 1955, 3 fledglings; in 1957 there were 8 fledglings; 7 in 1961, 10 in 1962; and a census in April 1962 counted 47 altogether. In 1957 Torishima was declared by the Japanese government to be a specific reserve for the Short-tailed Albatross; a meteorological station protects the colony from natural disasters.

Galapagos Flightless Cormorant
(Nannopterum harrisi)

Class: Aves Subclass: Neornithes
Order: Pelecaniformes Family: Phalacrocoracidae
Genus: *Nannopterum*
French: *Cormoran aptère* Italian: *Cormorano delle Galápagos* German: *Galapagos-Kormorane*

Description. This is the only species of cormorant unable to fly; it is also the rarest. It is around 96cm (3ft) long with very small wings measuring 25cm (10in); it weighs around 2kg (4½lb). The plumage is brown with shades of purple on the wings. The head and neck are covered with long hair-like feathers. The Galapagos Cormorant's diet consists of fish and molluscs, especially the octopus. It lays one to two eggs in nests made out of algae and twigs placed on rocks near the sea. The incubation period is 23–25 days.
Geographic distribution. Limited to Isabella Island in the Galapagos Archipelago.
Habitat. The rocky coast of Isabella Island.
Population. The species has fallen an easy prey to hunters because it is flightless. It has therefore been reduced to about 1,000 and its number is still declining. It is protected but the law is not respected. In the past, trapping for zoos has contributed to its decline. There are probably none in captivity today.

Japanese Crested Ibis
(Nipponia nippon)

Class: Aves Subclass: Neornithes
Order: Ciconiiformes Family: Ibis
Subfamily: Threskiormithinae Genus: *Nipponia*
French: *Ibis blanc du Japon* Italian: *Ibis del Giappone*
German: *Japanischer Ibis*

Description. The Japanese Crested Ibis has grey and white plumage on the body and a brick-red coloured head. The legs are dark red and the beak is black. It generally lays two eggs but occasionally one or three.
Geographic distribution. Until eighty years ago the species was common throughout Japan; it was also found in northern China, Manchuria and Korea, where the last was seen in 1936. Now it can be found on Sado Island and on Noto Peninsula, Japan. Whether it has survived in China and Manchuria is unknown. In 1974 four ibis were observed in Korea.
Habitat. Marshes where there are large groups of birds.
Population. Recent information has estimated the population to be only nine individuals in Japan; it is not certain if any inhabit the Asian continent (apart from the four observed in Korea). There are none in captivity. The species was greatly reduced as a result of its persecution by man between 1870 and 1890 and the degradation of its habitat during and after World War II.

Bald Ibis

(Geronticus eremita)

Class: Aves Subclass: Neornithes
Order: Ciconiiformes Family: Threskiornithidae (or Plataleidae) Subfamily: Threskiornithinae
Genus: *Geronticus*
French: *Ibis chauve* Italian: *Ibis eremita*
German: *Waldrapp*

Description. Known by its Bavarian dialectic name of waldrapp in Germany, Austria and Switzerland, this bird was one of the first creatures to be protected. In 1504, Archbishop Leonard of Salzburg decreed it a protected species, for the nestlings were a delicacy reserved for the tables of the rich and powerful. However, although the decree was renewed annually, it was virtually ignored so that the Bald Ibis disppeared from Europe in the space of a century and was forgotten, except as a creature of myth. When a colony was discovered in Syria in 1854, it was treated as a new species, and was not connected with the legendary Bald Ibis until 1906. The male is similar in size to a duck; the female is slightly smaller. The long, red beak curves downwards. The head is featherless and reddish with a grey cap. The legs are also red and are very long. When the long feathers covering the neck are blown in the wind they form a ruff around the head. Three or four eggs are laid in the first days of April and are incubated for about twenty-eight days; the young are able to fly by the beginning of June. Insects, larvae, worms, small reptiles and amphibians constitute the species' diet.

Geographic distribution. Until the seventeenth century the Bald Ibis was distributed and reproduced in various areas in Europe (the Alps, Danube, Rhône, and the Swiss Jura). Today, it survives only in parts of Morocco and in the Turkish city of Birecik on the Euphrates. It is only known for certain that it nests in Birecik although it may possibly nest in Morocco.

Habitat. The Bald Ibis builds its nest on rock overhangs but as the eggs are almost round they fall out of the nest very easily. This fate also happens to the nestlings who are dashed to death on the rocks or fall prey to cats.

Population. It probably numbers a few hundred. In 1953, the colony at Birecik was estimated to be 530 couples; 130 in 1962, and 39 birds in 1976. The Bald Ibis already had a very low level of reproduction due to the loss of eggs and young and it also seems that the birds cannot tolerate disturbance. The species is not protected but the World Wildlife Fund is preparing a project for its conservation; it also features prominently in the efforts of the Turkish National Appeal for the World Wildlife Fund, founded in 1975. Around 215 Bald Ibis are distributed among 30 zoos where they reproduce fairly successfully. The largest group of about 20 can be found at the National Zoo of Rabat, Morocco.

Hawaiian Goose

(Branta sandvicensis)

Class: Aves Subclass: Neornithes
Order: Anseriformes Family: Anatidae
Subfamily: Anserini Genus: *Branta*
French: *Bernache des îles Sandwich* Italian: *Oca delle Hawaii* or *Ne-ne* German: *Hawaiigans*

Description. The Hawaiian Goose belongs to the genus *Branta* (Sea Geese) and differs from the genus *Anser* (Field Geese) in the structure of the beak, which is short, black and without the horny covering on the outside of the upper half. The male Hawaiian Goose is 60–70cm (24–28in); the female is about 37cm (15in) long. Its plumage is brown, black, grey or white, and the head is covered with black feathers in the shape of a hood. The beak, legs and webbed feet are also black. This species inhabits the slopes of volcanic mountains between 1,500 and 2,500m (4,920 and 8,200ft) – an inhospitable grim territory, almost always surrounded by mist, and subject to frequent rainstorms. There are no meadows, only dry lava fields which are either in the process of cracking, or the old lava is disintegrating. However, where the lava has split, there are a few patches of grass and bushes, and pools with deep water which are the refuge of the Hawaiian Goose. Over the centuries, these geese, which the locals call 'Ne-ne', have adapted to living in such conditions: they now live almost exclusively on land and have developed very long legs and strong feet linked by membrane as an aid to swimming. The female lays four to six eggs in hollows in the ground protected by shrubs. The geese eat grasses and berries.

Geographic distribution. The island of Hawaii in the archipelago of that name; on the slopes of the volcano, Mauna Kea; the volcanoes Mauna Loa and Hualalai. In 1962, they were reintroduced to Haleakala Crater on the island of Maui where it was extinct.

Habitat. Semi-arid slopes of volcanoes, with grass and shrub pockets, between 1,500 and 2,500m (4,900 and 8,200ft).

Population. The Hawaiian Goose is the most valid example of a species which was reduced to the point of extinction but has been saved by man through captivity and reintroduction to its original territory. It represents the best example of encouragement for everybody who is interested and concerned with the conservation of nature. The species lived peacefully on the islands when they were inhabited only by the Polynesians, who hunted the geese without endangering their population. When the white people arrived on the islands of Hawaii and Maui, there were an estimated 25,000 geese. However, as happened to the major part of the original fauna of Hawaii, the geese were intensively hunted by the white man who also introduced mammals and destroyed the local habitat for the rearing of domestic livestock. By 1950, there were only 50 geese left on Hawaii Island. Although a number lived and reproduced in various zoos throughout the world, there was none in captivity after 1940. In 1950, one male and two females were captured and taken in by the Wildfowl Trust at Slimbridge, England, headed by Sir Peter Scott, Vice-president of the World Wildlife Fund International and of the World Wildlife Fund of Great Britain. The first nine goslings were born at Slimbridge in 1951. Meanwhile, the Department of Agriculture of Hawaii had set up another reproduction centre at Pohakuloa. To date, the World Wildlife Fund has raised at least 820 geese, 200 of which have been re-released in Hawaii and 180 have been given to 50 international zoos and private bird experts for breeding purposes. The total population of the Hawaiian Goose has now increased to over 1,000 examples, and it is considered out of danger of extinction. It is no longer necessary to transfer any geese from the Wildfowl Trust because the United States Wildlife Service has now reproduced a sufficient number for itself. The salvation operation cost a great deal of money; the transference of the 200 geese back to their original territory cost £5,000 sterling and the whole operation was only possible thanks to contributions from many people and organizations, among whom was the World Wildlife Fund. The Hawaiian Goose has been adopted as the symbol of the 49th State of the United States of America (Hawaii).

Trumpeter Swan
(Cygnus buccinator)

Class: Aves Subclass: Neornithes
Order: Anseriformes Family: Anatidae
Subfamily: Anserini Genus: *Cygnus*
French: *Cygne trompette* Italian: *Cigno trombettiere*
German: *Trompeterschwan*

Description. This is the largest of the Anatidae; it is 165cm (almost 5½ft) in length; the wings are 69cm (27in) long and the wingspan 3m (10ft); its weight is about 13½kg (30lb). The Trumpeter Swan is also distinguishable by the thin, reddish stripe which decorates the edge of the lower part of its black beak. The young have a greyish plumage and a patchy red beak. The Trumpeter Swan feeds off aquatic plants: it is able to obtain plants underwater by submerging either its long neck only, or the front of its body and the neck. Although a relatively sedentary creature, in winter the Trumpeter Swan flies to the southern parts of its area in search of mild weather and sufficient food. It reaches adulthood at three years and will then take a mate for life. Their nest is made of grasses and twigs and is built preferably on top of a mound of earth, but frequently on top of a musk-rat burrow. There the five or six eggs are laid and incubated by the mother only, while the male guards the nest and defends her. The cygnets hatch out after thirty-five to forty days and are reared by both parents; the mortality rate is quite high due to parasitical diseases, cygnets being crushed by their parents and, surprisingly, drowning.

Geographic distribution. North America; at one time extensively, but now limited to Alaska, Idaho, Montana, Wyoming, Alberta and British Columbia.

Habitat. Fresh inland water: lakes, pools and rivers.

Population. The species is seriously threatened with extinction due to the rapid decline in numbers since 1930. It is now estimated to total about 2,500. The decline was principally brought about by the hunting of it for food, although swan meat is not very tasty, and also by the demand for swan feathers. A protection system was effected by the United States and Canada, prohibiting the hunting and trading of the species, and the establishment of reserves (Red Rock Lake in the Yellowstone National Park, in 1935, and subsequently others). These measures probably saved the species from extinction. There are a few in captivity in the zoo at Berlin and at Slimbridge, although these officially belong to the government of the USA, as well as various examples in American zoos. The species is very adaptable in captivity and reproduced for the first time at Clères in 1965.

Cape Barren Goose

(Cereopsis novaehollandiae)

Class: Aves Subclass: Neornithes
Order: Anseriformes Family: Anatidae
Subfamily: Anatinae Genus: *Cereopsis*
French: *Céréopse de Nouvelle Hollande*
Italian: *Cereopside* German: *Hühnergans*

Description. The Cape Barren Goose is close to the Tadorninae but differs from them in the shape and colouring of its beak, which is short, placed high and a bright green colour; it also differs in the colouring of the legs, which are red with black toes. It is the only representative of its genus although, despite obvious somatic differences, it is classified with the Tadorninae. The species is not gregarious, preferring to live in pairs or small groups near water, although it does not take easily to the water as it is basically land-living. It is diurnal by habit and lives off grasses and shoots; while searching for food it occasionally emits an extraordinary squawk which is similar to a pig's grunt, and so the species has acquired the name 'pig-goose'. Reproduction occurs in summer when the pairs isolate themselves from other individuals in the group; the female, having found a suitable hollow in the ground, then makes a nest out of grasses which she completely covers with down. There are four to six eggs which are incubated for about a month; the goslings are able to follow the mother to find food shortly after birth. The male is extremely aggressive while the female occupies the nest, and is capable of killing any intruder that comes too close. This species is commonly found in zoos or private collections; in 1975, there were 450 in about 100 zoos. The species reproduces successfully in captivity.

Geographic distribution. The southern part of Australia, Tasmania, and a few islands in the Bass Straits. In 1915, four examples were introduced into New Zealand although by 1936 it was no longer seen there.

Habitat. The Cape Barren Goose prefers areas near water, but where grasses and shoots are easily available.

Population. The species is still very rare, although recently a slight increase has been noted. The estimated population in 1957 was about 6,000. In 1963, an investigation of the population at Furneaux, which is one of the most important areas for the species, produced a count of only 2,000 birds. The cause of the diminution of the species can be found in its slaughter by man for its meat. A few islands have been turned into sanctuaries – the Glennie Group which was already a sanctuary fifty years ago, and Goose Island in 1964 – but it is difficult for the police to control poaching, especially by local fishermen.

Californian Condor

(Gymnogyps californianus)

Class: Aves Subclass: Neornithes
Order: Falconiformes Family: Cathartidae
Genus: *Gymnogyps*
French: *Condor de Californie* Italian: *Condor della California* German: *Kalifornischer Kondor*

Description. The Californian Condor is one of the rarest of all North American fauna. Its fossil remains indicate that the species existed in America as long as 200,000 years ago; some scientists believe that it had at that point reached its final stage of evolution and that now it is really a prehistoric relic which will become extinct with or without the intervention of man. No one can say whether or not this vast bird of prey will survive, but it is in a serious and precarious situation and has become the centre of the conservationist movement in California. Its wing-span of 2.90m (9½ft) and weight of over 11kg (25lb) makes it one of the largest North American birds; however, its powers of reproduction are the lowest of all the birds there. It is similar in appearance and size to the more common and also more famous Andean Condor (*Vultur gryphus*), but without the characteristic crest of the latter. The Californian Condor has a dark plumage with large white triangles on the wings. It has a black and white collar similar to the Andean Condor's with a bald, pink head and neck. The powerful beak is a greyish-yellow. The condor can glide through the air without effort for hours on end. It does not have the manoeuvrability and speed of the smaller birds of prey, but it is undoubtedly the patriarch of the skies. The species nests in caves or cracks in the rock face, on precipices, or rock walls, without using twigs or leaves, so that the single egg is laid on the bare earth. The reproductive process is incredibly slow: the egg is incubated for up to fifty days and the young is reared by the parents for nearly two years; then, after it has learnt to fly, which takes a very long time, the young remains with its parents for a further period. Each couple therefore nests only once every two years. It takes six years for the young to develop adult plumage, but it does not reach sexual maturity until it is at least ten years old. Many eggs fall from the nests because they are rolled off by the parents when their attention is diverted or when they are frightened – in which case they inadvertently fly away with the eggs between their talons and drop them. In these precarious situations, the number of young that survive each year is extremely small and if the Californian Condor does survive, it will be due to its unique resistance to extreme conditions of its habitation, where the temperature ranges from 0°C (32°F) to 40°C (104°F), and also to its longevity, for some condors in captivity have lived for almost half a century.

Geographic distribution. During the nineteenth century the Californian Condor was distributed over a large part of western North America; British Columbia (Canada), Oregon, the state of Washington, and the northern part of the Mexican peninsula. Today, it is limited to the southern coastal areas of the state of California between Monterey and Los Angeles. It occasionally ventures west of the Sierra Nevada as far as Fresno.

Habitat. The mountain chains along the west coast of the United States.

Population. The main reasons for the species' decline are as follows: hunting, which began with the pioneers in search of gold and who collected the condor's long black feathers; the disturbance of their natural habitat by tourists and by the passage of air traffic, and the use of pesticides. The total population of the species for the last 100 years has remained between fifty and sixty; this is due to the fact that not more than one or two young manage to survive the incubation period each year and that an equal number of adults die or are killed. The species is strictly protected by the laws of the United States and the prime nesting area near the national forest of Los Padres has been declared a sanctuary. The only Californian Condor in captivity is in Los Angeles Zoo.

Bearded Vulture

(Gypaetus barbatus)

Class: Aves Subclass: Neornithes
Order: Falconiformes Family: Accipitridae
Subfamily: Aegypiinae Genus: *Gypaetus*
French: *Gypaète barbu* Italian: *Avvoltoio degli agnelli*
German: *Lämmergeier*

Description. The Bearded Vulture is the only representative of its genus, which has four sub-species. It is a
powerful-looking bird, measuring 1.50m (5ft) from the
end of its beak to the tip of its tail; it has a wing-span of
over 2.60m (8½ft) and a weight of 7kg (15lb). The female
is the same size as the male. There are certain characteristics which obviously differentiate the Bearded Vulture
from the true vulture species: the shape of the tail which
is long and cuneiform; the large head, which is covered
in white feathers and decorated by a black stripe running
from the upper part of the beak, across the eyes and
joining on the forehead, and the feathered beard which
forms around the base of the beak and on the sides of
the head and underneath the beak. Because the Bearded
Vulture lives at a great height and is affected by humidity, it gathers on its feathers a film of iron-oxide which
gives the bird a quite different colour from that of the
species when in captivity. The Bearded Vulture lives in
small groups or more usually in pairs. No other bird of
prey can match the sharpness of its sight or the speed
of its flight, travelling as it does high over valleys and
plains in search of carrion and prey. According to the
area that it inhabits, the Bearded Vulture feeds off
carrion of either wild animals or domestic livestock, and
in particular the placenta after the birth of lambs. It is
not unusual for it to eat tortoises and it cracks the
shell – using the same method for breaking bones to
eat the marrow – by flying at a great height in a rocky
area, with the creature in its talons, and dropping it.

Geographic distribution. Until several decades ago, this
species was distributed over the mountain chains of
central and southern Europe, from Spain and the
Balkans, across all central Asia as far as northern China,
and south to North and East Africa.

Habitat. Medium and high mountains.

Population. Exact population unknown, although there
are probably only a few couples due to the persecution
of shepherds and hunters who use traps to destroy it.
The species is therefore almost extinct in central Europe,
the Alpine mountains and Sardinia, where the last
couple was sighted only a few years ago. The species is
also in serious danger of extinction in its African
territory. Today, it is legally protected in many countries
where it lives, but it is very difficult to enforce the laws.

Monkey-eating Eagle

(Pithecophaga jefferyi)

Class: Aves Subclass: Neornithes
Order: Falconiformes Family: Accipitridae
Subfamily: Buteoninae Genus: *Pithecophaga*
French: *Aigle des singes* Italian: *Aquila delle scimmie*
German: *Affenadler*

Description. The Monkey-eating Eagle, which is the only representative of its genus, is a ferocious looking creature with a high, strong head and a large beak which in the males can be 51mm (2in) long and 21mm ($\frac{2}{3}$in) wide. This bird, which was first discovered in the Philippine archipelago in 1894, can be called the Old World Harpie because it looks similar to the Central and South American harpie. It is just under 1m (3ft) long and weighs just over 4kg (9lb). In the wild, its diet consists mainly of monkeys, but it will also eat domestic livestock and dogs. In captivity, the eagle easily adapts to being fed a diet of horse-meat, rabbit and poultry. The hunting ground of this species extends over an area of 30 sq km (12 sq miles). It reproduces every two years, but the number of eggs laid in each clutch is in dispute: according to the Red Data Book it is never more than one but according to other authorities it is never less than two. Fairly rare, it is still possible to see a few examples of this bird in European and American zoos. In 1975, there were five in five zoos: among these, the zoos of Antwerp, Frankfurt, Los Angeles and Tokyo have instigated a programme to aid reproduction of the bird in captivity. The species does not live for long in captivity, but there was one exceptional record of an example which lived 41 years 7 months in Rome Zoo, having arrived there in December 1934 and died in July 1976.

Geographic distribution. At one time distributed on the islands of Luzon, Samar, Leyte and Mindanao in the Philippine archipelago. Today is present only on the island of Mindanao. A small population has begun to rebuild itself recently on Luzon Island with one example having been killed there in 1963 and another in 1964.

Habitat. Woods, forests and densely tree-covered areas near villages and factories.

Population. According to the Red Data Book, there were no more than 100 couples in the wild in 1966. Today, this number has decreased to around 50. The principal causes of the decline of this species are to be found in the ambition of local tradesmen to obtain an eagle, embalm it and keep it as a trophy; also the efforts of various zoos to collect examples. All zoo directors have now been requested by the UICN to refrain from collecting further examples of this species.

Bald Eagle

(Haliaeetus leucocephalus)

Class: Aves Subclass: Neornithes
Order: Falconiformes Family: Accipitridae
Subfamily: Buteoninae Genus: *Haliaeetus*
French: *Pygargue à tête blanche* Italian: *Aquila di mare a testa bianca* German: *Weisskopf-Seeadler*

Description. The coat-of-arms of the United States of America bears a powerful imposing figure – a large eagle with a white head and white tail. This, the Bald Eagle, is related to the Euro-Asiatic Eagle, the White-tailed Sea Eagle (*Haliaeetus albicilla*) and differs from other eagles (of the genus *Aquila*) by its essentially aquatic behaviour. The head, upper part of the neck and tail of the Bald Eagle are covered in pure white feathers which contrast splendidly with the deep brown body, making this one of the most beautiful diurnal birds of prey. The length of the body varies from 50–90cm (20–35in), with a wing-span of 188–197cm (6ft) in the male and over 210cm (6½ft) in the female. The adult male weighs about 4kg (9lb) and the female about 6kg (13lb). The Bald Eagle is thus just as imposing as the Golden Eagle (*Aquila chrysaëtos*). The legs and beak are yellow, and the beak is extremely hooked. The species is more slender and agile than the Common Sea Eagle and has a rounded tail. Those Bald Eagles which live in the mountain regions nest between spring and the beginning of summer, while those inhabiting the southern regions nest from the end of winter to the beginning of spring. The nest is built by both sexes. The Bald Eagle mates for life and constructs its lonely nest near the water in high pine or mangrove trees, or high up among rocks. Two white eggs are laid which measure 7 by 5cm (2½ by 2in) and are incubated by both parents for 35 days. The young are born covered in grey feathers and develop their adult plumage after two months; only after three months do they venture from the nest. Even after they have learnt to fly, they will return to the nest in the evening. The young become independent in the autumn, leaving their parents and flying far away from the sea and lakes. After a few years they return to their original territory in order to build their first nest and settle down. There are two geographically defined strains of the Bald Eagle: the northern strain (*Haliaeetus leucocephalus alascanus*), which is still fairly common, and the southern Bald Eagle (*Haliaeetus leucocephalus leucocephalus*), which is much rarer and slightly smaller.

Geographic distribution. All North America, the island of Bermuda, and also the north-eastern part of Siberia. The southern sub-species inhabits all the southern United States and is most numerous in Florida, with 50 per cent of the population and nests there.

Habitat. The Bald Eagle inhabits the areas around sea coasts and the banks of lakes and rivers. It watches over its territory by perching on high trees or rocks, or circling over the water in order to pick up its prey. It feeds on small mammals – rabbits for instance – aquatic birds, fish, reptiles, amphibians and even tortoises.

Population. The main cause of the dramatic decline in numbers of the Bald Eagle has been chemical waste which either kills the birds or reduces their fertility. The rate of successful clutches has declined to 44 per cent. The growth of human settlement around its nesting areas has added to its decline. The total population of the Bald Eagle can be placed in the order of tens of thousands for the northern strain (between 30,000 and 55,000 in Alaska, but between 3,000 and 4,000 in the other states and a number in Canada). The southern strain has a current population of between 1,000 and 1,100. The species is protected by the law throughout its area of distribution, although a few are still killed by farmers. There are around 130 Bald Eagles in about 70 zoos, almost all of which are to be found in the United States; in captivity, the species is the property of the Federal Government.

Mauritius Kestrel

(Falco punctatus)

Class: Aves Subclass: Neornithes
Order: Falconiformes Family: Falconidae
Subfamily: Falconinae Genus: *Falco*
French: *Crécerelle de l'île Maurice* Italian: *Gheppio di Mauritius* German: *Mauritius-Turmfalk*

Description. This is the rarest bird in the world and it seems that its extinction is very close and inevitable, in spite of a difficult project which has been set up to save it through breeding in captivity. The species is directly linked to the African Kestrel (*Falco rupicoloides*) and the Madagascar Kestrel (*Falco newtoni*), although these are larger. The Mauritius Kestrel measures 23–25cm (10in) long. The plumage is similar to the female Old World Kestrel (*Falco tinnunculus*) although it does not have the dark stripes like moustaches on the side of the beak. The upper parts of the body are a reddy-brown colour with black flecks, and the underparts are whitish with reddy-brown or black flecks. The tail, which is decorated with dark bands is not as large as that of the Common Kestrel. The eyes are black and surrounded by a yellow circle of naked skin. The legs are yellow with black claws. The young are similar in appearance to the adults. The female lays three or four eggs which are incubated for around four weeks; the young are then reared by both parents. The species feeds on lizards.

Geographic distribution. It is believed that this species has always been limited to the island of Mauritius in the Indian Ocean.

Habitat. The forests of Mauritius.

Population. A century ago the Mauritius Kestrel was common throughout the island and even fifty years ago it was fairly common. The principal causes of its decline have been the destruction of its habitat and the introduction onto the island of rats and mice which have eaten the eggs or the nestlings. The kestrel is also killed by the local inhabitants who see it as a threat to their poultry. However, this does not entirely explain the species' almost complete disappearance in only a few decades. In 1965 it was estimated that there were still eight to ten couples left; today its total population is reduced to only three couples, with one of these in captivity in an attempt to reproduce the species, using the same methods as to reproduce the Common Kestrel: one of the three eggs laid in September 1974 by the couple was put into an incubator; all the conservationists and scientists throughout the world held their breath, but because of a technical breakdown in the incubator, the precious nestling died a few weeks after birth. It is hoped that the couple will lay an egg again and that the young will be successfully reared. Fortunately, shortly after the death of the nestling in captivity, two young were born in 1975 and another four in 1976 to the two couples in the wild. The total population throughout the world has now increased to thirteen – a small margin between survival and extinction!

Seychelles Kestrel
(Falco ararea)

Class: Aves Subclass: Neornithes
Order: Falconiformes Family: Falconidae
Subfamily: Falconinae Genus: *Falco*
French: *Crécerelle des Seychelles* Italian: *Gheppio della Seicelle* German: *Seychellen-Turmfalk*

Description. The Seychelles Kestrel is 18–20cm (7in) long, with a brown plumage on the upper parts of the body, black-flecked on the shoulder feathers, and bluish-grey and black remiges. The head is a bluish-black-grey with lighter cheeks. The underneath of the bird is pure white shading to a browny-pink. It nests all over available edifices and usually lays two eggs. It feeds off lizards.
Geographic distribution. Up to 1940 the species was distributed over the entire Seychelles archipelago; it is now only found on the island of Mahe.
Habitat. The coral sand dunes of this island.
Population. The reason for the species' decline is unknown although it is probably due to the introduction of barn owls, rats and mice. Its population is also unknown although it is very small and diminishing. The species is not protected.

Prairie Chicken
(Tympanuchus cupido)

Class: Aves Subclass: Neornithes Order: Galliformes
Suborder: Galli Family: Phasianidae
Subfamily: Tetraoninae Genus: *Tympanuchus*
French: *Poule des prairies* Italian: *Tetraone di prateria* German: *Präriehuhn*

Description. The Prairie Chicken is characterized by two tufts of slim feathers at the side of the head. These grow above two naked, hairless, orangy-red areas corresponding to air sacs. The species lives on shoots, seeds and small invertebrates. In spring, the female lays a dozen eggs which hatch out after eighteen days.
Geographic distribution. The two sub-species principally in danger are Attwater's Prairie Chicken (*Tympanuchus cupido attwateri*) and the Greater Prairie Chicken (*T.c. pinnatus*). The former is found in south-eastern Texas and the latter in central-southern Canada, as far as north-east Oklahoma and as far as the Missouri in the east. The typical sub-species, *T.c. cupido*, has been extinct since 1932.
Habitat. The open prairies of southern Canada and the central regions of the United States.
Population. In 1965, Attwater's Prairie Chicken numbered no more than 750 examples; the Greater Prairie Chicken is more numerous. In 1975, there were five Greater Prairie Chickens in captivity in two zoos in the USA with over 100 Attwater's Prairie Chickens reared in Illinois. The prime causes for the decline of the species have been predators and the transformation of its environment by man. The species is now protected.

Swinhoe's Pheasant

(Lophura swinhoei)

Class: Aves Subclass: Neornithes Order: Galliformes
Suborder: Galli Family: Phasianidae
Subfamily: Phasianiae Genus: *Lophura*
French: *Faisan de Swinhoe* Italian: *Fagiano di
Swinhoe* German: *Swinhoe-Fasan*

Description. Swinhoe's Pheasant, which is considered by
some authorities to belong to the genus *Hierophasis* and
by others to be part of the genus *Lophura*, can be classified with Edward's Pheasant and the Imperial Pheasant
as part of the group of 'blue pheasants', a name which is
gained by the characteristic colouring in the males of
these three species. Although the small group has
various similarities with the Swinhoe Pheasant, it differs
from them in the fertility of the hybrids and in its looks
and habits which are notably different.
Geographic distribution. At one time the species was
evenly distributed over the island of Formosa but now
it is found only in the mountains.
Habitat. Woods on hills and mountains.
Population. Due to the very limited area that the species
now inhabits, this pheasant has become extremely rare.
Until a few years ago there were several hundred in
various zoos throughout the world.

Edward's Pheasant

(Lophura edwardsi)

Class: Aves Subclass: Neornithes Order: Galliformes
Suborder: Galli Family: Phasianidae
Subfamily: Phasianinae Genus: *Lophura*
French: *Faisan d'Edwards* Italian: *Fagiano di
Edwards* German: *Edwards-Fasan*

Description. This pheasant is characterized by a short
white crest with black flecks; the rest of the plumage is
a dark blue except on the wings which have a beautiful
green silky colour.
Geographic distribution. In 1896 it was recorded that the
species could be found in the area of Quang Tri (the
central region) in Annam.
Habitat. Lives up to 1,000m (3,280ft) above sea-level in
thick undergrowth.
Population. Population of Edward's pheasant in the
wild is unknown. We do not have any records regarding
its reproduction except that in captivity it lays a clutch
of between four and seven eggs a year. The species has
been endangered as a result of the destruction of its
natural habitat and its persecution by hunters. It is
estimated that there are over 200 in captivity, with many
being highly prized in some twenty zoos.

White-eared Pheasant

(Crossoptilon crossoptilon)

Class: Aves Subclass: Neornithes Order: Galliformes
Family: Phasianidae Subfamily: Phasianinae
Genus: *Crossoptilon*
French: *Faisan oreillard blanc* Italian: *Fagiano orecchiuto bianco* German: *Weisser Ohrfasan*

Description. According to authorities all three species of the genus *Crossoptilon* are considered rare – the White-eared Pheasant with its three sub-species, *C.c. crossoptilon* (illustrated below), *C.c. drouynii*, and *C.c. harmani;* the Brown-eared Pheasant (*C. mantchuricum*), and the Blue-eared Pheasant (*C. auritum*). Those belonging to the first species, the White-eared Pheasant, are distinguished from the other species by their pure white plumage which is only black on the neck; by the rhachides of the remiges, and because the tip of the rectrices is shaded towards the centre with blue and metallic green. The exception to the species is the sub-species *harmani* which has slate-coloured plumage and resembles a cross between *C.c. crossoptilon* and *C. auritum*. None of the three sub-species of the White-eared Pheasant has the feathers on the auricular region which characterize the other species of the genus, giving it the name 'eared pheasant'. These large, mountain pheasants have much the same behaviour pattern as others of similar species: they are very gregarious and live together in large groups; they feed off the ground with their strong beaks which are in the shape of an upturned shovel. The species eats tubers, roots and bulbs as well as insects and worms. The groups split up in the spring when the male chooses a territory for himself and then finds a mate. Mating is preceded by a form of nuptial dance in which the male courts the female, following her and swirling around with his wings drooping towards the ground. The species spends the night in trees. Like the rest of the Galliformes, the White-eared Pheasant prefers to save itself in dangerous situations by following a crazy upward path bowling over any obstacle that comes in front of it. When forced to fly, it will plummet straight towards the nearest tree in order to hide among the leaves.

Geographic distribution. The sub-species *C.c. crossoptilon* inhabits the mountain chains of southern Tsinghai, central and western Szechwan and north-eastern Yunnan. The sub-species *C.c. drouynii* inhabits the region of the high Yangtze and Mekong in south-eastern Tibet. The sub-species *C.c. harmani* inhabits the Abor and Mishmi hills in south-eastern Tibet and also northern Assam. The Brown-eared Pheasant inhabits the mountains of north-eastern China in the province of Shansi and western Hopei.

Habitat. These pheasants all inhabit a similar area – mountain forests up to the highest line of tree growth, and the meadows beyond them.

Population. The populations of the species and sub-species are unknown. It is hoped to repopulate the original territories by rearing the pheasants in zoos. In 1975, there were 150 White-eared Pheasants in 14 zoos, and 145 Brown-eared Pheasants in 35 zoos.

Elliot's Pheasant

(Syrmaticus ellioti)

Class: Aves Subclass: Neornithes Order: Galliformes
Suborder: Galli Family: Phasianidae
Subfamily: Phasianinae Genus: *Syrmaticus*
French: *Faisan d'Elliot* Italian: *Fagiano di Elliot*
German: *Elliot-Fasan*

Description. Elliot's Pheasant (the male is illustrated below), which some authorities include in the genus *Calophasis*, is probably one of the small group of pheasants characterized by typical bars across the tail, giving it the name 'Band-tailed Pheasant'. Like the other species in this group, Elliot's Pheasant is also characterized by the absence of a quiff of feathers on the head, and by the tail – extremely long in the male – which is built up of sixteen rectrices, those in the middle being much longer than the others. Elliot's Pheasant is considered by those who rear it in captivity to be the most spectacular of all pheasants. The colouring of the male is especially brilliant, in contrast to the female's more subdued colours. It is possible to distinguish between the male and the female pheasant, even in the young, because the male's neck is decorated in the middle with transversal stripes, alternately white and chestnut-brown in colour; the female's tail is both shorter and an overall lead-grey colour. The eggs – generally a clutch of about a dozen – are laid towards the middle of March. The incubation period lasts twenty-five days; the eggs are small and pink, and the young hatch out with plumage flecked with chocolate-brown. It is very difficult to reproduce the species in captivity because their wild nature presents problems in teaching the chicks to feed themselves. Elliot's Pheasant was discovered in 1872 by the naturalist Swinhoe in Chekiang and in southern Anhwei. It was rediscovered the following year by Father David, at Kuatun in northern Fukien, who imported the first example of the species into Europe in 1874 where for several years it was on public view in a menagerie of a Parisian museum. Another couple was imported by W. Jamrach in 1879 and sold to a certain Signor Rodocanachi. This couple reproduced for the first time in Europe in 1890.

Geographic distribution. At one time distributed over a large part of south-east China in the provinces of Chekiang, Fukien, and Southern Anhwei. Today inhabits almost the same area, but in greatly reduced numbers.

Habitat. The preferred habitat of the species is thick mountain forest.

Population. Population of the species in the wild is unknown but it is estimated that a very small number inhabits a few restricted regions. The destruction of the forest and the persecution of the species by trappers have caused its decline. There are between 350 and 400 individuals in captivity, of which 120 are in about 50 zoos.

Mikado Pheasant

(Syrmaticus mikado)

Class: Aves Subclass: Neornithes Order: Galliformes
Suborder: Galli Family: Phasianidae
Subfamily: Phasianinae Genus: *Syrmaticus*
French: *Faisan mikado* Italian: *Fagiano mikado*
German: *Mikadofasan*

Description. The Mikado Pheasant is principally distinguishable from the other species of its genus by the dominant colouring of the male's plumage which is a beautiful blue-black, with a violet border on the back, rump and chest, and a white border on the shoulder and secondary feathers. The tail is black and transversely barred with white. The female differs from the females of the related species in the light dappling on the shoulder feathers and also in the yellow stripe on the rhachides of the rump; it differs from the female Elliot Pheasant primarily in the absence of black dappling on the throat. The Hume Pheasant also belongs to the genus *Syrmaticus* and has two sub-species, *S.h. humiae* and *S.h. burmanicus*. The male has a dark-brown head with white eyebrows, a steel-coloured neck and throat which are shimmered with green, and a chest and back in shades of mahogany-brown. The tail is grey decorated with transversal bars in black bordered by brown. The incubation period for both these species is twenty-six days. The Mikado Pheasant was discovered in 1906 by Goodfellow who brought it to Europe in 1912. The Hume Pheasant was not introduced into Europe until 1963.

Geographic distribution. The Mikado Pheasant is distributed in limited numbers over the mountain area of Taiwan (Formosa), over a height of 2,000m (6,500ft). The sub-species the Hume Pheasant (*humiae humiae*) is distributed over the mountains of Burma to the border of China, Tibet and India, to a height of between 2,000 and 3,000m (6,500 and 9,800ft); the sub-species *humiae burmanicus* is found only in the most northern parts of Burma although recent reports state that it also inhabits the southern part of Yunnan.

Habitat. These species inhabit mountain forest which is rich in undergrowth.

Population. The Mikado Pheasant probably numbers no more than a few hundred examples. The population of the sub-species *humiae* is unknown but *burmanicus* is fairly numerous in a confined area on the borders of the Yunnan. Information regarding protection measures are not available. Examples of these species in captivity guarantee their survival. It is hoped that when a certain number have been reared they can be returned to their original habitat and protected legally. The species is fairly well represented in various zoos.

Palawan Peacock Pheasant

(Polyplectron emphanum)

Class: Aves Subclass: Neornithes Order: Galliformes
Suborder: Galli Family: Phasianidae
Subfamily: Phasianinae Genus: *Polyplectron*
French: *Eperonnier Napoléon* Italian: *Speroniere di Palawan* German: *Palawan-Spiegelpfau*

Description. Most authorities would agree that the Palawan Peacock Pheasant is one of the most beautiful species of its genus. The plumage of the upper part of the male (illustrated below) is a metallic blue which shimmers with green and gold highlights. The wings and back are brown, but the wings are a lighter shade. The rump, tail and back are flecked with dark brown and red. Towards the tip of each tail feather are two 'eyes' in metallic green merging into gold, while the primary feathers have only one 'eye'. The head, which is adorned with a long quiff of occipital feathers, is green with blue highlights. A pure white eyebrow runs from the edge of the cheeks to the corner of the eyes. The female differs from the male in its overall brown plumage which is decorated with ocelli on the tail feathers only; morover, the head is not adorned with a quiff. The zoologist Ghigi believes that there are two strains of this species differentiated by their locality, and by the characteristic white eyebrow which is found in the typical sub-species described above but not in the second sub-species. In order to prove the claim that 'these have therefore developed a second genotype because it was not differentiated by geographical area', Ghigi carried out a number of experiments: in 1959 he imported from the Philippines two couples – one belonging to each strain – and when the male of the strain without the white eyebrow died, he crossed the male of the typical sub-species with the female of the second sub-species and this resulted in a pheasant with a light-brown stripe over the eye. This hybrid, from which five chicks were born in 1961 and ten in 1962 (only seven survived) consistently produced specimens with the white eyebrow. However, according to Ghigi, they were unable to differentiate the sexes. The Palawan Peacock Pheasant was imported for the first time to America in 1929, where the first reproduction in captivity was achieved. The first couple to be imported into Europe was taken from California in 1931.

Geographic distribution. Today the species is limited to a few areas on Palawan Island in the Philippine archipelago.

Habitat. Thick forest rich in undergrowth.

Population. Its numbers in the wild are unknown although it does not appear to be in danger of extinction. However, records show that there has been a significant decline in the last few decades. This pheasant can reproduce fairly successfully in captivity, but the number of births cannot guarantee the survival of the species. The causes of the rapid decline in numbers are deforestation and uncontrolled hunting. Information relating to local laws governing the protection of the species is not available. In 1975 there were 110 specimens in 23 zoos in Europe, Asia and North America.

Japanese or Manchurian Crane

(Grus japonensis)

Class: Aves Subclass: Neornithes Order: Gruiformes
Family: Gruidae Subfamily: Gruinae Genus: *Grus*
French: *Grue de Mandchourie* Italian: *Gru della
Manciuria* German: *Mandschuren-Kranich*

Description. Of all the species of crane that exist in Japan
and which appear in legends, history and superstition,
the Japanese or Manchurian Crane (*Grus japonensis*)
can be considered the 'true' crane. This stupendous bird
is probably the most beautiful of all the crane species.
The pure-white colour of its dense plumage is empha-
sized by the black remiges, and also by the two broad,
black stripes which extend down the sides of the head,
neck and throat. The top of its featherless head is bright
red, while the forehead and cheeks are surrounded by
long black feathers. The primary feathers and the tail
ones are white but the latter are usually hidden under the
long, black secondary feathers. The enormous legs are
black with a tarsal bone of 28–30cm (11in). The beak is
very long and greenish. The Manchurian Crane is one of
the largest in the species, measuring 1.30m (4ft) high and
with wings 65–70cm (26–28in) long. The female normally
lays one egg, but occasionally two. The incubation is
carried out alternately by both parents and lasts for
about thirty days; the young are born covered in a
reddish-brown down. They soon leave the nest and after
only nine or ten weeks are able to accompany their
parents on their course of migration.

Geographic distribution. The Manchurian Crane once
inhabited Manchuria, Korea, eastern China and Japan.
Now it nests only in two small areas on the Japanese
island of Hokkaido. There are also small nesting populations in China and Manchuria.

Habitat. The species nests in marshy terrain.

Population. The steady disappearance of the marshes
and intense hunting had almost exterminated the species
by the end of the nineteenth century. Its current population is not known exactly: in 1963, an investigation
carried out in Japan estimated it to be 147, but the
following year it increased to 180. In 1964, the Russians
estimated that their population of cranes was between
200 and 300, with 30–35 couples nesting on Hanka Lake
on the border between the USSR and Manchuria. The
Red Data Book considers the species to be 'very rare and
probably diminishing'. It is protected by law in Japan,
where it is considered a 'natural monument'; in 1921, its
nesting grounds were established as sanctuaries. The
species is also protected in Korea. In 1975 there were
52 Manchurian cranes in 20 zoos in Europe, North
America and Asia, with 17 of these in Peking Zoo. The
first Manchurian Crane to be reproduced in captivity
was born in Britain in 1918. There are fifty in captivity
in Korea, with at least ten in the zoo at Pyongyang, and
twenty among the four principal Chinese zoos (Shanghai,
Canton, Nanking and Hangchow).

Whooping Crane

(Grus americana)

Class: Aves Subclass: Neornithes Order: Gruiformes
Family: Gruidae Subfamily: Gruinae Genus: *Grus*
French: *Grue blanche américaine* Italian: *Gru urlatrice americana* German: *Schreikranich*

Description. The Whooping Crane is one of the rarest birds in North America. It is a very beautiful bird with white plumage over all the body apart from the ten primary remiges which are black. The forehead and the top of the head are featherless and red, with short, hairy bristles. The areas between the eyes, beak and cheeks are crimson and the throat has a form of rhombus which is a bright pink. The long legs and the feet are black. Being 125cm (4ft) high, the Whooping Crane is the tallest bird in North America. The species takes its name from the loud, sonorous cry which can be heard as far as 5km (3 miles) away. It nests in Canada and winters in southern Texas; at the beginning of January, it starts its characteristic nuptial dance. In spring and autumn the birds migrate about 3,000km (1,900 miles) in single file. The nests are built on the grass between reeds. The female lays two eggs which are incubated for about thirty-five days, although only one of the two young generally reaches maturity. The Whooping Crane are omnivorous and will eat any variety of food from roots to small reptiles, although their preferred food is crustaceans, which they kill with a blow from the beak. The Sandhill Crane (*Grus canadensis*) is similar to the Whooping Crane, although it is more refined and less in danger of extinction: it is smaller, measuring 110cm (3½ft) in height, has grey plumage on the head and a white throat. The crimson colour is limited to the featherless area on the forehead and top of the head. This species has five sub-species: *Grus canadensis canadensis* (the typical sub-species), *G.c. tabida*, *G.c. rowani*, *G.c. pratensis* (the Florida variety) and *G.c. nesiotes* (the Cuban variety). The Sandhill Crane's diet consists principally of insects.

Geographic distribution. Until the middle of the nineteenth century, the Whooping Crane nested throughout the major part of Canada in the provinces of Alberta, Saskatchewan and Manitoba, and far north of the Great Lakes; in the USA, in Illinois, Minnesota, Iowa, North and South Dakota, and probably in Montana and Nebraska. The species wintered on the coast of the Gulf of Mexico. One small population did not migrate but nested in Louisiana and probably in eastern Texas. Today, the species nests only in the Wood Buffalo National Park, in the southern part of the Mackenzie district in Canada, and it winters in the Aransas National Reserve, Texas. The Sandhill Crane with four of its sub-species is distributed from the extreme northeast of Siberia across Alaska, Canada, a large part of central-western United States as far as California, and in Texas and Florida. The fifth sub-species lives on Cuba.

Habitat. The Whooping Crane inhabits small marshy islands with many pools as are found on the many lakes throughout their area of distribution. The habitat of the Sandhill Crane is similar to that of the Whooping Crane, except that it lays its eggs close to water.

Population. Between 1860 and 1870 there must have been between 1,300 and 1,400 Whooping Cranes. Since then there has been a steady decline in the species. This has been caused by intense hunting, particularly when the birds are in flight, by the difficulty the birds experience in finding open, solitary spaces far away from human settlement. Between 1933 and 1942, the number decreased to thirty. However, there has been a small but steady increase ever since except between the years 1952 and 1957, when the species was again reduced to 30. Recently, the number has reached sixty and 10–15 per cent of the total are young birds. The species is strictly protected in Canada and the USA, and the law has been respected to a high degree. As the cranes arrive in Texas each autumn, they are counted, recorded and the number of young is estimated. The count is repeated at the beginning of spring in order to ascertain the mortality rate during the winter. An experiment is in progress in the Research Centre of Patuxent, Maryland, to reproduce them in captivity. Each year since 1967, a dozen of the second eggs, assuming that usually only one of the young will be brought up by the parents, are lifted from the nests in Wood Buffalo Park and are transported by air to the Patuxent Centre, where it is hoped to increase the number of Whooping Cranes by keeping them in captivity and that, in time, they will reproduce there naturally. There are currently twenty cranes at Patuxent, almost all of which have been raised from those eggs taken from the nests in the wild. There are Whooping Cranes in various zoos in the United States, with two in New Orleans Zoo and one in San Antonio Zoo, Texas. There has also been a serious decline in the Sandhill Crane, again due to intense hunting, but also because the eggs have been destroyed by rodents and snakes. While the first three of the sub-species are still fairly numerous with over 200,000 of the typical sub-species and *G.c. rowani*, and a further 6,000 in the sub-species *G.c. tabida;* the Florida strain, however, has a population of no more than 2,000–3,000, and the Cuban variety probably has a population of only 150. Although the species is protected in the United States and Canada it is not protected in Cuba. The sub-species which are numerous are also those most frequently found in zoos, above all in the United States and they do occasionally reproduce in captivity. In 1975 there were 100 examples of the Florida sub-species in 10 zoos (9 American and 1 English). None of the Cuban sub-species are known to be in captivity.

Takahe

(Notornis mantelli)

Class: Aves Subclass: Neornithes Order: Gruiformes
Family: Rallidae Subfamily: Rallinae
Genus: *Notornis*
French: *Takahé* Italian: *Takahe* German: *Takahe*

Description. This is the only representative of the genus *Notornis*. There were once two sub-species: *Notornis mantelli mantelli* which was limited to the northern island of New Zealand and *N.m. hochstetteri* which inhabited – as it does today – the southern island. The discovery of the bones of what was considered an extinct species was made in 1848. It was only in the second half of the nineteenth century that a few examples were captured and their bodies were embalmed and displayed in the Otago Museum of Dunedin, New Zealand. Following the capture of these four examples in 1898, all traces were lost of the species, and for the next fifty years it was held to be extinct. However, in April 1948, G. B. Orbell confirmed the existence of the southern takahe. The bird is the same size as a cock and, in fact, resembles a chicken: the beak, forehead and legs are red; the silky feathers on the chest and abdomen are a beautiful indigo colour, while the back feathers are a greenish shade; the underneath of the tail is white, and the rudimentary wings are unadapted to flying. The takahe eats seeds and shoots. The nest, which is constructed on the ground, is hidden between thick vegetation, and the chicks are born covered in dark, camouflaging down. With the onset of winter, the chicks, although hardly grown, follow their parents to more open regions.

Geographic distribution. The species is limited to South Island, New Zealand: the mountains of Murchison which rise up between the mid and southern fjords of Lake Te Anau; also on Keplero Mountains, situated between the southern fjords of Lake Te Anau and Lake Manapouri.

Habitat. Thick forest, undergrowth, humid mountain valleys above 1,000m (3,300ft).

Population. After many years' study, a modest increase has been recorded in the population of this species: it is estimated that there are about 500 adults living in small groups over an area of about 520sq km (200sq miles). The species has probably declined primarily as a result of the alteration of the habitat through climatic change; other causes are the importation of predators by European settlers, and hunting by the Polynesian peoples. An area of about 1,800sq km (700sq miles) has been declared a protected zone for the species, and it is hoped that the present colony may reproduce there. It is not known if there are any in captivity, although some are probably still held by the Wildlife Division in New Zealand, which was experimenting (as yet unsuccessfully) with breeding the species in captivity.

Kagu

(Rhynochetos jubatus)

Class: Aves Subclass: Neornithes Order: Gruiformes
Family: Rhynochetidae Genus: *Rhynocetos*
French: *Kagou* Italian: *Kagu* German: *Kagu*

Description. The kagu is a strange and timid bird which inhabits New Caledonia. It wanders during the night and at twilight joins up into small groups to search for food among the undergrowth. Its nest is built on the ground and the female lays three or four eggs which are incubated alternately by both parents; the eggs hatch after thirty-five days.
Geographic distribution. The island of New Caledonia.
Habitat. Thick forests of the island rich in undergrowth and moist soil.
Population. Exact numbers in the wild unknown, but it is definitely very rare. The prime causes of its steady decline have been the introduction on to the island of domestic predators, the transformation of its natural environment, and persecution by man. The species is rigidly protected. In 1975, there were ten kagu in captivity; of the four that are in the zoo at New Orleans, two were born in captivity in 1973.

Great Indian Bustard

(Choriotis nigriceps)

Class: Aves Subclass: Neornithes Order: Gruiformes
Family: Otididae Genus: *Choriotis* (*Ardeotis*)
French: *Outarde des indes* Italian: *Otarda indiana gigante* German: *Indische Trappe*

Description. The Great Indian Bustard is considered by some authorities to belong to the genus *Ardeotis*. Standing upright, it reaches 1m (3ft) in height to the top of its head; it has a wing-span of 2½m (8ft) and a weight of 20kg (44lb). The species lives in small groups which rarely exceed ten individuals. A single egg is laid, and incubation takes a long time. The bird performs a useful function in destroying grasshoppers and small animals that harm vegetation.
Geographic distribution. India: from the Punjab to Deccan and Sind in the south, and as far as the River Jumna in the east.
Habitat. Open, grassy areas.
Population. Exact population unknown although it is definitely an endangered species. The reasons for its diminution are the destruction of its habitat and the fact that it is still hunted despite legal protection. In 1975 there was only one couple in captivity, in Mysore Zoo, India.

Audouin's Gull

(Larus audouinii)

Class: Aves Subclass: Neornithes
Order: Charadriformes Family: Laridae
Genus: *Larus*
French: *Goéland d'Audouin* Italian: *Gabbiano corso*
German: *Korallenmöwe*

Description. Audouin's Gull, also known as the Corsican Gull, is considered by some authorities to be the link between the Slender-billed Gull (*Larus genei*) and the Herring Gull (*Larus argentatus*). Its total length reaches 50cm (20in) and the wings are 40cm (16in). The most obvious characteristic which distinguishes Audouin's Gull from the others of its genus is the black stripe across the beak towards the angle of the jaw. In the adult, the beak is yellow from the stripe down to the tip, and red from the stripe up to the base; the beak of the young is completely yellow except that the black stripe is already evident. Although the behaviour of this gull is similar to that of other gulls, it is wilder than the others, and during the winter it is more likely to take to the high seas. Gulls nest – as indeed do most sea birds – in colonies on the edges of isolated islands. During the nesting period and the rearing of the young, the parent gulls do not venture far from their base; it is only when the fledglings are able to fly away themselves that the parents fly with them over the open sea.

Geographic distribution. The central area for the species is Sardinia, but colonies have been noted on the islands of Spanish Morocco and Corsica, and throughout the Aegean as far as the Klidhes Islands to the east of Cyprus. In winter, the species widen its territory as far as the Atlantic coast of Morocco across to Agadir.

Habitat. During the nesting season, the coasts of solitary islands; during the rest of the year, the open sea and uninhabited coastlines.

Population. Estimated to be 1,200. The reasons for its progressive decline can be found in the increasing population of other gulls, such as the Herring Gull, which are less timid, and more adaptable when their nesting grounds are invaded by tourists. The species has also been attacked by fishermen who take the eggs and fledglings for food. Audouin's Gull has not been protected, but legal measures will probably soon be introduced to protect it in its area of reproduction. There are no recorded examples in captivity, nor is it possible to gauge whether the species would reproduce in this way.

Great Auk

(Pinguinis impennis)

Class: Aves Subclass: Neornithes
Order: Charadriiformes Family: Alcidae
Genus: *Pinguinus*
French: *Grand pingouin* Italian: *Alca gigante* or
Alca impenne German: *Riesenalk*

Description. The scientific name of this sea bird, which became extinct in 1844, is based partly upon the colouring of its plumage – black on the back, sides and throat, and white on the underparts – and partly on its almost completely erect stance. These characteristics, which are common to all of the Alcidae, make the bird very similar to the penguin. There were two white, oval spots between the eyes, and the beak was black, squat and hooked, with both halves marked with oblique furrows. The Great Auk was 80cm (30in) long and weighed up to 5kg (11lb). It was an excellent swimmer and diver but had lost its capacity to fly: the short wings, 20cm (8in) long, had become adapted for swimming. The legs and webbed feet were black. In June, the female laid one large egg which was 13cm (5in) long and weighed 400g (14oz) and was incubated by both parents about seven weeks. The fledglings were born with dark-grey plumage.

Geographic distribution. The Great Auk inhabited the islands and continental coasts of the North Atlantic and nested on Funk Island off Newfoundland; also the coast of Iceland, and the islands of St Kilda, Faroe and Orkney to the north of Scotland.

Habitat. The Great Auk travelled in large groups around coastlines or swam in coastal waters in search of food.

History and causes of extinction. In 1534, the French explorer, Jacques Cartier, landed on Funk Island where he saw a large number of Great Auks which he and his sailors slaughtered in half an hour – enough to fill two rowing boats. This was the start of the massacre of this unfortunate bird throughout its entire area of distribution. The Great Auk was killed for its meat, feathers, and even its use as firestuffs. Apart from man's destruction of the species, natural events in this area, such as the eruption of submarine volcanoes, destroyed the last nesting territories, so that the Great Auk's extinction was completed in the space of three centuries. The last Great Auks were killed in 1844 on Eldey Island which faces the south-western coast of Iceland; they were sold for 100 crowns and their embalmed bodies can be seen in Copenhagen Museum. Few other examples or skeletons are preserved in museums. In Italy, there are two embalmed Great Auks, one in the Zoological Museum in Rome and the other in the Civic Museum of Natural History in Milan. In 1971, one Great Auk was auctioned at Sothebys in London and was bought by the Natural History Museum of Reykjavik as a result of a national subscription from members of the Iceland people who felt that they would like to have at least one Great Auk, even if it was in a museum!

Dodo
(Raphus cucullatus)

Class: Aves Subclass: Neornithes
Order: Colombiformes Family: Raphidae
Genus: *Raphus*
French: *Dronte* Italian: *Dodo* German: *Dronte*

Description. Just as the Giant Panda, the symbol of the World Wildlife Fund, is regarded as the emblem of the conservation movement for nature throughout the entire world, so the dodo has become synonymous with extinction. The saying 'Dead as a dodo' – in other words, 'Gone forever' – accurately sums up the situation. The dodo was a very large bird, about the size of a well-built turkey; it reached a height of around 75cm (30in) and weighed 22kg (46lb). The wings were greatly reduced and the number of primary remiges was fairly limited. The plumage was downy with atrophied rectrices; the feathers on the rear part of the back looked very much like a fistful of quill pens. The bone structure of the legs and the pelvis became stronger with the bird's loss of flight: the heavy pectoral and sternum muscules had disappeared, leaving the sternum flat and the legs short and tough. The long, strong beak was sharply curved at the tip and covered with a type of horn, making it particularly adapted to cope with hard fruit and snails; the beak reached up to the eyes. The head was massive and featherless, and the front part was covered with bare skin; the eyes were placed well forward and had remarkably high powers of vision. The occipital feathers were blackish in colour, forming a sort of hood around the naked part of the head. The body plumage was greyish-brown and the remiges and tail were off-white. The colour of the female's plumage was generally duller and she was smaller in size. The dodo ate leaves, berries, seeds, hard fruit and snails. It laid one egg – directly onto the ground – which was then incubated by both parents.

Geographic distribution. The dodo was unique to Mauritius Island in the Indian Ocean. Many similar large birds were seen on neighbouring islands: *Raphus solitarius* on Reunion Island and *Pezophaps solitaria* on Rodriguez Island, neither of which had ever been seen in Europe. The entire Rafidae family are now extinct.

Habitat. The exact habitat of the dodo and other Raphidae is unknown, it was most likely the shrubby tropical forest covering the island they inhabited.

History and causes of extinction. When the Portuguese set foot on the islands to the north of Madagascar in the sixteenth century they discovered the various species of Rafidae. Among these, the dodo was fairly abundant on Mauritius Island. In the early 1600s, a few examples were carried to Europe: between 1605 and 1610 one managed to reach the court of the Emperor Rudolph II at Vienna; another in 1626 reached Amsterdam, and a third arrived in London in 1638. There were many pictures and illustrations of the dodo, but although there were well over twenty-five pictorial works based upon the species, they all sprang from a single description. The destruction of the dodo was brought about by man who ate it although the meat was so revolting to the taste that the unfortunate creature was named 'the sick bird'. Man also brought on to the island various domestic animals, such as dogs, cats and swine, who all ate the nestlings. These various factors brought the species into rapid decline, and its extinction was effected by 1681. One embalmed example was kept by Oxford University, but unfortunately it was destroyed in 1755. The eighteenth century witnessed the extinction of the dodo and the other members of the same family: the variety which inhabited Reunion Island was extinct by 1746 and those on Rodriguez Island suffered the same fate by 1791. In addition to pictorial representation, a few bone remains of the dodo are held by various museums: Oxford, London, Paris, Copenhagen and Prague.

Passenger Pigeon

(Ectopistes migratorius)

Class: Aves Subclass: Neornithes
Order: Columbiformes Family: Columbidae
Subfamily: Columbinae Genus: *Ectopistes*
French: *Pigeon migrateur* Italian: *Colomba migratrice*
German: *Wandertaube*

Description. The history of the disappearance of this bird is probably the most well known and discussed of all the stories of extinction. The Passenger Pigeon was once probably the most numerous species of bird in all North America. It was very beautiful and elegant; the wings were pointed, with the primary remiges longer than the others, and the graduated tail, half the body length, had thin fine, fanned feathers. The top part of the back was bluish-grey, and the bottom part as far as the tail was grey-brown; the chest was wine-coloured with a broad white patch; the neck had a beautiful bronzy plumage, highlighted with green and purple; the beak was black, the iris red and bright, and the legs were a deep dark red. The male was 41cm (16in) long and the female around 35cm (14in); their weight varied between 250 and 340g (9 and 12oz). The Passenger Pigeon was typically gregarious and lived in enormous groups. The species principally ate seeds and acorns, but also chestnuts, the seeds of pine, elm and other trees, hips and berries, and some invertebrates. The female laid a single egg which was incubated by the male during the day and the female by night. The incubation period lasted thirteen days after which followed the period of rearing the young. During the first week of life, the chicks were fed 'milk' secreted from the mucus in the parents' throats which was a mushy substance reconstituted from the food the adults had consumed.

Geographic distribution. The entire north-east of North America. In autumn, the pigeons migrated towards the south-east as far as Florida, Louisiana and Mexico.

Habitat. Vast forest regions and deciduous woods. After colonization when the land was cultivated, the Passenger Pigeon caused great damage.

History and causes of extinction. Until 1850, one could see clouds consisting of millions of Passenger Pigeons. The famous American naturalist, John James Audubon, (1785–1851) thought that in each cloud there must have been 100–115 million birds. The destruction of the species was effected by various methods: by shooting, cudgelling, the use of the bird as one of the main food sources for the United States, and by the exportation of the meat to Europe. Pigeon meat was included in pigswill and even used as manure. Towards the end of the nineteenth century, the destruction of the species was such that it was difficult to see even small groups of a few pigeons. When man did impose protective measures, it was already too late. In 1900, the last Passenger Pigeon in the wild was killed in Ohio; the last one born in captivity died of old age in 1914 in Cincinatti Zoo. Man had taken another step on the road to 'progress'.

162

Kakapo or Owl Parrot

(Strigops habroptilus)

Class: Aves Subclass: Neornithes
Order: Psittaciformes Family: Psittacidae
Subfamily: Strigopinae Genus: *Strigops*
French: *Perroquet-hibou* Italian: *Kakapo* or
Pappagallo notturno German: *Eulenpapagai*

Description. The Kakapo, or Owl Parrot, is the only species in the only genus belonging to the subfamily of Strigopinae. It is a massive bird, similar in size to other nocturnal birds of prey; it has short wings, a medium-length tail with a rounded edge, long tarsi and large feet ending in very strong, curved claws. The characteristics of the head also link the bird with other Strigopinae: the eyes are placed well in the centre of the face and are surrounded by a shaggy, feathered beard. The 'Kakapo', as it is called by the indigenous population, goes out in search of its food either at dusk, in the night or early morning, when it is still dark; its food consists of leaves, seeds, mosses, berries, fruit and other vegetation. It is an earthbound bird, flying only with difficulty and making its way from tree to tree on foot. In order to get into a tree, it climbs up the trunk. The species reproduces only once every two years and, very strangely, all the birds choose the same years. In the mating season, the males put on a show and emit strange shrieks like those of the bittern: they are, in fact, the only ones among the Psittacidae which have a throat sac. The Owl Parrot makes its nest either in decaying tree trunks, near the roots, or in a fallen tree. The bottom of the rough nest is covered with pieces of soft wood among which the female lays two to four eggs. Only a little is known of the habits of this bird in the wild, although attempts have been made to breed it in captivity, and in fact there are five at the Kelvin Grove Farm at Masterton, New Zealand.

Geographic distribution. This species at one time was widely distributed across the North and South Islands of New Zealand and the Chatham and Stewart islands. Today, it can be found only in a few restricted areas on the west of the northern island.

Habitat. Forest and the mountains up to 2,000m (6,500ft) above sea-level.

Population. According to the Red Data Book, in 1960 there were around 200; in 1961, the number had fallen to 100, with 30 of those confined to one area. There is reason to believe that the total is still diminishing. The species has progressively disappeared as a result of the destruction of its habitat by man and the introduction on to the island of various predatory animals which have found the practically defenceless kakapo 'good sport'. The species is now legally protected. There are no examples in any zoos.

Kaka

(Nestor meridionalis)

Class: Aves Subclass: Neornithes
Order: Psittaciformes Family: Psittacidae
Subfamily: Nestorinae Genus: *Nestor*
French: *Kaka* Italian: *Nestore meridionale*
German: *Kaka*

Description. According to various authorities the species *Nestor meridionalis* can be subdivided into 3 sub-species: the typical *Nestor meridionalis meridionalis*, the northern *N.m. septentrionalis*, and the third, which has been extinct since the middle of the nineteenth century, *N.m. productus*. Another species, the kea (*Nestor notabilis*), belongs to the same genus. The Nestorinae are similar to crows in behaviour, plumage, body size and the shape of the beak. Before the occupation of New Zealand by Europeans, the Nestorinae had a behaviour pattern very similar to the other Psittaciformes: it was primarily active at dusk, and ate seeds, fruits and shoots. When the white pioneers transformed and destroyed the natural habitat of the islands, as well as introducing domestic livestock, the customs of these parrots changed. There was no longer enough of the right sort of vegetation for them to eat and they quickly adapted to eating any sort of animal remains that they could get hold of and carry in their beaks – the placenta of sheep, carrion and even the meat that was thrown out by slaughterhouses. They also formed groups which could descend on sheep, kill them and devour the entire beast in a remarkably short time – a fact which did not endear the species to the local sheep-rearers. The Nestorinae, like the majority of the other parrots, nest in trees. There are two to four eggs; the young are reared by both parents until completely self-sufficient.

Geographic distribution. Before its extinction, *Nestor meridionalis productus* inhabited the Norfolk and Phillip islands; *N.m. septentrionalis* is found on North Island, New Zealand, while *N.m. meridionalis* is distributed over South Island.

Habitat. The mountains of New Zealand up to the tree line.

Population. The two sub-species of kaka are near to extinction. The birds are persecuted by sheep rearers who consider them a serious nuisance and, in fact, a reward is paid to anyone succeeding in killing one of them. It is to be hoped, however, that the possibility of extinction will outweigh the damage the birds cause and that they will soon become a protected species. Both sub-species of the kaka are on view in some of the New Zealand zoos.

Carolina Parakeet
(Conuropsis carolinensis)

Class: Aves Subclass: Neornithes
Order: Psittaciformes Family: Psittacidae
Subfamily: Psittacinae Genus: *Conuropsis*
French: *Perruche de Caroline* Italian: *Parrocchetto della Carolina* German: *Karolina-Sittich*

Description. This beautiful North American parakeet has been extinct since 1914. It measured 35cm (14in) long, had a slender shape and well defined, pointed wings and a long tail. The plumage was green on the back and greeny-yellow on the abdomen; the neck, head and the area immediately surrounding the wings were yellow; the forehead and cheeks were pink, and the high, squat beak was yellow. There were two strains: the Carolina (*Conuropsis carolinensis carolinensis*) and the Louisiana *C.c. ludovicianus*.
Geographic distribution. Virginia, Ohio, Indiana, Illinois, Missouri, eastern Texas, Louisiana and Florida.
Habitat. Forests and woods along river banks.
History and causes of extinction. The Carolina Parakeet was killed for its meat and feathers. Towards 1880 the diminution of the species was noted and attempts were made to protect it, but it was already too late. The last of the Louisiana variety were killed in 1912, and the last of the Carolina variety died in Cincinnati Zoo in 1914.

Splendid Parakeet
(Neophema splendida)

Class: Aves Subclass: Neornithes
Order: Psittaciformes Family: Psittacidae
Subfamily: Psittacinae Genus: *Neophema*
French: *Euphème resplendissante* Italian: *Parrocchetto splendido* German: *Glanzsittich*

Description. The Splendid Parakeet is one of the smallest, most beautiful and most brightly coloured of all parrots. It is approximately 20cm (8in) long, and has green feathers on the back, blue and black wings, a blue head, a yellow abdomen and scarlet chest. It has two related species which are also very rare: the Orange-stomached Parakeet (*Neophema chrysogaster*) and the Turkish Parakeet (*N. pulchella*).
Geographic distribution. The Splendid Parakeet was once distributed over a large part of southern Australia. Today, it is found only on the Eyre peninsula – apart from very occasional sightings in some regions in southern and western Australia.
Habitat. Semi-arid zones; it nests in dry tree trunks.
Population. Exact numbers unknown. The species has become rare due to the destruction of its habitat and capture for zoos and collections. It is now legally protected. The species is present in various zoos and private collections where it does reproduce.

Seychelles Owl

(Otus insularis)

Class: Aves Subclass: Neornithes
Order: Strigiformes Family: Strigidae
Subfamily: Buboninae Genus: *Otus*
French: *Petit Duc des Seychelles* Italian: *Gufo delle Seicelle* German: *Seychellen-Zwergohreule*

Description. The Seychelles Owl is 25cm (10in) long with wings reaching up to 28cm (11in); the tarsi are featherless. Like all owls, it is basically active at dusk, and eats insects and occasionally small reptiles.
Geographic distribution. Mahe Island, although probably at one time it also inhabited the other islands of the Seychelles archipelago.
Habitat. Moss-covered forest to a height of 1,000m.
Population. In 1906 the species was considered extinct, and research carried out between 1931 and 1936 reaffirmed this belief. In 1959, however, a small group was discovered in one of the mountain areas of Mahe where they were nesting. The species has declined as a result of the competition from other species introduced on to the island and the destruction of its habitat.

Seychelles Paradise (or Black) Flycatcher

(Terpsiphone corvina)

Class: Aves Subclass: Neornithes
Order: Passeriformes Family: Muscicapidae
Subfamily: Monarchinae Genus: *Terpsiphone*
French: *Gobe-mouche paradisier des Seychelles*
Italian: *Pigliamosche del paradiso delle Seicelle*
German: *Seychellen-Paradiesschnäpper*

Description. The genus *Terpsiphone* includes various species of flycatcher which have brilliant colours and very long tails, and are known as 'Paradise Flycatchers'. Among the most beautiful of these is the Seychelles Paradise Flycatcher and it is also the rarest. The male is a splendid black colour with blue highlights; it is 46cm (18in) long, of which 30cm (12in) account for the two central tail feathers. The back and wings of the female (illustrated below left) are brown, the underneath parts yellow-white and the head black. They eat insects which they catch among leaves and shrubs. The nest is a deep but tiny bowl into which two or three eggs are laid, followed by an incubation period of twelve days.
Geographic distribution. Originally distributed over almost all the Seychelles archipelago; until 1906 on Curieuse Island; until 1936 on Praslin and Felicité islands and, today, surviving only on La Digue Island.
Habitat. The tree-covered high plains of the Seychelles.
Population. The species was fairly numerous up to 1960, but has now become very rare.

Ivory-Billed Woodpecker

(Campephilus principalis)

Class: Aves Subclass: Neornithes
Order: Piciformes Family: Picidae
Subfamily: Picinae Genus: *Campephilus*
French: *Pic à bec d'ivoire* Italian: *Picchio dal becco avorio* German: *Elfenbeispecht*

Description. This beautiful woodpecker is one of the most notable birds in the USA although it is so rare that its very existence is in doubt. With a length of 50cm (20in), the Ivory-billed Woodpecker is one of the largest members of the family Picidae, and is only exceeded by the related and equally rare Imperial Woodpecker (*Campephilus imperialis*) which reaches 55cm (22in). The plumage is glossy black with two striking white stripes on the back and neck; the wings are also black and white and the legs are grey. The strong beak is chisel-shaped. The male (illustrated right) has a high crest of red feathers; the female, which is the same size and colour has a black crest which is slightly curved. As the name indicates, the beak is ivory white in both sexes. The female lays between one and four eggs (usually two to three) in a hole which has been dug out from a tree trunk. There are two known sub-species: the typical sub-species (*Campephilus principalis principalis*) and the Cuban variety (*C.p. bairdii*). They eat insects and larvae extracted from the barks of trees with the long beak.

Geographic distribution. The Ivory-billed Woodpecker was once distributed throughout the southern and western United States from North Carolina to Illinois, Missouri, Arkansas, and Oklahoma as far as western Texas and Florida. The last were seen in Florida, Louisiana, Texas, and primarily in South Carolina. The sub-species *C.p. bairdii* can now be found only in restricted areas in the eastern province of Cuba. The Imperial Woodpecker inhabits the Sierra Madre Mountains in Mexico.

Habitat. The most impenetrable parts of dense forest and marshy territory where there is an abundance of dead and decaying trees. The Imperial Woodpecker inhabits high mountain regions over 2,200m (7,200ft) in the northern part of its territory and over 2,700m (8,900ft) in the southern part.

Population. The Ivory-billed Woodpecker has always been rare and, as its habitat is almost impenetrable, its existence was for a long time known only by the Indians, woodsmen and a few naturalists. It has been highly prized by collectors because of its rarity. The major cause of its decline has been the destruction of its habitat through the felling of trees for timber. As the forests have disappeared, so have the woodpeckers. It was already thought to be extinct in 1925, but between 1930 and 1940 a few were discovered in Louisiana and South Carolina. The last recorded sighting was in 1972.

REPTILES AND AMPHIBIANS

Tuatara

(Sphenodon punctatus)

Class: Reptilia Subclass: Lepidosauria
Order: Rhynchocephalia Family: Sphenodontidae
Genus: *Sphenodon*
French: *Sphénodon ponctué* Italian: *Tuatara* or
Sfenodonte German: *Brückenechse*

Description. The tuatara is the only remaining member of an otherwise extinct order and it differs from all other living reptiles in various anatomical characteristics. It is 65cm (26in) long and its large, strong body easily weighs over 1kg (2lb). The Maori name 'tuatara' is not well chosen as it means 'sting-carrier' – in fact, the creature's only weapon is the horny lamellae half-way down the crest of its back. Its large eyes with vertical pupils suit the species' nocturnal habits. Because of the climate in its habitation, the tuatara, unlike most reptiles, has become adapted to low temperatures (optimum 12°C [54°F]). It has a slow metabolism and reaches maturity only at twenty years of age. The eggs, with paper-thin shells, are laid in clutches of fifteen and the young hatch out at thirteen to fifteen months. Although this long period of incubation is not unique, it is certainly exceptional. The tuatura's cry is a sad, tearful lament.

Geographic distribution. Originally distributed over all the New Zealand area but currently only found on some twenty islets off the New Zealand coast.

Habitat. Bushy or tree-covered terrain. Its lair is dug out from the ground, but where it finds a subterranean nest belonging to a sea bird, such as puffin or petrel, the tuatara will use it, chasing out the occupants and eating the nestlings if the nest is not already abandoned. The peaceful cohabitation between puffins and tuatara has frequently been stressed and described, but recent observations cannot confirm this.

Population. The reasons for the disappearance of this animal from the mainland of New Zealand seem to derive more from climatic change than from deliberate harm, for the Maoris have not actively hunted the tuatara (except to eat them occasionally) but the vegetation of the habitation has altered. The domestic animals introduced on to the island have substantially interfered with the species; sheep in particular have destroyed many of the plants which served as food for the various insects, which in turn, were a food source for the tuatara. The islets where the tuatara can still be found have been cleared of all life forms that are not autochthonal, including people, by the New Zealand government. It now seems that the *Sphenodon* population has reached a numerical constant. In 1964, a census estimated that there were about 10,000 individuals on some dozen islets. The species is strictly protected. In 1975 there were 21 in captivity in 11 collections.

Green Turtle

(Chelonia midas)

Class: Reptilia Subclass: Anapsida
Order: Testudines Suborder: Cryptodira
Family: Cheloniidae Genus: *Chelonia*
French: *Tortue verte* Italian: *Testuggine franca*
German: *Suppenschildkröte*

Description. Although this species can weigh as much as
400kg (882lb), the norm is between 150 and 250kg (330
and 550lb). The shell measures 95–120cm (35–47in) long.
Basically herbivorous, the Green Turtle also eats crustaceans, molluscs and jellyfish. It is a peaceful animal and,
unlike all its relatives which leave the sea only to lay
their eggs, it comes on to land in order to sleep and lie
in the sun.
Geographic distribution. Widely distributed throughout
seas in which the water temperature is no less than
20°C (68°F). It is occasionally carried by sea currents
into fresh water.
Habitat. Marine, with a preference for lagoons, bays and
gulfs, particularly when they are rich in vegetation.
Population. Fairly widespread, but the species is considered in danger due to the drastic reduction in
numbers. Although it is protected throughout almost all
its areas of distribution, the Green Turtle is still hunted
for its meat which is made into turtle soup, enjoyed by
gourmets worldwide. There are a number in captivity.

Hawksbill Turtle

(Eretmochelys imbricata)

Class: Reptilia Subclass: Anapsida
Order: Testudines Suborder: Cryptodira
Family: Cheloniidae Genus: *Eretmochelys*
French: *Tortue imbriquée* Italian: *Tartaruga
embricata* German: *Echte Karettschildkröte*

Description. The Hawksbill Turtle is fairly small, with a
shell usually measuring around 60cm (about 2ft). It has
large, variegated yellow and brown scales. The horny
sheath on the upper jaw forms a beak similar to a bird
of prey. It is omnivorous.
Geographic distribution. Mediterranean (although it has
disappeared from a few areas); the Atlantic, Pacific and
Indian Oceans. The eggs are laid only in warm regions:
South America, Africa, Australia, and southern Asia.
Habitat. Shallow coastal waters.
Population. No precise data is available because the
population fluctuates at different times in the different
areas of its distribution. Having been killed in large
numbers both on land and in the sea to obtain its scales
for fashioning into 'tortoiseshell' luxuries, it was hoped
that the invention of plastic materials would slow down
the pace of the hunting. However, it is as fierce as ever,
because the Hawksbill Turtle is now used in place of the
Green Turtle (see above) as the base of turtle soup.
Legal protection covering this species will have to be
more strict in order to save it from extinction. There are
several dozen examples in various zoos and aquaria.

Galapagos Giant Tortoise

(Testudo [Chelonoidus] elephantopus)

Class: Reptilia Subclass: Anapsida
Order: Testudines Suborder: Cryptodira
Family: Testudinidae Genus: *Testudo*
Subgenus: *Chelonoidis*
French: *Tortue éléphantine des Galapagos*
Italian: *Tartaruga gigante delle Galápagos*
German: *Galapagos-Riesenschildkröte*

Description. Although it is not the largest tortoise in the world – the Seychelles Tortoise (*Testudo [Aldabrachelys] aldabrensis*) is only about 10cm (4in) longer – the Galapagos Giant Tortoise is without doubt a 'giant' as it measures lengthwise a good 110cm (3½ft) and it weighs 150–200kg (330–440lb). The shell is highly arched and is covered in an almost black, horny shield. In the sub-species (the Saddlebacked Tortoise) this continues on to the underpart allowing the animal full extension of the long neck so that it can reach high branches. This tortoise is a good example of how a species adapts to its habitat. The Galapagos Giant Tortoise was described by Darwin in his *Diary of a Naturalist* and his observations – although recorded at a time when ecology and etho-logy were only words understood by fellow zoologists – are still highly valuable today and constitute a classic of biological literature. Because of the scarcity of warm water basins in arid climates, the species has been forced to adapt its behaviour. It has, in fact, developed a pattern whereby it journeys up from the sea to the high volcanic plains, finding there a large number of small lakes which give it the opportunity to drink and swim slowly, and to feed off the rich vegetation. These journeys back and forth have become an essential part of its way of life and over the centuries the paths carved out by thousands of tortoises have become built into the land-scape. This behaviour has become instinctive and is demonstrated by the fact that in environments where there is no chance of finding volcanic lakes, the tortoises will go through the same pattern. The Galapagos Giant Tortoise has numerous sub-species, each with its own population. However, by now the various facts and reports we have regarding these beasts are more a matter of history and sailors' stories than they are con-temporaneous reports. Of the fifteen known sub-species, one pair has been extinct for some time, another two (*Testudo elephantopus phantastica* and *T.e. wallacei*) are probably also extinct as they have not been seen for some time on the two islands (Narborough and Jervis respectively) which constituted their territory. *T.e. abingdoni* was also thought to be extinct but in 1972 one,

and traces of two or three, were discovered. The ten other sub-species are: *T.e. elephantopus*, which is the typical sub-species, *T.e. becki*, *T.e. chathamensis*, *T.e. darwini*, *T.e. ephippium*, *T.e. güntheri*, *T.e. hoodensis*, *T.e. microphyes*, *T.e. nigrita* and *T.e. vandenburghi*.

Geographic distribution. The centre of the Galapagos archipelago; of the living sub-species, five are found in Albemarle, six on each of the islands of James, Inde-fatigable, Duncan, Hood, Chatham and Abingdon, while the sub-species that are now considered extinct used to inhabit the islands of Narborough and Jervis. It is worthy of note that the other group of giant tortoises, or at least those which remain, also live on islands, in the Seychelles archipelago. It is also interesting that, while generally species and sub-species which inhabit islands are smaller than those found on mainlands, the Galapa-gos Giant Tortoise and the Seychelles Giant Tortoise prove the exception to the rule.

Habitat. The Galapagos Giant Tortoise prefers arid terrain with grassland, alternating with high volcanic plains with abundant water and vegetation.

Population. All of the sub-species are rare; a few are very rare and held to be in immediate danger of extinction. The sightings and recordings recently range from none (*T.e. becki*, *T.e. hoodensis*, *T.e. phantastica*, *T.e. wallacei*) to one (*T.e. abingdoni*, *T.e. elephantopus*) to around 1,000 (*T.e. nigrita*). The species has declined from the enormous numbers mentioned by the first explorers to the present state of near-extinction. This has principally been caused by the well equipped ships which, in the nineteenth century, carried traders and sailors to the 'tortoise islands', as they called the Galapagos. These crews slaughtered the tortoises for their meat without respite. The colonization of the island and the intro-duction of domestic animals, especially goats and pigs, was the final blow to hopes of the species' survival in large numbers. The species was protected in 1934 and the islands where the tortoises live are reserves and sanctuaries belonging to the government of Ecuador. The World Wildlife Fund financed the creation of the Charles Darwin Station which, together with others, has made steps towards ensuring the survival of the species and increasing its reproduction. In 1975, there were 322 in captivity from 5 of the sub-species, with 82 males, 86 females and 154 of unknown sex gathered in 68 collections. However, the Giant Tortoise has not yet reproduced in captivity, although Honolulu Zoo has succeeded in rearing a dozen young from eggs. This success has inspired the Bronx Zoo of New York to send their own examples of the Giant Tortoise to Honolulu in the hope of adding to what could be an effective reproducing group. Those reared in captivity prevent further numbers from being taken from the wild for zoos, and it is hoped eventually to reintroduce them to their natural habitat to increase the local populations.

Leatherback

(Dermochelys coriacea)

Class: Reptilia Subclass: Anapsida
Order: Testudines Suborder: Cryptodira
Family: Dermochelyidae Genus: *Dermochelys*
French: *Tortue luth* Italian: *Dermochelide*
German: *Lederschildkröte*

Description. This is the largest of all living tortoises
with a length of 2m (6½ft) and a weight of 700kg
(1,540lb). It is covered with bone plates inserted on to
the thick skin. The young are covered in scales growing
irregularly all over the body, but these are lost almost
immediately and are also very brightly coloured with
white or yellow blotches.
Geographic distribution. Temperate and tropical zones;
the eggs are laid only in the latter.
Habitat. Marine.
Population. The species is in grave danger of extinction,
although protected by the law. Partial counts have been
made of the total population based on the females which
lay their eggs in a given locality. Many of these females
are captured and killed for meat, and, if the eggs are
successfully laid, up to 100 per cent may be collected
for 'gastronomic' purposes. As far as the new-born
turtles are concerned, the effort of first getting out of the
egg, then out of the nest and down to the edge of the sea,
claims 70 per cent; their next test comes at the water's
edge when they have to launch themselves and swim to
safety while avoiding the predatory gulls and other sea
birds. It has been recorded that only one or two of the
1,000 new-born turtles reach their first year. There are
three Leatherbacks in captivity in two aquaria (Malta
and Miami).

(Galapagos) Land Iguana

(Conolophus subcristatus)

Class: Reptilia Subclass: Lepidosauria
Order: Squamata (scaly reptiles) Suborder: Sauria
Family: Iguanidae Genus: *Conolophus*
French: *Iguane* Italian: *Iguana terrestre delle
Galápagos* German: *Drüsenkopf*

Description. A quiet, inoffensive creature, the Land
Iguana has a squat heavy body with a bulky trunk,
strong limbs, cylindrical tail and a crest along its back
which stands up at the neck. It also has folds of skin
forming a pouch under the throat. The total length is
110cm (43in) of which 55cm (22in) are the tail. Its diet
consists of vegetables. During the mating season the
males fight ritual battles. The female lays her eggs in a
hole which she has dug in the ground and, having laid
them, she covers them with earth.
Geographic distribution. The species is exclusive to the
Galapagos archipelago.
Habitat. Terrain with sparse bush vegetation. The
destruction of this in order to make room for the
domestic goat has left the Land Iguana undefended from
the attack of buzzards.
Population. Extinct in a number of the Galapagos
islands, the species is very rare in others. Indiscriminate
hunting by man and persecution by the indigenous
birds of prey, together with the introduction of domestic
animals have all been responsible for the fall in numbers
of this species. There are no examples in any zoos, but at
San Diego Zoo there is one example of the related
Conolophus palligus.

Indian Gavial

(Gavialis gangeticus)

Class: Reptilia Subclass: Archosauria
Order: Crocodylia Suborder: Eusuchia
Family: Gavialidae Genus: *Gavialis*
French: *Gavial du Gange* Italian: *Gaviale del Gange*
German: *Ganges-Gavial*

Description. The order Crocodylia, which is rich in species from prehistoric times, can be divided into eight genuses with twenty-one species, subdivided into three families: Alligatoridae, Crocodilidae and Gavialidae. All, or very nearly all, these species are now rare and many among them are in grave danger of extinction principally because of intense hunting to obtain their highly prized skins for the world's luxury fashion market. The most threatened species are: the American Crocodile (*Crocodylus acutus*), the Nile Crocodile (*C. niloticus*), and the American Alligator (*Alligator mississipiensis*) (all these three are, however, well represented in captivity); the Morelet Crocodile (*Crocodylus moreleti*), the Cuban Crocodile (*C. rhombifer*), and the two species *Melanosuchus niger* and *Osteolaemus tetraspis* and the Indian Gavial. The latter is the species most in danger of extinction and it has morphological characteristics which make it different from all other crocodiles. This species, which is at least 7m (23ft) long, has a long and slender muzzle well away from the rest of the head; the muzzle is, in fact, 3½ times as long as it is wide. The upper jaw is armed with fifty-four teeth and the lower with forty-eight, all of which serve the purpose of seizing and holding prey. The gavial customarily feeds on fish and frogs. It is a dark olive colour with darker patches on the upper parts. Its flanks are shades of greeny yellow which becomes very pale on the underneath. The female lays the eggs directly on to the ground or on to sand banks. The young measure 40cm (16in) at birth.

Geographic distribution. The drainage basin of the Ganges and Brahmaputra in India; the Koladan and the mouth of the Maingtha in Indochina.

Habitat. Of all crocodiles, the gavial is the most truly aquatic, inhabiting deep and fast-running water in large rivers.

Population. The species was sacred to the god Visnu and for a long time was not harmed by man. It then fell prey to the hunters of crocodile skins, and by now has been eliminated from a large part of its original territory. It was also threatened by the construction of dams and artificial canals and was caught in the nets of fishermen who killed the creature out of fear. By 1958, the exportation of almost all crocodile skins was made illegal – hunting though continued, as a skin measuring 4m (13ft) could earn a native the equivalent of half a year's income. However, the gavial gained complete protection in India in 1972. This reptile was held to be one of the five species most in danger in all India. In 1973 an investigation took place along 5,000km (3,100 miles) of riverway formerly overrun with crocodiles – in three months only six gavials were sighted. It is thought that there are no more than 300 left in the world. In 1975 there were 35 in 21 zoos.

Komodo Dragon

(Varanus komodoensis)

Class: Reptilia Subclass: Lepidosauria
Order: Squamata Suborder: Sauria
Family: Varanidae Genus: *Varanus*
French: *Varan de Komodos* Italian: *Varano di Komodo* German: *Komodo-Waran*

Description. The Komodo Dragon is the largest saurian now living. A young adult male can reach a length of 3m (10ft) or more; however, the length is usually 2.40m (8ft) for the male and 2.10m (7ft) for the female. The komodo's length and the exceptionally massive shape of the body, weighing between 72 and 91kg (159lb and 201lb) in the male, with a record of 165kg (364lb), and between 68 and 73kg (150 and 161lb) in the female, give it an altogether imposing appearance. The muzzle, which is particularly wide across the jaws, the heavy trunk, the strong limbs armed with great claws, the powerful tail and the grey-black colour covered with lumps and pits in the skin justify the name of dragon. It is not surprising that the legendary descriptions by the local population and travellers have given such frightening reports of this great beast and its habits. Although legends had for a long time been related about fantastic reptiles that could be found on a few of the Sunda islands, or more precisely on Flores Island, it was only in 1912 that the species was actually scientifically described. Since then, a number of accurate observations over a long period have been carried out on the species, and its habits studied in its local habitat. This large heavy saurian is lethargic for it will hide away in vegetation, which makes it difficult to observe, or will spend many hours lying immobile in the sun; however, once jerked into action it becomes surprisingly agile. The Komodo Dragon is basically carnivorous, feeding off medium-sized vertebrates, with a particular predeliction for deer. It will also come out into the light in order to eat dead animals. These have been used as bait to bring the dragon to a position where it can be easily observed by researchers. It also, of course, provides a way of killing them as illegal hunting has never slackened. The power of the Komodo Dragon's jaws is noteworthy: while holding the beast down, it can, with the aid of the powerful neck muscles, tear off a deer's hind limb – the leg thigh and pelvic belt – without any apparent difficulty; this morsel is then entirely consumed. Among other stories of the Komodo Dragon's battles with various large animals is one which relates its combat with a horse but the conditions of the incident were, in fact, totally unnatural. While ferocious in its natural habitat, it is docile in captivity.

Geographic distribution. The distribution of this dragon is not totally limited to Komodo Island. Also found on the small islands of Rintja and Padar, and the western coast of the large island of Flores, the species is threatened with very rapid extinction on Padar and Flores Islands.

Habitat. The Komodo Dragon is of necessity limited to an area with a large amount of trees and the accompanying vegetation, as it requires them for refuge and protection. Furthermore, its customary prey also inhabits wooded or forest areas. In some regions, such as Padar, the habitat is suddenly transformed to such an extent that it no longer offers sufficient protection for the survival of species.

Population. It is estimated that the population of this species fluctuates between 2,000 and 5,000; however, currently compiled data indicates that the figure is now closer to 2,000. The population has a conspicuous prevalence of males which may account for the species' decline. There are probably about 400 adult females, with a smaller number capable of laying eggs; only a small proportion of the eggs actually hatch out. The phenomenon of the preponderance of males can be reckoned as a biological factor indicating that the species has not adapted to the conditions of its habitat and will gradually die out. Another reason for the species' decline is found in the degradation of its habitat (illustrated opposite with the example of Padar Island); the vegetation has gradually been removed taking away the animal's protection and source of food. The species is protected by the General Decree of Protection for Wild Animals published by the Indonesian Government; the islands of Rintja and Padar have been declared nature reserves. The unfavourable conditions of Padar Island have led the Forestry and Conservation Department to intervene with a project to re-create the characteristic vegetation of the island. Illegal hunting of the species has also contributed to its decline. In 1975, there were 6 males, 4 females and 7 individuals of unknown sex in 9 zoos. Reproduction in captivity is exceptionally rare, if not impossible, according to Djakarta Zoo. It is not possible to take any examples from the tropical zone for experimental purposes.

Giant Salamander

(Andrias japonicus)

Class: Amphibian Subclass: Urodelomorpha
Order: Urodela (urodeles)
Suborder: Cryptobranchoidea
Family: Cryptobranchidae Genus: *Andrias*
French: *Salamandre géante* Italian: *Salamandra gigante* German: *Riesensalamander*

Description. In 1831 this salamander was described as one species with the common name of Giant Salamander, but in 1871 it was divided into two sub-species (*Andrias japonicus japonicus*, illustrated below) and the Chinese variety, (*A.j. davidianus*). It had belonged to the *Megalobatrachus* genus (the giant amphibians) but when a description was found from an earlier date of the similar species *Andrias scheuchzeri*, which could be seen in Europe, the Giant Salamander was included in the genus *Andrias*. It is 1.60m (5ft) long, heavy and with a massive body. The skin is dark and covered in warts, and an overall purplish-brown. The head is wide and large, rather flat and shapeless, with a wide mouth and small eyes. The male incubates the eggs for between fifty-two and sixty-eight days. The salamander treats the day and night equally, dividing its time into periods of rest and periods of food-hunting activity. The reptile's diet consists of fish, frogs and insects, which it stalks and suddenly pounces upon before consuming. The Giant Salamander prefers to remain in one area, frequently staying there for years and making its birthplace its own home for life, only venturing outside the immediate territory if forced to or to breed and reproduce. Although extremely inert, the salamander will fight with great tenacity to death when provoked, without, however, greatly harming its adversary.

Geographic distribution. The typical sub-species inhabits western Honshu, part of central Kyushu, and the upper part of the Oia and Yakkan rivers; the Chinese sub-species inhabits the provinces of Szechwan, Shansi, Shensi, Kweichow, Hupeh and Kwangsi.

Habitat. The sub-species inhabit the areas around rivers that flow through mountains, with a preference for fresh-running water. In order to lay the eggs, the male goes to higher regions first, followed by the female shortly after.

Population. No precise information is available but the typical sub-species has definitely declined, particularly in Kyushu. In 1927, in Japan, the species was declared a 'national monument of wild life' and in 1952 a 'natural monument'. However, it is difficult to impose controls throughout the mountain areas and consequently the Giant Salamander continues to be captured and used either as food or for medicinal products. In 1975, there were 145 examples in 33 collections.

Olm

(Proteus anaguineus)

Class: Amphibian Subclass: Urodelomorpha
Order: Urodela (urodeles) Suborder: Salamandroidea
Family: Proteida Genus: *Proteus*
French: *Protée anguillard* Italian: *Proteo*
German: *Grottenolm*

Description. The olm is a very strange looking creature because of its eel-shaped body, short legs with three digits, cylindrical muzzle and eyes buried in slits in the skin. The usual length is 20–30cm (8–12in). The external ears are blood-red and extend from the side of the neck. This amphibian can reproduce either viviparously or oviparously, according to the water temperature. Strictly cave-dwelling and aquatic, it occasionally comes out to rest on the slimy banks of subterranean waters, or is carried out into the open current as a result of flood waters from violent rain.
Geographic distribution. The Karst regions of Venice and Slovenia; the Dalmatian coast.
Habitat. The typical habitat of the olm is subterranean waters within Karst caves.
Population. Although not in grave danger of extinction or even particularly scarce, the olm is very rare because it is restricted to living in a particular area.

Golden Frog

(Atelopus zeteki)

Class: Amphibian Subclass: Anuromorpha
Order: Anurans (anura) Suborder: Procoela
Family: Atelopodidae Genus: *Atelopus*
French: *Grenouille de Zetek* Italian: *Rana dorata*
German: *Panama-Stummelfussfrosch*

Description. This little frog has justly received its name from its splendid golden colouring. It has three large, black patches across the back and dark blotches on the legs. The Golden Frog is similar in looks to the Tree Frog, but the long slim legs give it a more slender appearance. The first two digits on the feet are atrophied. The females are attracted by the mating cry of the male. They lay their eggs in rain puddles where, adapted to the natural danger of evaporation of the water, they develop extremely quickly, hatching out after only twenty-four hours.
Geographic distribution. The Anton Valley in the Central American republic of Panama.
Habitat. A territory only 3km (1.2 miles) in diameter completely surrounded by mountains, except at the point where the River Anton flows out of the valley.
Population. Having been continually sought as souvenirs for the many tourists that visit the Anton Valley, the species has become rare.

APPENDICES

Fulco Pratesi

MAN AND ANIMALS IN THE NATURAL WORLD

The decree of Genesis

'And God said: "Let the earth bring forth living creatures according to their kind: domestic animals, reptiles and beasts of the earth, according to their kind." And so it was. And God saw that it was good.' This, according to Genesis, was the fifth day of the Creation. After this, in the instructions given by God to Noah after leaving the Ark, the situation changed, but not to the advantage of the animals: 'Be fertile and multiply, fill the earth and instill fear and terror in to all the animals of the earth and birds of the sky.' There is no doubt that the patriarch's successors carried out these orders scrupulously. As the human population increased, the animals diminished. The lions of the great hunts of Assur disappeared as did those of the feats of David and Samson, the black aurochs, the wild bulls of the European forests, the crocodiles and hippopotami of the Euphrates and the Nile delta. As if inspired by a divine mission, man has attempted to create desert around himself. And not merely metaphorically.

Efficient extermination

A system of efficient and precise extermination is rapidly leading to the disappearance of wild fauna, and, as a direct consequence, to the destruction of the human race:

1650 450 million men on earth: 7 species became extinct in the seventeenth century.
1750 550 million men on earth: 11 species became extinct in the eighteenth century.
1850 900 million men on earth: 27 species became extinct in the nineteenth century.
1975 3500 million men on earth: 67 species became extinct in the first three-quarters of the twentieth century.

This book draws attention to 144 species either already extinct or currently becoming extinct in the world. Many more species are in some way endangered and, in fact, all species, including man, have embarked on a road from which there is no return.

For those still living out of the 144, the situation is extremely serious – without immediate intervention their situation will be hopeless. One hope remains, however, for the attitude of humanity (the finer part of it) towards wild fauna has slowly changed in recent years. The enlightened and generous actions of men, **Hope** associations and governments, have improved the situation, as the following figures show. According to the statistics of the International Union for the Conservation of Nature and its Resources (UICN), during the last seventy-five years the progress of wildlife extinction has been as follows:

1900–1919: 23 species extinct
1920–1939: 27 species extinct
1940–1960: 14 species extinct
1960–1974: only 3 species extinct

These figures illustrate the growing preoccupation of man over the last thirty-five years with the fate of nature.

WHY PROTECT THEM?

It is helpful at this point to give some explanation of the importance of wild animals and why they need to be protected from extinction.

Apart from the ethical considerations forbidding us to destroy any form of life, we must recognize the reasons for which a species is of great interest for the life and survival of man himself.

The ancient relationship between man and animal

For a millennium, man and wild animals have evolved together on this planet. The relationship between the paleolithic hunter and the wild fauna was very close, so much so that man could not have survived without having at his disposal abundant wild fauna to provide him with food, clothing, implements, assistance in his agricultural efforts, etc. As man changed from being a hunter-gatherer and nomadic shepherd to farmer, citizen and worker, so his relationship with animals diminished in importance. Until the eighteenth century, the only form of harnessed energy was the domestic animal, apart from the limited use of air and water power in windmills, wind saws and textile mills. With the progressive abandoning of the countryside and the increase in population, the growth of urban and industrial society has provoked an attitude of indifference towards the species of wild animals unable to take any part in this development. Furthermore, they have been used and exploited in ever greater numbers to supply the needs of an increasing population and to furnish raw materials for industry. Thus we have seen the slaughter of the American Bison to feed the workers on the Transamerican Railway (which, incidentally led to the starvation of the Indians who relied on the bison for every source of livelihood), the

The great slaughter

slaughter of whales for the cosmetics and soap industry, and of fur-skinned animals for the clothing and fashion business. Nowadays, since the direct and immediate economic interest in animals has ceased, it would seem a matter of indifference that they should disappear completely to allow the unbridled expansion of cultivation and cities. But it has not been so. The direct and indirect causes which lead to the disappearance of animal species (pollution, destruction of habitat, etc.) also damage in the long-term those who are responsible. By rendering the planet uninhabitable for animals, we will not be able to avoid extinction ourselves. In spite of the fact that we do everything to ignore the fact, we also belong to nature and have the same strong links that bind every one of its creatures. If we destroy a few links in the chain, we shall inevitably destroy ourselves as well.

Even apart from the generally negative attitude of man towards animals, there are many reasons for the disappearance of the species; and some, we must remember, not due at all to man's actions.

NATURAL CAUSES OF EXTINCTION

Apart from man's efforts to eliminate wild animals from his territory, it cannot be denied that even before his arrival (about 2 million years ago) species were subject to extinction. No one would deny the fact – proved by centuries of research – that right

The end of dinosaurs

from its first beginnings (traces of life appeared about 2 billion years ago) the life of animal species has had a cycle similar to that of organisms. Species have appeared then lived populating entire continents for millennia and finally disappeared: the ammonites, large Cephalopoda of the Devonian Era (roughly $1\frac{1}{2}$ billion years ago) multiplied in the seas for nearly 300 million years, and dinosaurs, which appeared on earth about 200 million years ago, dominated both land and sea becoming extinct for unknown reasons after almost 100 million years. These great reptiles give us the opportunity to speak of the natural causes of extinction. How is it possible that such animals, endowed with considerable strength and strong physical constitution (the largest animals ever to exist on earth belonged to this species) became extinct in the space of a few millennia? Some researchers attribute this fact to unexpected changes in climate to which they could not adapt without thermo-regulation; others claim that it was brought about by a change in vegetation and the substitution of their preferred diet (giant ferns and evergreens) by phanerogams which today cover most of the earth. It has also been thought that their eggs were increasingly subject to predators such as mammals and the newly arrived marsupials which, being extremely agile and no bigger than large rats in comparison, were not noticed by the parent dinosaurs.

Extinction means forever

Whatever the cause, the natural extinction of this species does not assume the tragic importance of the extinctions treated in this book, mainly because, in accordance with natural laws, the extinction of one species was immediately followed by the appearance of another in a perfect and continuous cycle. However, in the disappearance of a species through lack of forethought, or worse by man's wickedness, no new species apart from *Homo sapiens* and his domestic animals can fill the gap. Thus, every extermination is a loss in absolute terms. The disappearance of a species represents enormous damage to all life on earth in the loss of that treasure of natural selection, of genetic adaptation, of ecological relationships with other species and with the environment which only events happening over millennia could produce. If the Colosseum and the Basilica of St Peter's was destroyed it would even be possible, having the plans and drawings, to reconstruct it; the reconstruction of a species, once destroyed by lack of human forethought is now, and always will be, impossible.

Another important difference between natural extinction and that caused by man is the relative speed at which they take place: as Vinzenz Ziswiler remarked, 'In the process of evolution one can consider the extinction of a species as a rare event.' To illustrate this we can see that following the 'unexpected' disappearance of the dinosaur (over the course of a million years) one thousand species disappeared; thus the rate of extinction was

200 exterminated in 300 years

once every thousand years. Man's destruction, on the other hand, has eliminated more than 200 species of birds and mammals in the last 300 years – species which were in prime condition and very far from natural extinction.

Even recent and imminent extinctions which are said to be from 'natural causes' have directly or indirectly a human cause. Let us take, for example, Audouin's Gull (*Larus audouinii*): similar

Audouin's Gull: a case in point

in size and habits to the Herring Gull its numbers are declining alarmingly over the whole Mediterranean; it is thought that the cause of this is competition with the latter with whom both habitat and sources of food are shared. Man apparently has no part in it. But, looking closer, we find that the Herring Gull has increased notably in numbers in the last years thanks to the increase of fishing at sea and the increase of fish refuse following a general cut-back in the numbers of varieties of fish landed. Access to the remote islands where the Audouin's Gull nests has become increasingly easier for boats and small craft, thus damaging this shy and wild species more than the Herring Gull. These are indications that man is involved in the plight of these two species which have lived together for millennia.

MAN'S RESPONSIBILITY

Direct and indirect destruction

The greatest single cause in the extinction of wild animal species in the last centuries has come, as we have seen, from the thoughtless and egotistical action of man. Ways and means by which this has been accomplished have been various. We can roughly divide these into two categories: direct destruction (hunting, capturing, indiscriminate extermination for various reasons) and indirect destruction (alteration of habitat, introduction of new species, poisonings, traffic, etc).

Hunting

The principal cause of the extinction of wild animal species is, of course, any direct action towards their physical elimination. Thus hunting, in whatever way and for whatever reasons (pure amusement, to provide meat, furs, feathers or trophies), has acted in a negative manner on the survival of animals ever since man's creation. Some experts, for example, attribute the disappearance of some species to destruction perpetrated by our predecessors; the large-scale slaughter of herbivorous creatures

The harassed bison

(especially wild horses), apparently forced over precipices in herds, is indicated by the immense deposits of bones at the bottom and could have contributed greatly to their disappearance. This is little different from what happened 100 years ago to the American Bison. It was calculated that around 1700 there were 60 million head of bison in North America, and they were all but destroyed in a few years of relentless and brutal hunting. Armed with rifles butchers who specialized in wholesale slaughter, like the famous Buffalo Bill, killed in one day alone about 250 head – then only the animal's tongue was consumed and the rest of the body was left to rot. The company which managed the Atlantic Pacific Railroad organized 'hunting trips' providing passengers with rifles and carbines to shoot continuously from the windows at the peaceful beasts feeding in the prairie. As a result, by 1890 there were only a few dozen left. But fortunately the species was saved and, thanks to rigid protection laws, and prudent governments regarding conservation, there still exist today tens of thousands of American Bison in national parks and reserves in the United States and Canada. A similar story, but one with a tragic conclusion, concerns the Migrating Dove. The responsi-

The end of the Migrating Dove

bility for this bird's extinction undoubtedly lies with the hunter. Relentless human action brought about the extinction of the species of which billions existed. In 1855, a New York merchant was selling daily 18,000 doves; in 1869, over $7\frac{1}{2}$ million were caught in one area; in 1879 a billion were killed in Michigan alone.

The American naturalist painter, John James Audubon, described one of these massacres in the following way: 'Already some thousands had been killed by the blows of men armed with sticks; but fresh flocks came without cease. One could barely hear the rifle shots; I would not have noticed the shots fired had I not seen them reloading their weapons. The hunters stood in piles of dead, dying or wounded animals. The doves were piled up, everyone took as many as he wanted and then the pigs were let loose to eat the rest.'

The naturalist, Figuier, who also reported the event, affirmed: 'This carnage does not compromise at all the existence of the species, in fact, according to Audubon, the number of these doves doubles and even quadruples in the same year.' This comment was quickly contradicted by events: already in 1860 there were no important colonies in existence, in 1894 the final nest was found and in 1899 the last bird in the wild. In 1914, in Cincinnati Zoo, the last Migrating Dove died.

The Blue Whale is undergoing a similar fate as, indeed, are all species of whale: every year, of the various species, between 60,000 and 70,000 individuals are killed. Unbridled hunting for fat (used in cosmetics), for meat (used in dog food) and for other substances, is leading to the disappearance of the largest animal which ever existed.

The martyred animal

Victims of other 'irresponsible raids', as Ziswiler defines them, have been numerous in the last centuries, for example the dodo, a large dove no longer able to fly, which lived on the island of Mauritius. Sailors, stopping on the island to provision themselves with meat used to kill them in their hundreds. Then, in 1589, Mauritius became a Dutch penal colony and with the establishment of a convict colony came pigs and rats which destroyed the nests of the peaceful bird. Around 1681, the species disappeared.

The same fate overtook the Great Auk. This bird was also slaughtered by sailors and fishermen who stopped in the islands where it nested; Figueir tells us that they were so abundant that 'Captain Mood, in one fell swoop was able to collect more than 100,000 of their eggs'. In 1844, the last examples still living were killed on an island close to the coast of Iceland.

Let us cite as an epitaph what the great naturalist Figuier said when talking about the extinction of the dodo: 'The dodo, fat and squat, would never weigh less than 25 kilos. This fat body held up by short legs and furnished by ridiculous wings was as incapable of running as of flying and thus found itself condemned to rapid destruction. Finally, to add to the singular appearance, it had a stupid physiognomy which did not make it in the least attractive to the onlooker. This bird did not even have the merit of being useful after its death since its flesh was repugnant and of a bad taste. There is thus no reason to mourn its disappearance.'

The philosophy of extinction

In these few phrases nearly all the philosophy of extinction is contained: and it is not at all by chance that these words were written during the years of the worst slaughters. These are the concepts: an animal which is not useful to man and moreover not sympathetic and beautiful has not the merit to live; therefore remove it from the face of the earth. But if these absurd concepts were valid for animals which were simply useless or ugly, they were even more valid towards those which were considered, almost always wrongly, to be harmful. And this is the case of the large carnivorous beasts. The Asiatic Lion, whose domain in ancient times stretched as far as Greece and Albania is today reduced to not more than 250 examples in a forest in West India. The tiger also is on the point of extinction; so also is the White Bear, the leopard and other mammal predators.

The reason for this is a mistaken attitude towards those animals which occupy the summit of the food chain. Until fairly recently, traditions or superficial and unsupported beliefs attributed the carnivorous animals with merely a negative function towards other species; even today, despite the modern theory that predators exercise a useful selecting function by eliminating sub-standard and weak animals, many carnivorous animals are accused of 'ferociousness', 'blood lust' and 'killing for the sake of killing'.

Thus, the real killer is let loose: exterminating the puma, the coyote, the Grizzly Bear and wolves with doses of strychnine and cyanide in North America (bringing to the point of extinction the North American Jaguar and the Grizzly Bear); eliminating with beatings, traps and poisoned bait, tigers, lions and leopards in Asia and Africa; destroying wolves in Germany, Austria, Switzerland, Belgium, France, Denmark, Holland, Sweden, bringing to extinction the lynx in Italy, France, Germany, Austria, Switzerland, etc.; sweeping away the Barbary Lion and the Cape Lion (the first in 1920, the second in 1865); and reducing to its last legs any animal which could in any way at all be suspected of threatening the domestic beast.

The misdeeds of fashion

There exists a form of hunting which bases itself on that most futile of human passions – fashion. For the sake of the questionable concepts of elegance and to give work to a superfluous industry – the condemnable needs of our over-populated world – hundreds of species are, or are about to be, in danger of extinction. The Marine Otter, the Plate Otter and all animals of the cat family with spotted skins are condemned in the name of a fashion which is shocking and vulgar; the small, white seals of the arctic coasts are skinned alive to adorn exacting wives and costly mistresses; the egrets, the herons and the Birds of Paradise were in danger of extinction at the beginning of the century only so that their feathers could adorn the horrible hats of elegant ladies of that time. In 1912 when the fashion of the boa and ostrich feather hat was at its height, 146,371 kilos (161 tons) of ostrich feathers were sold in France alone. In 1913, according to Ziswiler, the market for feathers for the clothes industry in London cost the hide of 86,315 cranes and herons, 26,618 Bird of Paradise and 27,650 Crown Doves. This does not even include the crocodiles, alligators, pythons and iguana killed in millions for bags, shoes and watchstraps, or the tortoises torn alive from their shells because of a fashion for tortoiseshell objects.

The mania for souvenirs

Other forms of usage more or less absurd are contributing to the drastic reduction of many animals – the mania for souvenirs which menaces the ivory-carrying animals (walruses, elephants, hippopotami), the dik-dik (horns for key-rings), butterflies and beautiful coleopters, molluscs with bright shells and colonies of coral, etc. Then there are superstitions which attribute medicinal powers to parts of animals (rhinoceros horn was believed to prevent the killing of a legal possessor or restore the sexual vigour of the old Chinese), and the necrophiliac mania for trophies and stuffed animals – for this reason every year in Italy tens of thousands of most useful hunting or rare birds are killed. Finally, no less shocking or cruel, the collection of live animals for private zoos.

Indirect causes

The indirect causes are also numerous: they range from the destruction of woods (in Italy, for example, 50 per cent of the territory was covered in woods in 1500 compared to 20 per cent today), to the drainage of swamps (we have gone from more than 2 million hectares of swamps in ancient times to only 150,000 hectares today), and to the breaking up of grassland. Such alterations condemn animals to live strictly bound to one environment.

The tragedy of pollution

Other indirect causes can be seen in pollution: the continuous deterioration of the Volga is posing serious questions about the survival of the sturgeon in that river, and the blankets of crude oil spilled by petroleum tankers seriously menace the populations of marine birds worldwide. When, in 1959, the American steamer *Armouk* unloaded 360 tons of petroleum into the Weser estuary, it caused the death of at least 15,000 aquatic birds, of which 8,000 were teal and 1,000 were merganser (Ziswiler). The effects of the sinking of the *Torrey Canyon* in the English Channel with 115,000 tons of crude oil on board were proportionately greater. Further, there is the traffic which kills millions of animals every year: in 1968, for example, in the United States alone, 365 million – 1 million a day – wild animals died because of traffic.

Insecticides like DDT accumulate in animals' bodies and induce sterility and finally death. According to recent studies, the frightening rarity of many species of hunting birds (for example, the Bald Eagle which is the symbol of the United States, and the kingfisher) is to be attributed, apart from hunting, to the accumulation of DDT in the skin tissue which induces excessive fragility in the eggshell, causing the loss of entire nests.

THE IMPORTANCE OF ANIMALS FOR THE LIFE OF MAN

Even without having recourse to rhetorical and sophisticated images, there is no doubt that the presence of wild fauna in the human environment is of fundamental importance to the quality of life and to man's physical well-being. Quite simply, an environment in which many species of wild animals live is an environment which is ecologically clean and therefore suitable also for the habitation of man. Besides, even without following this indicative function of animals, they have a value in the enrichment of the countryside.

A world without animals

A marsh without the flight of wild duck loses half its rustic fascination; thus the African savannah without its splendid population of herbivorous creatures would be nothing but arid and tree-covered steppe. In the same way, seagulls are an integral part of marine landscapes, and the eagle and chamois are indivisible from the image of the mountain environment; so are woods and countryside without the song of birds, ponds and marshes without the croaking of frogs and the flight of dragonfly, and rivers without the splash of trout and the call of the river nightingale. A countryside without wild animals is a dead countryside – static, monotonous and rather like a picture postcard.

But even without having an effect on the five senses, it is enough to consider the idea of satisfaction and appeasement. To walk through the tracks of the Abruzzo National Park and to know that bears still live there, to admire an Indian jungle and be certain of the presence of a tiger, offer sensations and emotions so deep that they give value to life itself.

THE NATIONAL PARKS

A large part of the fascination and emotion which a wild animal can arouse depends, as we have just said, on finding it in its own environment. An elephant in a circus ring or a lion in a zoo enclosure evoke different feelings which are not at all to be compared with those aroused by the same animal seen in the Indian jungle or in the African savannah. These concepts, purely aesthetic and emotive, can be compared to those of an ecology which refuses to consider flora and fauna and inanimate environment as facts alone, but which puts them together and integrates them into nature itself. From this idea comes the concept of integrated conservation. The idea of saving a species which is on the road to extinction by putting it into a zoo or special enclosure to reproduce (as is the case for the stag or the American bison) shows that we have turned, thanks to the importance of ecology, to the nurturing of the environment, at one with the animals and plants which compose the whole. This concept is best illustrated in the national parks. For 100 years (the first national park in the world, that of Yellowstone, was founded in 1872) the ever-greater importance given to national parks has made it possible for many species to be saved from extinction. For example, the Mountain Gorilla is protected in the National Park of Alberta, the Steinbok of Abyssinia is guarded in the National Park of Simien, and in South Africa and last 'bontebok' antelope has been saved from extinction (in 1931 there were only about 17 but the population now is about 750 head, thanks to Bontebok National Park). The examples go on continuously. The puma of Florida survives in the Park of the Everglades, the Californian Condor is protected in the Rifugio di Los Padres, the tiger and the Indian Lion today live only in national parks, the Steinbok of the Pyrenees is protected in the National Park of Ordesa in Spain, and the European

Salvation by all means

The function of national parks

Bison, saved at the eleventh hour, survives in the National Park of Bialowieska in Poland.

THE BIRTH OF THE PROTECTIONIST CONSCIENCE

It is almost impossible to obtain from politicians provisions in favour of nature in general and fauna in particular until a diffused protectionist conscience is created throughout the population.

Fashion and destruction

The difficult task of creating this awareness, today quite well consolidated in most of the more civilized and advanced countries of the world from the United States of America to the Soviet Union, can take its strength and indeed purpose from some particularly grave facts about the destruction of animal species (or to a lesser degree vegetable species). One of the facts which had the greatest effect on arousing protectionist sympathies in Western countries has been, during the years 1800–1900, the incredible massacre of birds for their plumage to go towards the making of women's dresses and hats. The news of crazy slaughters to satisfy these frivolous demands (in Venezuela in 1848, 500,000 herons were killed and in 1909 in the island of Laysan, 300,000 albatrosses) aroused the indignation of people already concerned about this activity especially in the Anglo-Saxon countries: thus at the end of the nineteenth century there grew up, in order to prevent the massacre of egrets in the Everglades of Florida, the 'National Audubon Society': the first martyr to the

The first societies

ecological cause was an inspector of that society who was killed by a group of poachers who operated in the marshlands. Hard on their heels there grew up in England the 'Royal Society for the Protection of Birds' and in 1904 the 'Society for the Preservation of the Fauna of the Empire', today the 'Fauna Preservation Society'. The taking of such positions succeeded, to some extent, in putting an end to the slaughters and laid the base for the modern theories of the protection of nature. A lack of scientific foundation in the activity of conservation, a lack which often saw the societies unprepared to confront ever new and growing menaces to the patrimony of world fauna, brought about the creation in 1948 of a scientific organization on an international base whose inspiration was clearly protectionist – the International Union for the Protection of Nature – which became in successive years the International Union for the Conservation of Nature and Resources (UICN) based at Morges in Switzerland. After a few years of activity with exceptional importance from the scientific point of view, but with financial difficulties of every type, it was decided to found another organization which would have as its principal goal the collection of funds to distribute to conservation operations the world over.

THE WORLD WILDLIFE FUND (WWF)

The World Wildlife Fund was founded in 1961 and, like the UICN, its headquarters are at Morges, Switzerland. Its intention is quite unequivocal, as is its name, and its plans were set out in the Manifesto of Morges by the founders of the UICN so that it could be a fund for the financing of actions proposed by that organization.

Sir Peter Scott, Chairman of the WWF, explains the four basic considerations of its work as follows:

> that mankind bears a moral responsibility to guarantee freedom of existence for the animals and plants which share the earth with us;
> that the raw material of biological science must not be destroyed or allowed to die out as a result of man's interference with the environment, least of all before it has been properly studied;
> that the maintenance of renewable wildlife resources can and should complement the kind of development needed to bring adequate standards of life to the greatly increased population; and
> that the beauty and diversity of natural life should be preserved for its own sake, and held in trust for future generations.

The WWF, which embraces many hundreds of organizations all over the world, has spread its activities into every sector of the complex field of conservation: in the education sector, in propaganda and publicity, and in conservation itself.

In the first of these sectors, the WWF considers that the education of young people in particular is of crucial importance. A major step forward was made in 1973 with the adoption of a Declaration of Intent between the WWF and the World Organization of the Scout Movement 'to introduce and to use their best endeavours to develop a close and long-term co-operation and partnership in the conservation of nature and the natural environment of man.' With the aid of a series of practical manuals which were translated into many languages, this provided an opportunity to promote conservation among some 13 million young people in more than 100 countries.

However, the field of conservation absorbs the greatest part of the fund's financial resources: from 1961 until 1977, the WWF has spent £15 million ($30 million) following the indications of the UICN and of the various national sections on worldwide projects. They range from the protection of the environment (buying parks, taking them on a concessionary basis, obtaining the institution of national parks from respective governments) to that of animal species. A guide to this last activity are the famous Red Data Books, huge directories and schemes compiled by the UICN which give information as accurate and complete as possible on the state of the animal species which are rare or in danger.

Red Data Books

From the first years of its foundation, the WWF made itself clear as a leader in the field, coming forward with operations of great public acclaim – for example in the acquisition of a large territory of the mouth of the Guadalquivir in Spain. Research and numerous studies, particularly of the UICN, underlined the exceptional importance of this marshy territory (called Coto

Doñana) for rare fauna (the very rare Imperial Spanish Eagle nests here and it is one of the last refuges of the Leopard Lynx on the Iberian peninsula), with the result that the WWF invested a vast sum to buy 6,500 hectares of this marshy paradise. Once the acquisition had taken place, the land was given with solemn ceremony to the Spanish government which, stimulated by this fact, set up in the region and peripheral areas covering in total 30,000 hectares, a marvellous national park – and certainly the most beautiful in a marshy area that Europe possesses.

Positive actions

A representative operation in another field, in the protection of the species, had for its subject the White Oryx of Arabia. This splendid antelope, one of the few species surviving after centuries of hunting and overfeeding in the Arab peninsula, was still living in small herds in the most lonely and inaccessible areas of Arabia. In spite of this the species was hunted by rich sheiks and emirs in jeeps and desert vehicles, helped by falcons and greyhounds, in an undignified slaughter of such rare animals.

The operation financed by the 'Fauna Preservation Society' and by the WWF consisted of the following: a few oryxes were captured and transported after a sufficient period of acclimatization in Italy to a zoo in a desert of Arizona where the climatic and environmental conditions were not too dissimilar from those which they originally enjoyed. Here, the animals began to reproduce and the flourishing herd has since been split with other zoos, such as San Diego. Meanwhile, preparations are well advanced to reintroduce the oryx in the Azraq National Park in Jordan, with the prospect of reintroductions elsewhere later.

The vicuña of the High Andes was another animal which was almost wiped out through man's lack of foresight, for within twenty years it had been decimated for its extremely valuable wool. With the assistance of Peru and other Andean countries, the WWF was able to save this elegant creature from extinction and its numbers are now increasing in special reserves, such as Pampa Galeras in Peru.

One of the more sophisticated initiatives was made on behalf of the flamingos which nest in the Camargue at the mouth of the Rhône in France. It was observed that, for various reasons – not least the disruption of the eggs by wolves and wild pigs – these splendid birds were not nesting on a small island where they had always built their nests. The WWF therefore provided a new island in the area – safe from predators – to facilitate the task of the flamingos' reproduction.

Project Tiger

In 1969 the WWF launched what was then its biggest ever campaign – Project Tiger, India – in an attempt to save this rapidly declining species which by then had an estimated total population of only 1,800. With WWF assistance, the governments of India, Nepal, Bangladesh and Indonesia quickly responded and initiated their own projects. Within seven years their strict protection measures saw results, for the Director of Project Tiger, India, was able to announce with confidence that the tiger had been saved.

The elephant

The situation of another well known animal, the elephant, is not so assured, however. Apart from heavy poaching for ivory, the elephant has suffered most severely from the destruction of its habitat for agriculture, so that its migration routes have been disrupted and it frequently finds itself in conflict with man.

Moreover, an ironic situation has arisen in reserves set aside especially for elephants, where their increasing numbers may effect the destruction of the vegetation; consequently, the elephants will suffer from malnutrition and may even become extinct in the areas reserved for their conservation.

Despite widespread fears of its extinction, no one really knows the exact number of elephants in Africa and Asia. The WWF and the UICN, with the active association of the New York Zoological Society, have therefore launched a three-year project to establish the true picture of the elephant situation and to work out conservation measures.

By means of questionnaires and detailed studies, the intention is to obtain both a broad picture of the elephant situation and a detailed knowledge of population and the effects of range contraction, expanding human settlement and poaching. A survey of the ivory trade will be undertaken and it is hoped that the information will help to develop proposals for legislative action to end illegal ivory trading and to rationalize elephant exploitation.

Survey of the WWF's activities

A large part of the WWF's resources are devoted to protecting animals' natural habitats and the establishment of national parks and reserves. Having achieved this, follow-up action includes the survey of specific areas, the provision of equipment for guards, training of park personnel, preparation of literature to bring greater public awareness, and the refinement of conservation legislation.

Africa

An example of this work can be seen in Africa, where a major effort is being made to ensure the survival of all known habitats. A number of national parks or reserves – usually in areas which have remained undeveloped or have outstandingly spectacular wildlife and scenery – have been established to protect the country's natural heritage. In order to identify the species in need of protection and the critical factors affecting their conservation, surveys have been carried out in eastern, central and western Africa. It is then planned to set out priorities for action on a regional basis.

The Bia National Park in Western Ghana, which was established in 1974, is representative of the many projects carried out in Africa. This park protects undisturbed rain forest inhabited by animals such as elephants, bongos, leopards, chimpanzees and Colobus Monkeys. Projects which are under way include one to save the Simen Fox, the Gelada Baboon and the Walia Ibex which live in the Simen Mountains National Park, and studies are being carried out to form a basis for conservation measures in north-west central Africa to protect the Mountain Lion, Damara Dik-Dik, Black Rhinoceros, the Black-faced Impala and a species of elephant – the largest in Africa.

North and Central America

In the United States of America, the WWF is supporting the activity of the Nature Conservancy, a private organization, which is establishing a programme in North and Central America to identify species, natural features and ecosystems which are the rarest, least protected and most endangered. The Nature Conservancy plans to establish a system of conservation areas and to create and promote model management systems for the maintenance of important natural lands.

South America

With tropical rain forests being cut and cleared at the alarming rate of 50 acres a minute, the WWF's priority in equatorial countries is the establishment of reserves. Work has already started in the area, and the first reserve of its kind in tropical rain forest is the Amazon National Park, Brazil, which will receive specialist assistance with surveys. In south-western Brazil, the Emas National Park is being helped to protect the Marsh Deer and the Pampas Deer, two rare and highly endangered species. Provision is also being made for the management and conservation of the Monteverde Cloud Forest Preserve in Costa Rica, which contains 2,000 plant species and over 320 birds and 100 mammals; moreover, it is the only place in the world where the Golden Toad is found.

In Argentina, the WWF is providing a game specialist and equipment to protect the remaining populations of the Argentinian Pampas Deer which is highly endangered due to the destruction of its habitat, competition with livestock and agriculture, and excessive hunting. Two small populations numbering no more than 100 specimens now survive in isolated localities.

Asia

The WWF's work in Asia is diversified. In India, the forest area in the coast range of the Western Ghats is now menaced by plantation projects, threatening the wildlife population, including the Lion-tailed Macaque. Studies are therefore being set up as a basis for a conservation programme. The Jaldapara Wildlife Santuary in West Bengal, which is one of the last strongholds of the Great Indian One-horned Rhinoceros, apart from harbouring the tiger, leopard and elephant among other species, is extremely vulnerable to poaching. A radio network is therefore being established to strengthen the guard system, which will also help animal behaviour studies.

The Gunung Leuser Reserve in Sumatra harbours the Sumatran Rhinoceros, one of the most endangered species in the world. Conservation measures are in effect to protect its habitat, and two units are to be established for a captive breeding project to boost the present critically low population.

Among the many other projects to protect endangered species in Asia the WWF hopes to set aside more areas for national parks in the tropical rain forests of south-east Asia, which are the richest and most diversified in the world. It is hoped to set up new reserves in East and West Malaysia, Indonesia, Papua New Guinea and Melanesia in the South-west Pacific.

In Indonesia, the WWF's work consists mainly of preserving natural habitats – many of which are threatened with the effects of a growing human population, shifting cultivation, and industrial development, such as timber exploitation – and protecting species from poaching and illegal trade in animals. A programme has been prepared to support the Indonesian authorities in their efforts to establish a representative network of reserves to ensure the continued existence of viable rain forest areas on the major Indonesian islands where several animals are on the verge of extinction.

Of its activities in Europe, the WWF has devoted the largest portion of its funds to the Ruggeler Ried, one of the last remnants of a once extensive area of swamp and marshland in Liechtenstein. The area, which has steadily been taken over for agriculture, harbours a great variety of rare wetland plant communities and offers feeding and breeding grounds for several endangered animal species. It is planned to set up a Wetland Reserve through a long-term land acquisition programme.

A number of projects have been set up to protect bird species, including the Griffon Vulture, of which there are about thirty-five pairs in Sardinia; the White-tailed Sea Eagle, which is rapidly declining in Scandinavia, Northern Germany and Greenland due to the effects of toxic chemicals in its food and loss of breeding areas, and the Peregrine Falcon in North-west Europe, which has also been sharply decreasing due to the spread of environmental poisons, intentional killing, collecting of eggs and young, and changes of breeding habitat. Conservation measures include protection of nest sites, studies of the toxic chemical problem and a ringing programme.

There are several projects to protect the wolf in Europe, where it is an endangered species, and in fact has already been exterminated in some areas. Protection measures are to be established in Norway, Sweden and Finland; the species is to be protected in conservation areas throughout the Apennines, and Poland, where the wolf population is declining, has been chosen for a model project designed to convince other governments of the possibilities of wolf conservation.

The smallest animal to benefit from WWF protection in Europe is the wood ant, an essential element of coniferous forests. A large sum has been devoted to setting up an ant conservation programme in Germany and Switzerland, which includes the protection of existing heaps with wire nets, artificial breeding of queens, and translocation and artificial establishment of new nest heaps.

In Britain, over £1 million ($2 million) has been spent by the WWF on conservation, much of this on over 100 nature reserves, including woodland, marsh, coast and upland areas. Important surveys and protection work has been carried out on some of the most rare and threatened wildlife species, including the Mouse-eared and Greater Horseshoe Bats, the Natterjack Toad and the coastal seabirds of north-east Scotland.

Endangered plants

Apart from its work to protect endangered animal species, the WWF is equally concerned with the plant world for human impact on this area has been as devastating as on the animal kingdom. Over 25,000 wild flowering plants worldwide are now in danger of extinction – in Britain alone there are 21 threatened species. The collection of cacti – particularly from Mexico – has meant that several species are almost extinct in the wild. Orchids have suffered similar ravages and their growing areas are very restricted. Apart from their beauty, however, plants are essential to all higher forms of life since man depends on them for food, drugs, timber and other materials. A Threatened Plants Committee has therefore been established by the UICN at the Royal Botanic Gardens, Kew, London. Its intention is to work with similar institutions and botanists throughout the world to compile data on endangered botanical species.

The Seas Must Live

In recent years, the WWF has become increasingly concerned with the condition of marine life, and the seas themselves – which occupy almost three-quarters of the earth's surface. Pollution, over-fishing, coastal development, mining and dredging have combined to pose a major threat to the oceans, at a time when their resources are needed more than ever to support the growing human population.

The WWF has therefore launched a £5 million ($10 million) campaign, The Seas Must Live, to establish a programme to safeguard the most vulnerable animals, protect the most critical habitats and stimulate governments and inter-governmental agencies to act on a wider scale.

The whale has been massacred for the products which can be made from its blubber – notably catfood, cosmetics, soap, margarine, lubricants and fertilizer – so that its population has been decimated to a critical degree. The whale conservation programme has two separate problems to deal with for the protection of this species: first, although many of the major whaling nations have reduced or stopped hunting this mammal, it is still threatened by other nations who hunt it along their coasts; secondly, the whale's feeding, calving and resting grounds are increasingly disturbed and man is competing with it for food, such as the krill. The WWF plans to promote an international system of whale sanctuaries and to support research to provide a firm scientific basis for conservation measures.

The dolphin and porpoise are also hunted for food and oil, but an estimated 100,000 are uselessly slaughtered every year as a result of tuna fishing. It was discovered long ago that dolphins and porpoises leaping about on the surface often have tuna shoals beneath them, and the huge purse nets which catch the tuna also trap the dolphins which drown because they cannot breath. The United States of America is the only country where tuna fishermen are being controlled and pressured to adopt methods to save the dolphin, and a project is under way to develop and promote fishing gear and strategies aimed at reducing or eliminating the useless slaughter of dolphins, porpoises, turtles, sea cows and seabirds.

Although seals are less severely threatened than whales, they are nevertheless harassed by fishermen and suffer from the effects of pollution. The Monk Seal, the only warm-water species, is seriously in danger of extinction and sanctuaries are planned in the main areas of its concentration, such as Greece, Algeria, Turkey and other places where the conservation climate is favourable.

Most otter populations are diminishing throughout the world as a result of skin hunting, pollution and habitat destruction – in fact, five of the nineteen known species are already in immediate danger of extinction. Authorities on otter species have therefore been nominated to identify conservation priorities and action requirements and to develop otter conservation projects.

The crocodile has also suffered as a result of over-exploitation for commercial purposes and its future is now seriously in doubt.

An action plan is being developed and it is hoped that conservation measures will include the banning of the sale of crocodilian hides for luxury items.

The Seas Must Live programme includes plans for the conservation of turtles, sea and coastal birds as well as large varieties of molluscs, corals, and other invertebrates, mangroves and sea grasses, all of which contribute in some way to the life of the others.

CONCLUSION

This rapid survey on the conservationist activities in the world has a precise aim: to stimulate the reader who has enough belief in the possibility of changing the present disturbing situation of animals and plants. This possibility can be realized only if an individual is prepared to become part of an organization which has, for its end, the protection of nature. But not in any sense rhetorical, or even worse, egotistical: the conservation and protection of nature, of its irreplacable environments, of its fascinating and useful species, cannot come before the conservation of man himself.

As we remarked at the beginning of this Appendix, man, who now finds himself as the major cause of the destruction of nature, must be conscious of the fact that the world which surrounds him, in spite of the assurances made by Jehovah to Noah, is not his private property, and not at all the area for his irrational and blind exploitation: it constitutes, on the other hand, his home (the only one, as it turns out, which exists in all the universe) to share with other human beings, his minor brothers, who also have the same right to life that he requires; and only by abandoning his attitude of king of the universe and by feeling himself an integral part of nature (a thing which too often has been forgotten with unfortunate and serious results) may he administrate and manage the immense heritage at his disposal with careful prudence, with rational conscience and with intelligent love. So that only by loving nature and its creatures, respecting them and helping them, *Homo sapiens* can avoid the already imminent destiny which threatens him.

BIBLIOGRAPHY

GENERAL

BURTON, JOHN H., *Conservation of Wild Life*, Blackie, Glasgow, 1974

BURTON, MAURICE and ROBERT (Editors), *International Wildlife Encyclopaedia*, New Caxton Library Service, London, 1972

CARAS, ROGER A., *Requiem on Wild Life: Last Chance on Earth*, Shocken, New York, 1972

DUPLAIX-HALL, N., *International Zoo Yearbook*, Vols 15 (1975) and 16 (1976), Zoological Society of London

EDINBURGH, DUKE OF, and FISHER, J., *Wildlife Crisis*, Hamish Hamilton, London, 1970

FISHER, J., SIMON, N., and VINCENT, J., *The Red Book*, Collins, London, 1969

MARTIN, R. D., *Breeding Endangered Species in Captivity*, Academic Press, London, 1975

MELLANBY, HELEN, *Wildlife in Danger*, Wayland, London, 1972

SITWELL, NIGEL, *Wild Life Now*, David & Charles, Newton Abbot, 1976

SMITH, DAVID, and NEWTON, DEREK, *Wildlife in Danger*, Longman Young Books, London, 1972

STREET, P., *Animals in Captivity*, Faber & Faber, London, 1965

WOOD, G., *The Guinness Book of Animal Facts and Feats*, Guinness, London, 1976

MAMMALS

Red Data Book, Vol 1 (*Mammalia*), UICN, Morges, France

BUCKLES, MARY PARKER, *Mammals of the World*, Bantam Books, London, 1977

CRANDALL, L. S., *The Management of Wild Mammals in Captivity*, University of Chicago Press, 1964

FITTER, R., *Vanishing Wild Animals of the World*, Midland Bank, London, 1968

HANZAK, JAN, *Mammals of Britain and Europe*, Hamlyn, London, 1975

LYDDEKKER, R., *The Deer of All Lands*, Rowland & Ward, London, 1898

MORRIS, R. and D., *Men and Pandas*, Hutchinson, London, 1966

PEMBERTON, JOHN LEIGH-, *Disappearing Mammals*, Ladybird Books, Loughborough, 1973

PEMBERTON, JOHN LEIGH-, *European Mammals*, Ladybird Books, Loughborough, 1971

RIDE, W. D. L., *Native Mammals of Australia*, Oxford University Press, 1966

SCLATER, P. L., and THOMAS, O., *The Book of Antelopes*, Vol 4, R. H. Porter, London, 1894-1900

VAN DEN BRINK, F. H., *A Field Guide to the Mammals of Britain and Europe*, Collins, London, 1967

WALKER, E. P., *Mammals of the World*, Vols 1 and 2, John Hopkins Press, Baltimore, 1964

BIRDS

Red Data Book, Vol 2 (*Aves*). UICN, Morges, France

Catalogue of the Birds in The British Museum, Vol 3, London, 1877

ANDREWS, JOHN, *Birds and Their World*, Hamlyn, London, 1976

AUSTIN, OLIVER L., *Birds of the World*, Hamlyn, London, 1968

BEEBE, W., *Pheasants, their Lives and Homes*, Robert Hall, London, 1937

BROWN, LESLIE, *African Birds of Prey*, Collins, London, 1971

BROWN, LESLIE, *British Birds of Prey*, Collins, London, 1976

BROWN, PHILIP, *Birds of Prey*, Hamlyn, London, 1976

BRUUN, B., *Concise Encyclopaedia of Birds*, Octopus Books, London, 1974

BRUNN, *Birds of North America*, Hamlyn, London, 1973

DELACOUR, J., *The Pheasants of the World*, Country Life, London, 1951

FISHER, JAMES, and PETERSON, ROGER TORY, *Birds: An Introduction to General Ornithology*, Aldus, London, 1971

FORSHAW, J. M., *Parrots of the World*, Lansdowne Press, London, 1973

GREENWAY, J. C., *Extinct and Vanishing Birds of the World*, Dover Publications, 1968

GROSSMAN, M. L., and HAMLET, J., *Birds of Prey of the World*, Cassel, London, 1965

HOSKING, E., and NEWBERRY, C., *Birds of the Night*, Collins, London, 1945

LITTLEWOOD, C., *The World's Vanishing Birds*, W. Foulsham & Co., London, 1972

MACKWORTH-PRAED, C. W., and GRANT, C. H. B., *African Handbook of Birds*, Vols 1 and 2, Longmans, Green & Co., London, 1952

PETERSON, ROGER TORY, *Birds*, Time-Life International, 1965

SHARROCK and SHARROCK, *Rare Birds in Britain and Ireland*, Poyser, Berkhampsted, 1976

WILLIAMS, J. G., *The Birds of East and Central Africa*, Collins, London, 1963

REPTILES

Red Data Book, Vol 3 (Reptilia & Amphibia), UICN, Morges, France
DITMARS, R. L., *Reptiles of the World*, MacMillan, New York, 1940
JAMES, ALAN, *Reptiles and Amphibians*, Blackwell, Oxford, 1973
POPE, C. H., *The Reptile World*, A. Knopf, New York, 1955

PERIODICALS/JOURNALS

AAZPA Newsletter, American Association of Zoological Parks and Aquariums, Wheeling, West Virginia
Animal Kingdom, New York Zoological Society, New York
International Wildlife, National Wildlife Federation, Washington
International Zoo News, Zoo Centrum, London
National Wildlife, National Wildlife Federation, Washington
Oryx, Journal of the Fauna Preservation Society, London
UICN Bulletin, UICN, Morges, France
Wildlife, Wildlife Publications Ltd., London
World Wildlife News, World Wildlife Association, London

INDEX

Abbe Lake, 96
Abingdon Island, 172
Abor, Mount, 149
Abruzzo Chamois, 125
Abruzzo National Park, 58, 125
Abu Dhabi, 120
Abyssinian Ibex, 128
Acinonyx jubatus, 82
Acinonyx jubatus rex, 82
Acinonyx jubatus venaticus, 82
Addax, 122
Addax nasomaculatus, 122
Aegean Sea, 158
Aepyornis maximus, 132
Afghanistan, 76, 78, 82, 129
Africa, 35, 46, 68, 73, 74, 78, 82, 84, 88, 92, 105, 110, 114, 119, 122, 123, 124, 142, 171
Africa, South-west, 68
African Convention of 1969, 35, 84, 89, 96, 105, 124
African Kestrel, 146
African Manatee, 89
African Wild Ass, 96
Agadir, 158
Ailuropoda melanoleuca, 62
Ailurus fulgens, 62
Alaska, 52, 86, 138, 144, 154
Albania, 70, 188
Albemarle Island, 172
Alberta, 64, 138, 154
Alberto National Park, 191
Aleppo, 94
Aleutian Island, 66
Alfedena 58
Algeria, 73, 78, 110, 122, 124
Alligator mississipiensis, 175
Alpine Chamois, 125
Alpine Ibex, 128
Alps, the, 58, 135
Altobello, 58
Amazon, River, 30, 89
Amazon, the, 40, 65
America, 32, 42, 52, 56, 64, 69, 81, 89, 99, 116, 138, 140, 143, 144, 152, 154, 162, 171
American Alligator, 175
American Bison, 116
American Crocodile, 175
American National Appeal for the WWF, 89
Ampasindava Bay, 26
Amsterdam, 93, 160
Amur, River, 76
Amur Leopard, 78
An-an, 62
Anatolian Leopard, 78
Anazah, 94
Andean Condor, 140
Andes, the, 40, 43, 99, 105, 140
Andohahela Reserve, 23
Andrias japonicus, 178
Andrias japonicus davidianus, 178
Andrias japonicus japonicus, 178
Andrias scheuchzeri, 178
Angola, 68, 89, 92, 104
Anhwei, 150
Ankarafantsika Reserve, 23
Annam, 148
Anoa, 114
Anoa depressicornis, 114
Anshi Ghat, 32
Antarctic, the, 47
Antelope, roan, 119
Antilles, the, 89
Antilope leucophaea, 119
Antongil Bay, 24
Anton, River, 179
Antwerp, 38, 118, 143
Apennines, the, 52, 58, 125
Aquila, 144
Aquila chrysaëtos, 144
Arabia, 74, 88, 94, 120, 127

Arabian Oryx, 120
Arabian Tahr, 127
Aransas National Reserve, 154
Arctic Walrus, 86
Ardeotis nigriceps, 157
Argentina, 40, 42, 43, 54, 69, 106
Arizona, 64, 81, 120
Arkansas, 69, 167
Arctic Sea, 50, 60, 86
Asia, 44, 52, 68, 73, 74, 76, 78, 80, 82,103, 116, 142, 171
Asia Minor, 74, 114
Asiatic Lion, 73, 74
Asiatic Wild Ass, 94
Assam, 100, 103, 126, 149
Assam Takin, 126
Atbara, River, 96
Atelopus zeteki, 179
Atjeh, 36
Atlantic Ocean, 47, 48, 49, 50, 89, 96, 159, 171
Atlas Mountains, 124
Atopogale cubana, 22
Auasc, River, 96
Auckland, 14
Audouin's Gull, 158
Audubon, John James, 162
Aurochs, 114
Australia, 15, 16, 17, 19, 20, 88, 139, 165, 171
Australian Chamois, 16
Austria, 52, 135
Aye-aye, 28

Baco, Mount, 114
Bagrach Kol, Lake, 108
Bahamas, 89
Bahia, 31
Baird Tapir, 99
Baitag-Bogdo, 90
Balaena mysticetus, 50
Balaenoptera musculus, 46
Balaenoptera musculus brevicauda, 47
Balaenoptera physalus, 48
Bald Eagle, 144
Bald Ibis, 135
Balek, River, 36
Bali, 76, 115
Bali Tiger, 76
Balkans, 70, 142
Balui, River, 36
'Bamboo Bear', 62
'Band-tailed Pheasant', 150
Bangkok, 31
Bangladesh, 102
Bannikov, Professor, 108
Banteng, 115
Baram Kalimantan, River, 36
Barbary Leopard, 78
Barbary Lion, 73
Barbary Stag, 110
Barcelona, 128
Barnard's Hairy-nosed Wombat, 19
Barrea 58
Basilea, 102, 105
Basle Patronage Committee for the Udjung-Kulon, 102
Bass, Strait, 139
Bearded Vulture, 142
Bedford, Duke of, 112
Bei-shung, 62
Belgium, 52
Beluchistan, 129
Bengal, 100
Bengal Tiger, 76
Berenty, 23
Bering Island, 87
Bering Sea, 86, 87
Bering, Vitus, 87
Berlin, 40, 112, 115, 118, 126, 138
Bermuda, 144
Betampona Reserve, 24

Bhutan, 126
Bialowieska Forest, 116
Birecik, 135
Bisegna, 58
Bison bison, 116
Bison bison bonasus, 116
Bison bison caucasicus, 116
Bison bonasus, 116
Black-footed Ferret, 64
Black Lemur, 26
Black Rhinoceros, 104
Black Sea, 84
Black Whale, 50
Bluebuck, 119
Blue-eared Pheasant, 149
'Blue pheasants', 148
Blue Whale, 146
Bolivar, Simon, 106
Bolivia, 43, 54, 56, 106
Bombay, 74
Bombetoka, Bay of, 26
Bonavides, Felipe, 106
Bonin Islands, 133
Borneo, 36, 72, 103, 115
Borneo Banteng, 115
Bos grunniens, 118
Bos javanicus, 115
Bos javanicus birmanicus, 115
Bos javanicus javanicus, 115
Bos javanicus lowi, 115
Bos primigenius, 114
Botswana, 68
Bowhead, 50
Brachyteles arachnoides, 31
Brachyurus, 54
Brahmaputra, 100, 175
Branta sandvinensis, 136
Brazil, 30, 31, 40, 42, 54, 65, 89
Brazilian Manatee, 89
Brenta-Adamello-Val di Genova-Val di Tovel, Parco del, 58
Bridied Nailed-tailed Wallby, 15
British Columbia, 138, 140
Bronx Zoo, 34, 126, 172
Broome, 18
'Brown Bear in Abruzzo National Park, Italy', 58
Brown-eared Pheasant, 149
Brown Hyena, 68
Bubalus [Anoa] mindorensis, 114
Budorcas taxicolor, 126
Budorcas taxicolor bedfordi, 126
Budorcas taxicolor taxicolor, 126
Budorcas taxicolor tibetanus, 126
Buenos Aires, 56
Bulgaria, 84
Buller, Ken, 18
Burchel Zebras, 93
Burma, 72, 76, 102, 103, 115, 126, 151
Burma Banteng, 115
Burundi, 38
Butant Lupar, River, 36
Butler, Harry, 18

Cacajao rubicundus, 30
Cagliari, 110
Calavita Mountains, 114
Calcutta, 103, 109
California, 54, 66, 84, 120, 124, 140, 152, 154
Californian Condor, 140
Calophasis, 150
Cambodia, 76, 102
Cametus bactrianus ferus, 108
Campephilus principalis, 167
Campephilus principalis bairdii, 167
Canada, 38, 52, 60, 64, 138, 144, 147, 154
Canary Islands, 84
Canis lupus, 52
Canis lupus irremotus, 52
Canis lupus italicus, 52
Canis lupus rufus, 52
Canton, 153
Cap Blanc, 84
Cape Barren Goose, 139
Cape Lion, 73
Cape Mountain Zebra, 92
Cape Province, 68, 73, 92, 93, 104, 123
Capoterra, 110
Capra falconeri, 129

Capra falconeri chiltanensi, 129
Capra falconeri falconeri, 129
Capra falconeri jerdoni, 129
Capra falconeri megaceros, 129
Capra ibex ibex, 128
Capra ibex walie, 128
Capra pyrenaica lusitanica, 128
Capra pyrenaica pyrenaica, 128
Carolina, 89, 165, 167
Carolina Parakeet, 165
Carpathians, 70
Carthaginians, 132
Cartier, Jacques, 159
Caspian Tiger, 76
Castor canadensis, 44
Castor fiber, 44
Catskill, 90
Caucasian Bison, 116
Caucasian Lynx, 70
Caucasus, 70, 116
Celebes, 114
Ceratotherium simum, 104
Ceratotherium simum cottoni, 104
Ceratotherium simum simum, 104
Cereopsis novaehollandiae, 139
Cervus elaphus, 110
Cervus elaphus berberus, 110
Cervus elaphus corsicanus, 110
Cervus elaphus hippelaphus, 110
Cervus eldi, 109
Cervus eldi eldi, 109
Cervus eldi siamensis, 109
Cervus eldi thamin, 109
Cervus nippon, 109
Cervus nippon grassianus, 109
Cervus nippon keramae, 109
Cervus nippon kopschi, 109
Cervus nippon mandarinus, 109
Cervus nippon taioanus, 109
Chad, 89, 96, 122, 124
Chapman Zebra, 93
Charles Darwin Station, 172
Chatham Island, 163, 172
Cheetah, 82
Chekiang, 150
Chelonia midas, 171
Chester, 38
Chicago, 19, 40, 62, 72, 74
Chi-chi, 62
Chile, 43, 106
China, 62, 76, 78, 80, 90, 108, 109, 112, 114, 134, 142, 149, 150, 151, 153
China Sika, 109
Chinchilla, 43
Chinchilla laniger, 43
Chinese Salamander, 178
Chinese Tiger, 76
Choeropsis liberiensis, 105
Choriotis nigriceps, 157
Chrysocyon brachyurus, 54
Cincinnati, 62, 165
Cyrenaica, 84
Citta del Messico, 62
Civic Museum of Natural History, Milan, 110
Clères, 138
Clermont, 19
Clouded Leopard, 72
Coastal Gorilla, 38
Colombia, 40, 56, 65, 99
Colonia, 38, 74
Colorado, 43
Columbus Zoo, 38
Commodoro Island, 87
Common Rorqual, 48
Cormorin, Cape, 32
Congo, River, 35
Connochaetes gnou, 123
Conolophus pallidus, 174
Conolophus subscristatus, 174
Conuropsis carolinensis, 165
Conuropsis carolinensis hudovicianus, 165
Copenhagen, 103, 159, 160
Corna, Mount, 58
Corsica, 110, 158
Corsican Gull, 158
Corsican Red Deer, 110
Costa Rica, 42
Costa Verde, 110

Coto Doñana National Park, 70
Crocodylus acutus, 175
Crocodylus moreleti, 175
Crocodylus niloticus, 175
Crocodylus rhombifer, 175
Crocuta crocuta, 68
Crossoptilon auritum, 149
Crossoptilon crossoptilon, 149
Crossoptilon crossoptilon crossoptilon, 149
Crossoptilon crossoptilon drouynii, 149
Crossoptilon crossoptilon harmani, 149
Crossoptilon mantchuricum, 149
Cuba, 22, 154, 167
Cuban Crocodile, 175
Cuban Solenodon, 22
Cutervo National Park, 56
Cygnus buccinator, 138
Cynailurus, 82
Cyprus, 158

Dakota, 64, 154
Dalmatia, 179
Dama dama, 108
Dama mesopotamica, 108
Dampier Land, 15, 18
Danube, 135
Darling, River, 15
Darwin, Charles, 172
Dasht-e-Naz, 108
Dasyurus quoll, 16
Daubentonia madagascariensis, 28
David, Armand, 62, 112, 150
Dawbin, W. H., 170
Dawson, River, 15
Deccan, 157
Delphin Strait, 86
Denmark, 52, 60
Derby, 18
Dermochelys coriacea, 174
Devil's Tower National Monument, 64
Dez, River, 108
Diary of a Naturalist, 172
Diceros bicornis, 104
Didermoceros sumatrensis, 103
Didermoceros sumatrensis lasiotis, 103
Didiereacea, 23
Dinornis maximus, 132
Diomedea albatrus, 133
Djakarta, 176
Dnieper, River, 92
Dodecanese, 84
Dodo, 160
Don, River, 92
Douc Langur, 31
Dublin, 72
Dugong dugong, 88
Duisburg, 40
Duncan Island, 172
Dunedin, 156
Durham, 23

Eastern Native Cat, 16
Ectopistes migratorius, 162
Ecuador, 56, 65, 99, 106
Edgar, J. H., 62
Edmonton, 38
Edward's Pheasant, 148
Egypt, 124
Elaphurus davidianus, 112
Elbe, River, 44
Eldey, Island, 159
Eld's Deer, 109
Elephant Bird, 132
Elliot's Pheasant, 150, 151
Endangered Species Research Station, Maryland, 64
England, 72, 112, 136, 153 *see also* United Kingdom
Enhydra lutris, 66
Equus asinus, 96
Equus [Asinus] asinus africanus, 96
Equus [Asinus] asinus atlanticus, 96
Equus [Asinus] asinus somalicus, 96
Equus burchelli, 93
Equus burchelli antiquorum, 93
Equus burchelli bohemi, 93
Equus gmelini, 92
Equus hemionus, 94

Equus hemionus hemionus, 94
Equus hemionus hemippus, 94
Equus hemionus khur, 94
Equus hemionus kiang, 94
Equus hemionus onager, 94
Equus przewalskii, 90
Equus quagga, 93
Equus zebra, 92
Equus zebra hartmannae, 92
Equus zebra zebra, 92
Eretmochelys imbricata, 171
Eritrea, 96
Espirito Santo, 31, 34
Ethiopia, 96, 104, 128
Eubalaena, 50
Eubalaena glacialis, 50
Euphausia superba, 46, 48
Euphorbia, 23
Euphrates, 135
Euro-Asiatic Eagle, 144
Europe, 44, 60, 70, 92, 100, 114, 116, 124, 135, 142, 150, 151, 152, 160, 162, 178
European Beaver, 44
European Bison, 116
Eyre Peninsula, 165

Falco ararea, 147
Falco newtoni, 146
Falco punctatus, 146
Falco rupicoloides, 146
Falco tinnunculus, 146
Fallow Deer, 108
Farallones de Cali National Park, 56
'Father David's Bear', 62
Fauna Preservation Society, 120
Félicité Islands, 166
Felis, 72, 80
Felis lynx orientalis, 70
Felis lynx pardina, 70
Felis pardalis, 69
Felis pardalis albescens, 69
Felis pardalis pardalis, 69
Fernandina Island, 133
Fezzan, 73
Finback Whale, 48
Flores Island, 176
Florida, 89, 124, 144, 154, 162, 165, 167
Formosa, 50, 72, 109, 148, 151
Formosa Sika, 109
France, 44, 52, 70, 82, 84
Frankfurt, 54, 72, 115, 143
Fresco, 140
Fukien, 150
Funk, Island of, 159
Furneaux, 139

Galapagos, 133, 134, 172, 174
Galapagos Flightless Cormorant, 134
Galapagos Giant Tortoise, 172
Galapagos Land Iguana, 174
Galapagos Penguin, 133
Gambia, 118
Ganges, 45, 175
Ganges Dolphin, 45
Gavialis gangeticus, 175
Gazella leptoceros, 124
Gebidebo, 96
Germany, 44, 52, 92, 108
Geronticus eremita, 135
Gewani, 96
Ghat Mountains, 127
Ghig, Alessandro, 152
Giant Anteater, 42
Giant Armadillo, 40
Giant Eland, 118
Giant Moa, 132
Giant Otter, 65
Giant Panda, 62
Giant Salamander, 178
Giarabub, oasis, 96
Gir, Forest of, 74
Glennie Islands, 139
Goa, 32
Gobi Desert, 90, 108
Golden Eagle, 144
Golden Frog, 179
Golden Lion Marmoset, 34
Golden Panda, 62

Gondar, 128
Goodfellow, 151
Goose Island, 139
Gorilla Game Reserve, 38
Gorilla gorilla beringei, 38
Gorilla gorilla gorilla, 38
Gosford, 14
Gran Chaco, 42, 54
Grand Canyon, 43
Gran Sasso, 125
Grant Zebra, 93
Great Auk, 159 -
Great Indian Bustard, 157
Great Khan, 82
Great Lakes, 154
Great White Mountain, 126
Greece, 70, 84
Greenland, 86
Greenland Right Whale, 50
Green Turtle, 171
Grus americana, 154
Grus canadensis, 154
Grus canadensis canadensis, 154
Grus canadensis nesiotes, 154
Grus canadensis pratensis, 154
Grus canadensis rowani, 154
Grus canadensis tadida, 154
Grus japonensis, 153
Guadalquivir, 70
Guanabara, 34
Gudda, dams, 45
Guinea, Gulf of, 89
Guinea, 89, 105, 118
Gujarat, 94
Guyana, 65
Gymnogyps californianus, 140
Gypaetus barbatus, 142

Hagenia, 38
Hainan, 31, 109
Haiti, 22
Haleakala, volcano, 136
Haliaeetus albicilla, 144
Haliaeetus leucocephalus, 144
Haliaeetus leucocephalus alascanus, 144
Haliaeetus leucocephalus leucocephalus, 144
Hamburg, 65
Hangchow, 153
Harkness, Ruth, 62
Hartmann Zebra, 92
Hatiyet, marshes, 96
Hauraki Maritime Park, 14
Hawaii, 84, 136
Hawaiian Goose, 136
Hawksbill Turtle, 171
Hellabrunn Park, 96
Hemitragus hylocrius, 127
Hemitragus jayakari, 127
Hemitragus jemlahicus, 127
Herre, W., 52
Herring Gull, 158
Hierophasis, 148
Himalayan Tahr, 127
Himalayas, 129
Hindu Kush, 100
Hippopotamus amphibius, 105
Hippotragus equinus, 119
Hippotragus equinus leucophaeus, 119
Hippotragus leucophaeus, 119
Hokkaido, 153
Holland, 52
Honolulu, 172
Honshu, 178
Hood Island, 172
Hopei, 149
Hualalai, volcano, 136
Hudson Bay, 86
Huesca, 128
Hume Pheasant, 151
Humpback Whale, 49
Hungary, 52
Hun Hoo, River, 112
Hupeh, 178
Hyaena brunnea, 68
Hyaena hyaena, 68
Hydrodamalis stelleri, 87
Hypericum, 38
Iceland, 159
Ice Whale, 50

Idaho, 138
Iglit, Mount, 114
Ilangurra, 18
Illawarra, Lake, 14
Illinois, 147, 154, 165, 167
Imperial Woodpecker, 167
Incas, 106
Indefatigable Island, 172
India, 72, 73, 74, 76, 80, 82, 88, 94, 100, 102, 114,
    151, 157, 175
Indiana, 165
Indian Gavial, 175
Indian Ocean, 47, 88, 146, 160, 171
Indian Rhinoceros, 103
Indian Wild Ass, 94
Indochina, 72, 109
Indo-Chinese Tiger, 76
Indonesia, 36, 76, 88
Indri indri, 24
Indris, 24
Indus, 45, 100
Indus Dolphin, 45
International Association for the Conservation of
    Bisons, 116
International Fur Trade Federation, 80, 82
International Union for the Conservation of
    Nature, 60, 73, 99, 103, 110, 114, 143
International Union of Directors of Zoological
    Gardens, 36
International Whaling Commission, 50
Iowa, 154
Iran, 74, 76, 78, 80, 82, 108, 129
Iraq, 74, 94, 108
Isabella Island, 133, 134
Italian Association of the WWF, 52, 58, 84
Italy, 52, 58, 70, 82, 84, 159
Itatiaia, 31
Ivory-billed Woodpecker, 167
Ivory Coast, 105, 118

Jafuani Reserve, 22
Jaguar, 81
Jalan Shar Keeyeh, 127
Jaldapara Reserve, 100
James Island, 172
Jamrach, W., 150
Japan, 50, 66, 82, 109, 112, 134, 153, 178
Japanese Ibis, 134
Japanese Salamander, 178
Java, 76, 102, 115
Java Tiger, 76
Javan Banteng, 115
Javan Rhinoceros, 100, 102
Jersey, 74
Jervis Island, 172
Jobal Hafit, Mount, 127
Jugoslavia, 84
Jumna, River, 157
Junagardh, 74
Jura, 135

Kadra, 32
Kagu, 157
Kahuzi, Mount, 38
Kahuzi-Biega National Park, 38
Kaibab Plateau, 43
Kaibab Squirrel, 43
Kaka, 164
Kalahari Desert, 93
Kamchatka, 86, 87
Kansu, 118
Karkheh, River, 108
Karoo, 123
Kashmir, 100, 129
Kasi, River, 35
Kawau Island, 14
Kaziranga Wildlife Sanctuary, 100
Kea, 164
Kelvin Grove Farm, 163
Keplero Mountains, 156
Kiang, 94
Kimberley, 18
Klidhes Islands, 158
Kodiak Bear, 60
Koladan, 175
Komodo Dragon, 176
Korea, 78, 134, 153
Krill, 46, 48
Kronberg, 108

Kruger National Park, 68
Kuala Lumpur, 74
Kuatun, 150
Kuen-lun, 118
Kulan, 94
Kumbharwada, 32
Kunmunya, mission, 18
Kuwait, 120
Kwangsi, 178
Kweichow, 178

Ladakh, 118
La Digue Island, 166
Laga, Apennines, 125
Lama, 106
Laos, 31, 76, 102
Laptev Walrus, 86
Larus argentatus, 158
Larus audouinii, 156, 168
Larus genei, 158
Las Anod, 96
Lasiorhinus barnardi, 19
Lasiorhinus latifrons, 19
Leatherback, 174
Leiden, 119
Lemur macaco, 26
Lemur macaco fulvus, 26
Lemur macaco macaco, 26
Lena, River, 116
Leonard, Archbishop of Salzburg, 135
Leontopithecus rosalia, 34
Leontopithecus rosalia chrysomelas, 34
Leontopithecus rosalia chrysopygus, 34
Leontopithecus rosalia rosalia, 34
Leopard, 78
Lesser Panda, 62
Leuser Reserve, 102
Leyte Island, 143
Liberia, 105
Libya, 124
Li-li, 62
Linceus, 70
Lin-lin, 62
Lion-tailed Macaque, 32
Lisbon, 84
Lob Nor, Lake, 108
Lokobe Reserve, 26
London, 20, 62, 112, 120, 160, 166
Lophura edwardsi, 148
Lophura swinhoei, 148
Los Angeles, 120, 140, 143
Los Padres National Forest, 140
Louisiana, 69, 154, 162, 165, 167
Love, J. R. B., 18
Luzon, island of, 143

Macaca silenus, 32
Macarena Reserve, 40, 65
Macedonia, 70
Mackenzie district, 154
Macropus eugenii, 14
Macropus parma, 14
Madagascar, 24, 26, 88, 132, 160
Madagacar Kestrel, 146
Madeira, island of, 84
Madras, 32
Madre de Dios, 30, 65
Madrid, 65, 128
Mahambo Reserve, 28
Mahe Island, 147, 166
Maiella, 125
Maingtha, River, 175
Majabat-al-Kubra, 122
'Major Panda', 62
Malacca, 98, 103, 115
Malayan Tapir, 98
Malaysia, 76, 88, 98
Mali, 118, 122
Malta, 174
Mananara, 23
Manapouri, Lake, 156
Manatee, 89
Manchuria, 109, 112, 134, 153
Manchurian Crane, 153
Mandapan, 88
Maned Wolf, 54
Manila, 114
Manipur, 109

Manipur Eld's Deer, 109
Manitoba, 154
Manu, River, 65
Manu National Park, 56
Markhor, 129
Maroansetra, 28
Morocco, 73, 78, 135, 158
Maryland, 64, 154
Masoala Reserve, 24
Masora, River, 24
Massaua, 96
Masterton, 163
Mato Grosso, 40, 54
Maui, island of, 136
Mauna Kea, 136
Mauna Loa, 136
Mauritania, 84, 122
Mauritius, 146, 160
Mauritius Kestrel, 146
Mediterranean, 84, 171
Mediterranean Monk Seal, 84
Megalobatrachus, 178
Megalopteryx didinus, 132
Megaptera novaeangliae, 49
Mekong, 149
Melanosuchus niger, 175
Melva, marshes, 96
Memphis, 127
Menlaboh, 36
Mesopotamia, 74, 120
Mexico, 69, 89, 99, 162, 167
Mexico City, 62
Mexico, Gulf of, 154
Miami, 174
Mikado Pheasant, 151
Milan, 159
Milne-Hedwards, 112
Minas Gerais, 31
Mindanao, 143
Mindoro, 114
Ming-ming, 62
Minnesota, 154
Mirmecophaga tridactyla, 42
Mishmi, 149
Missouri, River, 147
Missouri, state, 165, 167
Monachus monachus, 84
Monachus schauinslandi, 84
Monachus tropicalis, 84
Mongolia, 80, 90, 100
Monkey-eating Eagle, 143
Montana, 64, 138, 154
Montecristo, 84
Monterey, 140
Morelet Crocodile, 175
Moscow, 62
Mosul, 94
Mountain Gorilla, 38
Mountain Tapir, 99
Mountain Zebra, 92
Mozambique, 68
Munich, 93, 96, 108, 114
Mup-ing, 62
Murchison Mountains, 156
Murray River, 15
Musk-ox, 126
Mustela nigripes, 64
Myrmecobius fasciatus, 17
Mysore, 157

Nagar Parkar, 94
Na-Hai-Tzu Imperial Park, 112
Namoroka Reserve, 23
Nanking, 153
Nannopterum harrisi, 134
Napo, Rio, 30
Narborough Island, 172
Natal, 68, 73, 123
Nebraska, 154
Neofelis nebulosa, 72
Neophema chrysogaster, 165
Neophema pulchella, 165
Neophema splendida, 165
Nepal, 100, 126
Nestor meridionalis, 164
Nestor meridionalis meridionalis, 164
Nestor meridionalis productus, 164
Nestor meridionalis septentrionalis, 164
Nestor notabilis, 164

Neuwied, 40
New Caledonia, 157
New Delhi, 109
Newfoundland, 159
New Guinea, 20, 88
New Mexico, 64
New Orleans, 154, 157
New South Wales, 14, 15, 16
New York, 34, 126, 172
New Zealand, 14, 132, 139, 156, 163, 164, 170
Niger, 122
Nigeria, 105
Nile, 124
Nile Crocodile, 175
Nilgiri, 127
Nilgiri Tahr, 127
Niokolo-Koba National Park, 118
Nipponia nippon, 134
Norfolk Island, 164
North African Wild Ass, 96
North American Grey Squirrel, 43
Northern Manatee, 89
Norway 60
Nossi-Be Island, 26
Nossi-Komba Island, 26
Nossy-Mangabe Island, 28
Noto Peninsula, 134
Notornis mantelli, 156
Notornis mantelli hochstetteri, 156
Notornis mantelli mantelli, 156
Nova Lombardia Reserve, 31
Nubian Wild Ass, 96
Nullabor Plain, 20
Numbat, 17

Ocelot, 69
Odobenus rosmarus, 86
Odobenus rosmarus divergens, 86
Odobenus rosmarus laptevi, 86
Odobenus rosmarus rosmarus, 86
Ohio, 162, 165
Oia, River, 178
Oklahoma, 147, 167
Oklahoma City, 38, 40
Old World Harpy, 143
Old World Kestrel, 146
Olm, 179
Oman, 120, 127
Onager, 94
Onychogalea fraenata, 15
Onychogalea lunata, 15
Onychogalea unguifera, 15
'Operation Oryx', 120
'Operation Tiger', 76
Orange-stomached Parakeet, 165
Orang-utan, 36
Orbell, G. B., 156
Oregon, 140
Orinoco, 89
Orso bruno delle Alpi *verdi Ursus arctos*
Oryx dammah, 122
Oryx leucoryx, 120
Oryx tao, 122
Osteolaemus tetraspis, 175
Otago Museum, 156
Otus insularis, 166
Ovibus muschatus, 126
Owl Parrot, 163
Oxford, 160

Pacific Ocean, 47, 48, 49, 50, 66, 86, 171
Pacific Walrus, 86
'Paco-vicuña', 106
Padar Island, 176
Pakistan, 80, 94, 129
Palawan, 152
Palawan Peacock Pheasant, 152
Palestine, 74, 94, 108
Pallas, Peter Simon, 119
Pampa Galeras Reserve, 106
Panama, 179
Pan paniscus, 35
Panthera, 72, 80
Panthera leo leo, 73
Panthera leo melanochaita, 73
Panthera leo persica, 73, 74
Panthera onca, 81
Panthera onca ariconensis, 81

Panthera onca hernandesi, 81
Panthera onca veracruensis, 81
Panthera panthera chui, 78
Panthera panthera jarvisi, 78
Panthera panthera nimr, 78
Panthera panthera orientalis, 78
Panthera panthera panthera, 78
Panthera panthera tulliana, 78
Panthera pardus, 78
Panthera tigris, 76
Panthera tigris altaica, 76
Panthera tigris amoyensis, 76
Panthera tigris balica, 76
Panthera tigris corbetti, 76
Panthera tigris sondaica, 76
Panthera tigris sumatrae, 76
Panthera tigris tigris, 76
Panthera tigris virgata, 76
Panthera uncia, 80
Pan troglodytes, 35
Paraguay, 40, 54, 65
Paris, 24, 62, 109, 118, 119, 132, 150, 160
Parma Wallaby, 14
Passenger Pigeon, 162
Patuxent, 64, 154
Pechino, 62, 108, 112, 126, 153
Peoples Republic of Mongolia, 90
Perace National Park, 56
Perdido, Mount, 128
Père David's Deer, 112
Periyar Wildlife Sanctuary, 32
Persia, 74
Persian Fallow Deer, 108
Peru, 30, 40, 42, 43, 56, 65, 89, 99, 106
Peshawar, 100
Pestchanyi Island, 86
Petrogale xanthopus, 16
Peureulak, River, 36
Pezophaps solitaria, 160
Philadelphia, 36, 82, 90
Philippines, 88, 143, 152
Phillip Island, 164
Phoenix, 120
Piaui, 54
Picinisco, 58
Pigmy Chimpanzee, 35
'Pig-goose', 139
Pigmy Hippopotamus, 105
Pigmy Moa, 132
Pinguinus impennis, 159
Pithecophaga jefferyi, 143
Pizzone, 58
Plains Zebra, 93
Platanista gangeticus, 45
Platanista indi, 45
Plata, Rio de la, 54
Poco das Antas, 34
Pohakuloa, 136
Poland, 44, 92, 116
Polar Bear, 60
Poljakov, I. S., 90
Polo, Marco, 82
Polyplectron emphanum, 152
Pongo pongo abelii, 36
Pongo pongo pygmaeus, 36
Pongo pygmaeus, 36
Popular Chinese Republic, 62
Portugal, 70
Portuguese Ibex, 128
Prague, 90, 160
Prairie Chicken, 147
Praslin Island, 166
Pretoria, 104
Priodontes giganteus, 40
Propithecus verreaux coquereli, 23
Propithecus verreaux coronatus, 23
Propithecus verreaux deckeni, 23
Propithecus verreauxi, 23
Propithecus verreaux majori, 23
Propithecus verreaux verreauxi, 23
Proteus anguineus, 179
Przewalskij, Nikolaj Michajlovič, 90
Przewalski's Wild Horse, 90
Pteronura brasiliensis, 65
Punjab, 157
Putorius, 64
Putumayo, 30
Pygathrix nemaeus, 31

Pyongyang, 153
Pyrenean Ibex, 128
Pyrenees, 44, 128

Qatar, 120
Quagga, 93
Quang Tri, 148
Queensland, 15, 16, 19
Queensland Hairy-nosed Wombat, 19

Rabat, 73
Rajang, River, 36
Rangoon, 126
Raphus cucullatus, 160
Raphus solitarius, 160
Rapti, River, 100
Red Data Book, 68, 78, 86, 96, 104, 136, 143, 153
Red Rock Lake, 138
Red Sea, 82, 88, 96, 122
Red Uskari, 30
Red Wolf, 52
Réunion Island, 160
Reykjavik, 159
Rhinoceros sondaicus, 102
Rhinoceros unicornis, 100
Rhodesia, 68, 82
Rhynochetos jubatus, 157
Riad, 120
Right Whales, 50
Ring-tailed Rock Wallaby, 16
Rintjia Island, 176
Rio de Janeiro, 31, 34
Rio Doce, 31
Rio Grande do Sul, 54
Rocky Mountains, 64
Rodocanachi, Signor, 150
Rodriguez Island, 160
Rome, 26, 73, 82, 124, 143, 159
Rotterdam, 115
Royal Cheetah, 82
Ruanda, 38
Rudolph II, 160
Rupicapra ornata, 125
Rupicapra rupicapra, 125
Rupicapra rupicapra ornata, 125
Ryukyu Sika, 109

Sabah, 36
Sablayon, 114
Sado Island, 134
Sadong, River, 36
Sahara, 73, 82, 122
Sahel, 122
Saint Kilda, 159
Samar, 143
Sambirona, 26
San Antonio, 154
Sandakan, 36
Sandhill Crane, 154
San Diego, 54, 120, 124, 174
San Domingo, 22
Sankuru, 35
San Pasqual, 124
São Paulo, 31
Sarawak, 36
Sardinia, 70, 84, 110, 142, 158
Sardo, Lake, 96
Saskatchewan, 154
Saudi Arabia, 120
Scaly-tailed Phalanger, 18
Scandinavia, 44, 82
Schenkel, R., 102
Scimitar-horned Oryx, 122
Sciurus kaibabensis, 43
Scotland, 159
Scott, Sir Peter, 136
Sea Cow, 88
Sea Otter, 66
Senegal, 89, 118
Settefratelli, 110
Seychelles, 147, 166, 172
Seychelles Kestrel, 147
Seychelles Owl, 166
Seychelles Tortoise, 172
Shamnar, 94
Shanghai, 62, 153
Shansi, 126, 149, 178
Shansi Sika, 109

Shansi Takin, 126
Shensi, 178
Shetland, Australia, 46
Short-tailed Albatross, 133
Siamese Eld's Deer, 109
Siberia, 76, 78, 86, 116, 144, 154
Siberian Tiger, 76
Sicily, 70, 84
Sierra de Guadalupe, 70
Sierra de la Macarena Reserve, 56
Sierra de Mar, 31
Sierra dos Orgaos, 31
Sierra Leone, 105
Sierra Madre, 167
Sierra Mantiqueira, 31
Sierra Morena, 70
Sierra Nevada, 140
Sierra Nevada de Merida Park, 56
Sika, 109
Silva Jardim, 34
Simien, Mount, 128
Simpang-Kanan, River, 36
Sinai, 78, 120
Sinai Leopard, 78
Sind, 45
Singkel, 36
Sinkiang, 62
Slender-horned Gazelle, 124
Slimbridge, 136, 138
Slovenia, 179
Snow Leopard, 80
Solenodon paradoxus, 22
Somalia, 96
Somalian Wild Ass, 96
Sotheby, 159
South Africa, 68, 73, 82, 93, 119, 123
South Arabian Leopard, 78
South China Sika, 109
South Russian Plains Tarpan, 92
Spain, 70, 82, 142
Spanish Lynx, 70
Spectacled Bear, 56
Spheniscus mendiculus, 133
Sphenodon punctatus, 170
Splendid Parakeet, 165
Spotted Hyena, 68
Square-lipped Rhinoceros, 104
Sri Lanka, 78
Steller, Georg Wilhelm, 87
Steller's Sea Cow, 87
Stewart Island, 163
Stockholm, 119
Strigops habroptilus, 163
Striped Hyena, 68
Suakin, 96
Sudan, 122, 124
Su-lin, 62
Sumatra, 36, 72, 76, 98, 102, 103, 115
Sumatran Rhinoceros, 103
Sumatran Tiger, 76
Swinhoe's Pheasant, 148
Switzerland, 44, 52, 135
Sydney, 14, 17, 74
Syria, 94, 108, 120, 135
Syrmaticus ellioti, 150, 151
Syrmaticus humiae, 151
Syrmaticus humiae burmanicus, 151
Syrmaticus humiae humiae, 151
Syrmaticus mikado, 151
Szechwan, 62, 149, 178
Szechwan Takin, 126
Szpakowicz, Bartlomeus, 116

Tailandia, 76, 98, 102, 103, 115
Taiwan *see* Formosa
Takahe, 156
Takhin Shar-nuru, 90
Takin, 126
Talbot, L. M. and M. H., 114
Tamarau Conservation Program, 114
Tamaru, 114
Tammar, 14
Tampa, 124
Tapirira guianensis, 34
Tapirus bairdi, 99
Tapirus indicus, 98
Tapirus pinchaque, 99
Tapper, John, 18
Tasmania, 16, 20, 139

Tasmanian Pouched Wolf, 20
Tasmanian Tiger, 20
Taurotragus derbianus, 118
Te Anau, 156
Teheran, 82
Tendaho-Sardo Reserve, 96
Tenerife, 23, 28
Teo, 96
Terai, 100
Testudo [Aldabrachelys] aldabrachelys, 172
Testudo [Chelonoidis] elephantopus, 172
Testudo elephantopus abingdoni, 172
Testudo elephantopus becki, 172
Testudo elephantopus chathamensis, 172
Testudo elephantopus darwini, 172
Testudo elephantopus elephantopus, 172
Testudo elephantopus ephippium, 172
Testudo elephantopus guntheri, 172
Testudo elephantopus hoodensis, 172
Testudo elephantopus microphyes, 172
Testudo elephantopus nigrita, 172
Testudo elephantopus phantastica, 172
Testudo elephantopus wallacei, 172
Testudo elephantopus wandenburghi, 172
Texas, 64, 69, 154, 165, 167
Thamin Eld's Deer. 109
Thylacine, 20
Thylacinus cynocephalus, 20
Tibesti, 96
Tibet, 62, 94, 149, 151
Tiger, 76
Tijuca National Park, 34
Tijuca Park of Lion Marmosets, 34
Toa Baracoa, 22
Tokyo, 62, 143
Toledo, monte de, 70
Torishima, island of, 133
Transvaal, 68, 93, 123
Tremarctos ornatus, 56
Trichechus inunguis, 89
Trichechus manatus, 89
Trichechus senegalensis, 89
Trumpeter Swan, 138
Tsinghai, 149
Tuatara, 170
Tunis, 110
Tunisia, 73, 78, 110, 124
Turkestan, 108, 129
Turkey, 78
Turkey Creek, 18
Turkish National Appeal for the WWF, 135
Turkish Parakeet, 165
Turkmenistan, 82
Tympanuchus cupido, 147
Tympanuchus cupido attwateri, 147
Tympanuchus cupido cupido, 147
Tympanuchus cupido pinnatus, 147

Ucayali, Rio, 30
Udjung-Kulon Reserve, 102
Uebiscebeli, 96
Uganda, 38
Uganda Leopard, 78
Ukraine, 90, 92
United Kingdom, 23, 24, 26, 28, 31, 32, 34, 35, 36, 52, 69, 72 *see also* England
Uppsala, 119
Ursus arctos, 58

Ursus arctos marsicanus, 58
Ursus arctos middendorfi, 60
Ursus maritimus, 60
Uruguay, 54, 65
US Wildlife Service, 136
USA, 23, 24, 26 28, 31, 32, 34, 35, 36, 38, 47, 60, 62, 64, 69, 72, 81, 82, 89, 90, 106, 124, 127, 138, 140, 144, 147, 154, 162, 167
USSR, 44, 52, 60, 80, 82, 92, 108, 116, 129, 153

Valley Station, 18
Varanus komodoensis, 176
Venezuela, 40, 56, 65, 99
Venice, 179
Vera Cruz, 99
Vernon, D. P., 19
Verreaux's Sifaka, 23
Victoria, 15, 16
Vicugna vicugna, 106
Vicuña, 106
Vienna, 119, 160
Vietnam, 31, 76, 102, 103
Virginia, 165
Virunga Reserve, 38
Visnu, 175
Volcans, Parc des, 38
Vultur gryphus, 140

'Waldrapp', 135
Walrus, 86
Walvis Bay, 46
Wampoe, River, 36
Warsaw, 114
Washington, 22, 54, 62, 73, 90, 110, 140
Western Australia Museum, 18
West Indies, 89
White-eared Pheasant, 149
White Rhinoceros, 104
White-tailed Gnu, 123
Whooping Crane, 154
Wild Animal Park, 120
Wild Camel, 108
Wildfowl Trust, Slimbridge, 136
Wildlife Division of New Zealand, 156
Wild Yak, 118
Wind Cave National Park, 64
Woburn Abbey, 112
Wolf, 52
Wollongong, 14
Wood Bison, 116
Wood Buffalo National Park, 154
Woolly Spider Monkey, 31
World Herd, 120
World Wildlife Fund (WWF), 62, 76, 102, 103, 110, 120, 128, 135, 136
Worora, 18
Wotjulum, mission, 18
Wyoming, 138
Wyulda squamicaudata, 18

Yang-tse, 62, 149
Yavari, Rio, 30
Yellow-footed Rock Wallaby, 16
Yellowstone National Park, 138
Yunnan, 149, 151

Zaire, 38
Zungaria, 90